An Introduction to Vernacular Culture in America: *Society, Region, and Tradition* by Keiko Wells & Lisa Gabbert

多文化理解のための
アメリカ文化入門

社会・地域・伝承

ウェルズ 恵子，リサ・ギャバート 著

丸善出版

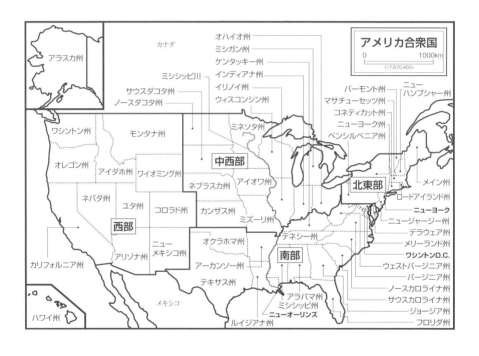

はじめに

　ロサンゼルス郊外で，私はバスを待っていました．夏の夕方，私はひとりでした．21歳でしたか留学したばかりで，あらゆることにドキマギしていました．アメリカでは，路線バスを利用する人はほとんどいません．そこへ14, 5歳の少年が現れ，私に尋ねました．"Do you have time?"（え？ 時間ありますか，って？ この子，何のつもり？）するとまた，"Do you have time?" と彼は言って，私の腕時計を指さしました．（あ，時間が知りたいのか）あのね，いまは……．

　あのとき，私は「アメリカ」に出会った気がします．大げさですけど，もっと知りたいな，この国に住んでいる人のこと，と思ったのでした．あの少年もそうですが，アメリカの人は，概して抵抗なく他人に話しかけます．特に西海岸では．

　ところがニューヘイブンという歴史ある東海岸の町へ行くと，すれ違う人が目を合わせることもなく西海岸とは別の国のようでした．また圧倒されたのが，西と東の諸都市の間に漠と存在する内陸部の広大な国土．360度の地平線を見渡せる広さと自然の威力は，私の想像を絶する「地球の顔」とも思えました．

　この大きな国を，「アメリカ」という単純な枠内で観察するのは無理なのではないか．こんなに多様な人々を，ひとまとまりに「アメリカ人」と呼ぶのは，法律上は可能でも，生活のレベルでは取り落としが多すぎはしないか．この疑問をひとつのきっかけとして，私は文化研究をすることになりました．

　本書ではまず第一に，文化のダイバーシティ（多様性，雑多性）を伝えるよう努めました．ですがもちろん，ここに著せたのはアメリカ文化のごく一部にすぎません．また本書は，アメリカに限らない文化の研究入門書でもあります．本書を始発駅に，読者のみなさんが文化のダイバーシティ探究へと旅立つことを願っています．

*

　生きるということは，何かが動き変化することでしょう．細胞が死滅し再生することも，思考や感情が働くことも，消化がすすんでお腹が空くことも，生きている証拠です．文化は人間の生活の営みとともに存在しますが，文化を生かし続けるいくつかの特色のうち，大事なものに「価値観」があります．私たちは何かを選びながら生きています．この瞬間に何をするのかがすでに選択ですが，選択内容を左右するのが価値観です．そして価値観がいちばん正直に現れるのが，「日々の生活に生きている文化」です．

　これを「ヴァナキュラー文化」とも，「フォークロア」とも呼びますが，本書

の大部分では，単に「文化」として述べています．

　本書が目指した二つ目のことは，文化から人々の価値観を読み取る方法を示すことです．個人の価値観が一朝一夕ではできないように，価値観を支える文化には長い歴史があります．国民の多くが移民やその子孫であるアメリカ合衆国でも，文化に長い歴史があることには変わりありません．それで，文化のルーツを知る方法も示したいと私たち著者は考えました．「いま」の文化と「伝統」文化との関係や，「伝統」をどう考えるのかということも書きました．第V部では，インターネットが普及した現代の文化はどのように観察できるかを述べています．2016年のアメリカ合衆国大統領選挙なども，14章を参考にしていただければ，みなさん独自の文化分析ができるでしょう．

*

　著者であるリサとケイコの二人は，この本を書きながらいくつかの文化的ショックを経験しました．

　そのうちの一つは，エイズの話題がリサの記述に加わったときです．アメリカでは，エイズは高校生レベルであれば共有可能な話題でしたが，日本の教室で文化研究の素材として扱いきれるかどうかに疑問があり，割愛しました．同様な理由で割愛した素材が2，3あり，広げてさらして議論したがるアメリカの文化土壌と，畳んでしまって見ずにすごしたい日本の違いを感じました．

　もう一つは，ケイコが文化を「アメリカ」の枠組みからはずして，普遍的要素に着目して記述したいのに対し，リサは，アメリカの多様なアイデンティティを見せることでむしろ「アメリカ」を日本の読者に知らせたいという強い希望を持っていたことでした．

　これは，考えてみれば，それぞれの文化土壌に対する反動としての研究姿勢です．アメリカの文化があまりにも多様で議論も拡散しがちであればこそ，リサは自分の思う「アメリカ文化」を示したいと思うのでしょう．一方ケイコは，雑多性を抱擁し楽しむ習慣が根付かない日本にいて，文化に国境のないことを積極的に訴えたいと思ったのでした．

　ですから本書そのものが，多様な文化の出会いと衝突と共存の成果なのです．この本が，文化に興味を持つ人や文化研究を志す人の，最初の友になれば嬉しいです．

2017年3月

ウェルズ恵子

A Message to the Reader

Hello! You are about to read a book on the United States that is likely quite different from other textbooks you have seen or read. While this is a book about culture, it does not directly cover traditional subjects such as government, national history, the economy, politics, or transportation systems. It doesn't even cover popular culture, like books, movies, or television shows. Instead, this book focuses on some of the traditional forms of culture that many Americans encounter in their everyday lives. You will be reading about stories, songs, celebrations, monsters, Internet culture, and other offbeat topics not found in conventional textbooks. Scholars sometimes call these forms of culture "**folklore**" or "**vernacular culture**." The term "vernacular culture" simply means the ordinary, everyday forms of culture that exist in people's lives. These ordinary and traditional aspects sometimes are overlooked by scholars because at first glance, they seem unimportant or insignificant. What we discover, however, is that not only are these aspects of culture useful for providing insights in culture and society, but they intersect in interesting ways with broader and more customary topics, like government, history, or economics. Political themes emerge in songs; American history is implicated in celebrations; and themes of transportation are found in legends. All topics overlap with contemporary forms of popular culture, since vernacular culture and pop culture form an interlocking loop. We hope you enjoy it. And please, come visit!

Early spring, 2017

Lisa Gabbert

目　　次

第Ⅰ部　お話とストーリーテリング——文化の中の不安と教訓
- 1 章　アメリカの民話——伝統を知り教訓を学ぶ ………………………2
- 2 章　同時代伝説(都市伝説)——不安を洞察する ………………………16
- 3 章　大災害の脅威——経験を伝える ………………………29

第Ⅱ部　歌——価値観の反映として
- 4 章　仕事の歌——働く辛さと生きる喜び ………………………44
- 5 章　ヒーロー・バラッド——本音の価値観 ………………………57
- 6 章　アメリカ人の愛唱歌——生活に大事なこと ………………………71

第Ⅲ部　モンスター・幽霊・ファンタジー——想像力と文化
- 7 章　怪物の伝承——環境と創造 ………………………86
- 8 章　幽霊話——社会問題と幽霊 ………………………99
- 9 章　子どもの遊びと文化——未来を創造する ………………………113

第Ⅳ部　祝祭と地域——地域共同体の営み
- 10 章　ハロウィン——地域で異なる文化 ………………………128
- 11 章　マルディ・グラ——文化の重層性を理解する ………………………138
- 12 章　カントリーフェアとロデオ——農村の価値観を知る ………………………150

第Ⅴ部　デジタル時代に生きる伝統文化と新世代文化　——未来への文化を透視する
- 13 章　インターネット・ミーム——越境する文化を把握する ………………………164
- 14 章　デジタル時代のヴァナキュラー・カルチャー
　　　　——これから文化を学ぶ人のために ………………………175

参考文献 ………………………187
図版出典一覧 ………………………194
索　引 ………………………198

Part I Stories and Storytelling

Chapter 1　Folk Tales: Teaching Traditional Lessons and Values ········· 2
Chapter 2　Contemporary Legends: Reflections of Current Anxieties ····· 16
Chapter 3　Disaster Stories: Narrating Experiences and Morals ·········· 29

Part II Songs and Singing

Chapter 4　Work Songs: Expressing Hardship, Lifting Sprits ············ 44
Chapter 5　American Hero Ballads: What Do People Value? ············· 57
Chapter 6　Best-Known Songs: What Is Important in Life? ·············· 71

Part III Monsters, Ghosts, Fantasy

Chapter 7　Monsters: Landscape and the Creation of Culture ············ 86
Chapter 8　Ghosts: Social Issues ······································· 99
Chapter 9　Children's Traditions: Creating the Future through Play ···· 113

Part IV Festivals and Celebrations

Chapter 10　Halloween in New York City and California:
　　　　　　Regional Variations of a Single Celebration ················ 128
Chapter 11　Mardi Gras: Cultural Diversity ···························· 138
Chapter 12　County Fairs and Rodeos:
　　　　　　Agricultural Roots and Rural Communities ·················· 150

Part V Living Traditions in the Digital Age

Chapter 13　Internet Memes: Investigating Borderless Culture/s ········ 164
Chapter 14　Vernacular Culture in the Digital Age:
　　　　　　For Those Who Study Culture, a Conclusion ················· 175

References ··· 187
List of Photograph Attributions ······································· 194
Index ·· 198

この本の使い方

　和文は英文テキストを理解するための補助として書きました．英文の翻訳ではありません．英語の教科書として使うときは，英文を日本語で要約する練習の参考にしてください．

　英文テキストと参考文献をあわせると（日本語部分を除くと），各章はほぼ，学生の英語論文モデルになっています．Introduction（導入）－Body（本文．2つか3つのセクションに分けてある）－Discussion［Conclusion］（結論）－References（参考文献）です．既存研究の報告は含められませんでしたが，記述のベースに研究動向の把握が欠かせないことを，学べるようにしました．本文中の論証部分では，研究調査による一次資料を引用しています．扱う資料の質や引用の仕方などを含め，英語論文執筆学習の助けになれば幸いです．注のつけ方は，各自の専門分野に従って学んでください．

　この本を文化研究クラスの教科書として使うなら，本文は宿題として読み，教室では各自のリサーチトピック検討や研究発表および議論を中心にしてほしいと思います．そこで，ACTIVE LEARNING のための研究課題例や討議項目を掲げました．充実した議論をするには，事前の調査と分析が不可欠です．読者が本書で文化研究の方法を学び，ご自分のテーマで研究をしてくださるのが著者の願いです．

　本書の専用ウェブ（http://pub.maruzen.co.jp/space/tabunka_america/）には，インタビューのマナーなど文化研究に必要な基礎知識や研究テーマ案，本書に関連する話題やニュースが掲載されています．学習や指導のためにご活用ください．

第I部
お話とストーリーテリング
――文化の中の不安と教訓

Part I
Stories and Storytelling

1章
アメリカの民話——伝統を知り教訓を学ぶ

Chapter 1
Folk Tales: Teaching Traditional Lessons and Values

1 フェアリーテイルの基本の形

　伝承物語の呼び方は，日本語でも「おとぎ話」「昔話」「民話」などと複数ありますが，英語でもいくつかの用語があり，それぞれの区別や定義は明確ではありません．最も包括的な呼び方は"folk tales"（フォークテイル）で，普通「民話」と訳されます．フォークテイルは娯楽として言い伝えられてきた話やそれを元に書き留められた話のことで，人々の価値観が表れていて，してはいけないことやしたほうがいいことなどを伝える教訓も含まれています．よく知られるのが"fairy tales"（フェアリーテイル）で，「魔法物語」と同義に使われることがよくあります．必ずしも妖精（フェアリー）が出てくる話とは限らず，不可能と思われる役目を担わされたり，きわめて困難な立場に置かれた主人公が，魔法を使える援助者のおかげで，物語の開始時よりもずっと優れた状態に飛躍するのが基本の流れです．結末は結婚で終わることが多く，困難を通過した主人公が大人になったことを示唆しています．

INTRODUCTION

Folk tales are fictional stories that are told for entertainment, although often folk tales have an educational or moral lesson as well, or they teach a particular value.

　One of the most common types of folktales is called a "fairy tale," although the name "fairy tale" is imprecise—scholars may use the term "magic tale" to describe this type of story. Despite the title, fairy tales are not necessarily about fairies, which are small human-like magical beings that play tricks on people. **Some fairy tales contain fairies, but the term "fairy tale" refers more broadly to coming-of-age stories that are set in the** distant past, and contain magic or elements of fantasy, such as talking animals, monsters, and wondrous objects. The protagonist, who is usually human, endures some kind of quest or trial. Heroes and heroines leave home to complete seemingly impossible tasks and overcome adversaries. They may also set out on a quest to find something that they lack, and they frequently are **aided by magical helpers**. The story usually ends in marriage, signifying the protagonist's successful entrance into the adult world.

　「シンデレラ」は伝統的な物語の代表格でしょう．何百年にもわたって伝わり，地理的にも広く知れわたっています．「伝統」とは，動かない古い文化のことではなく，ダイナミックに変容する創造的な文化プロセス，ないしはその創造物をさします．「伝統」の性質には，古いものを守ろうとする「保守的な部分」と，時代の流れに合わせて変わろうとする「躍動的な部分」の相反する二つの性質があると研究者は指摘しています．「シンデレラ」を例にとって，今述べたことを確認していきましょう．

....

　One of the most well-known fairy tales in the United States and indeed throughout many parts of the world is "Cinderella." Cinderella is an excellent example of a **traditional tale** because it is both widespread and has endured over a long period of time. It is hypothesized, for example, that Cinderella may have emerged in China during the fifth century, although it is largely known as a European tale. **Although many people think of "tradition" as being located in a static, unchanging past, in reality tradition is a dynamic and creative process**. Traditions stem from the past but they also constantly change and update themselves in order to be relevant and useful. Scholars identify this dual aspect of tradition as conservativism (meaning "unchanging") and dynamism (meaning "changing") (Toelken 1996). Let's see how this process works—along with the lessons and values taught—by examining the tale of Cinderella.

2　ディズニーとペローの「シンデレラ」

　ある文化が「伝統的」かどうかを見極める一つの目安は、多くの変種（バージョン）が存在するかどうかにあります。伝統的な物語は何十年何百年にもわたって伝承されつつ、広範囲の地域にバリエーションが生まれています。「シンデレラ」の場合、1951年の研究で700以上の異話が確認されています。アメリカで最もよく知られているのは、1950年に公開されたディズニー映画です。シンデレラが継母や継母の連れ子の姉たちにいじめられながらも、魔法を使うやさしい婦人（フェアリー・ゴッドマザー）に助けられて、ついに王子と結婚します（もっと詳しいあらすじは英文を読んでくださいね）。さて、伝統的な文化を研究するときは、「フォーミュラ」と呼ばれる共通する型を読み取り、それが保持されているものを同類の（ここでは「シンデレラ」の）物語とみなします。フォーミュラには2種類あって、一つはその物語が属するジャンルを決める型、もう一つはその物語を他の物語と区別するような特有の型です。「シンデレラ」物語の場合、これを魔法物語に分類するフォーミュラは、虐待されている主人公を魔法を使う者が助けるという点です。他方、「シンデレラ」を他の魔法物語と区別するフォーミュラにはいくつかあり、学説も一定しませんが、たとえば「靴」のように身に付けるものの一部が彼女の運をひらくきっかけとなることがあげられます。そしてこの場合の靴は、彼女の精神の高貴さを具現化するシンボルとして使われています。

....

CINDERELLA ACCORDING TO WALT DISNEY AND CHARLES PERRAULT

One way to identify whether or not an example of culture is traditional folklore is to identify whether or not it has **multiple versions**. A "version" refers to one example of some aspect or form of culture (such as the story of Cinderella). **Traditional forms of culture have multiple versions that can be documented over time and across space**. Each version will not be exactly the same as the others, but the group of examples, or **texts**, will be similar enough to each other that people know it belongs to the same story. (This holds true for other traditional forms of culture, such as songs, dances, holidays, etc.)　It is not known exactly how many versions of Cinderella there are, but one study produced in 1951 examined over 700 different versions of the story (Rooth 1951).

The most well-known version of Cinderella in the United States is the one produced by Walt Disney Studios in 1950. Walt Disney Studios is well known for adapting traditional folk and fairy tales to the big screen. In Disney's version of the story, Cinderella lives in a large mansion with her wicked stepmother and stepsisters, who are jealous of Cinderella's beauty. Cinderella's only friends are mice and other animals, and she is forced into a life of poverty and drudgery. One day, her family receives notice that the prince of the kingdom will hold a ball and all the women in the kingdom are invited to attend. Her stepmother and stepsisters go, leaving Cinderella behind. Heartbroken, Cinderella is helped by her fairy godmother, who magically transforms a pumpkin into a carriage, mice into horses, and other animals into a driver and footman. She also transforms Cinderella's shabby clothing into a beautiful gown. At the ball, the prince dances with Cinderella and falls in love with her, but Cinderella is forced to leave at midnight when the magic spell ends. She leaves behind a glass slipper as the only clue to her identity. The prince searches the entire kingdom, looking for the girl who fits the shoe. The shoe fits Cinderella; the couple marry and live happily ever after.

Folklore usually follows **recognizable patterns or formulas**. These patterns or formulas are what makes the text seem "the same" or "familiar" to examples that have come before. Cinderella, for example, follows two patterns: **a pattern for the particular story of "Cinderella," and the more general pattern for the genre of fairy tale** (discussed above). Scholars differ in exactly what constitutes the pattern for a Cinderella story, but it is generally agreed that Cinderella is the story about an abused or neglected child (sometimes called a "persecuted heroine") who is forced into a way of life beneath her status. She suffers misfortune but is eventually recognized for her worth by nobility, often by means of a shoe.

アメリカの伝統文化の多くは，ヨーロッパに起源があります．ディズニーの「シンデレラ」は，シャルル・ペローが1697年にフランス語で出版した物語に基づいています．ペローのおとぎ話集は，みなさんもよく知っている「赤ずきん」や「長靴をはいた猫」などを有名にした，文学史上とても重要なものです．ディズニー映画は，ペローの「シンデレラ」から複数のモチーフをうまく使っています．「モチーフ」とは，複数の作品に共通するナラティブのごく小さい単位のことで，歌

詞や笑い話や物質文化にも存在し，これをたどって文化の類似や相違を観察することができます．「シンデレラ」物語でいえば，魔法を使う援助者である婦人，魔法で馬車に変えられるカボチャ，魔法で御者になる動物たち，そしてあの印象的なガラスの靴などが，ディズニーの「シンデレラ」がペローの「シンデレラ」から受け継いだモチーフです．

....

Many forms of traditional American culture have origins in Europe. The Walt Disney version of Cinderella is based on a much earlier European version of the **story published in French in 1697 by Charles Perrault**. This book included many well-known folk and fairy tales, such as "Little Red Riding Hood" and "Puss in Boots." Many of the motifs that appear in the Disney version can be found in this version of Cinderella. **A motif** is a small narrative unit and can be useful for doing **comparative research**, that is, identifying similarities and differences among stories. Additionally, motifs exist not only in stories, but also in songs, jokes, and even material culture. Motifs found in both Perrault and Disney versions of "Cinderella" include **a magical godmother as helper, the transformation of animals into coachmen, a pumpkin that becomes a coach and, of course, a glass slipper**. The excerpt below is from Perrault's version and contains several identifiable motifs.

> Cinderella went at once to pick the best one she could find, and took it to her godmother, but could not guess how the pumpkin would get her to the ball. Her godmother scooped out the inside, and when only the skin was left, she tapped it with her wand, and suddenly it was transformed into a beautiful golden coach. Then she went to look in the mousetrap, and found six mice all alive. She told Cinderella to lift the trap-door a tiny bit, and as each mouse ran out, she touched it with her wand, and the mouse changed instantly into a beautiful horse, which made a fine team of six horses, with prettily dappled mouse- grey coats.
>
> (Perrault［1697］2009)

ディズニーの「シンデレラ」はたいへん人気がありますが，主人公に主体性がなさすぎるという批判もあります．研究者や批評家たちは，これは 1950 年代の

アメリカ女性の状況を反映していると指摘します．1975 年に，ストーンは論文で次のようなことを書きました．「太平洋戦争で男性の労働力が戦場に奪われている間，アメリカの女性たちは社会に出て働いていたが，終戦で男性が職場へ戻ると女性は家庭内に押し戻されることになった．シンデレラが王子の用意する城に入ったのは，彼女の主体的な意志によるものではなく，従順で無条件に寛容な性格と魔法という外部の力によって誘導されたのだ」と．事実，他のバージョンの「シンデレラ」の主人公は，もっと異なる性質を備えています．それを次に詳しく見ますが，こうしたバリエーションこそが，伝統文化のダイナミックな側面なのです．

....

Cinderella tries on the slipper

Although Walt Disney's *Cinderella* is quite well loved, **it also has been the subject of much criticism because the character of Cinderella is quite passive**: she is dutiful, obedient, sweet, hardworking, and accepts her difficult situation without complaint. Scholars and critics suggest that **this excessively submissive and compliant portrayal of Cinderella reflects a conservative ideological vision of American women and domesticity in the 1950s**. Prior to the 1950s, during World War II, many women worked outside the home because so many men were out of the country fighting the war. When the soldiers returned from war, however, women were expected to give up their jobs and return to domestic duties as housewives and mothers, much like Cinderella's own transformation in the Disney film from working girl to wife. Kay Stone (1975), for example, points out that Walt Disney's Cinderella is a heroine because of her temperament and beauty, not because of her actions. She relies on her fairy godmother for help, rather than helping herself. In both the Disney and the Perrault versions of the story, Cinderella also forgives her wicked stepmother and stepsisters because of her sweet disposition. **Other versions of the story, however, suggest a different kind of heroine**, which is why it is useful to compare and contrast different versions of the same story in order to obtain a more full understanding of the range of the Cinderella story—that is, the conservative and dynamic aspects of this traditional tale.

3 グリム童話のシンデレラ

　ヤーコプ・グリムとヴィルヘルム・グリムの兄弟は，1812 年に「シンデレラ」を含む『グリム童話集』（原題では『子どもと家庭のための物語』）を出版しました．『グリム童話集』は世界的なベストセラーとなり，ヨーロッパで民話の比較研究が盛んになるきっかけを作りました．グリムがこの話につけたタイトル（伝承物語にはタイトルがありませんから）は，「灰だらけの少女」というものでした．グリム版の物語のあらすじは，下の英文を読んでくださいね．グリムの物語では，主人公の少女は現状の打開に向かって積極的に行動しています．実母を亡くしたシンデレラは継母に酷く扱われているのですが，母の遺言に従って墓地に木を植えます．この木がシンデレラを助け彼女は王子との結婚に至ります．何度かの魔法の援助を受けられたのはシンデレラが母を弔ったからで，彼女の自発的な行動が結果を導いています．また，彼女はディズニー映画の主人公とは異なり，残酷な継母と義姉を無条件に許すようなことはせず，義姉たちの虚偽の行動が発覚する機会を待っています．そのようにして，自分の幸福を自分の手でつかんでいます．グリムは出版後に物語を書き変えていて，1857 年の版では，王子との結婚式で鳥が姉たちの目をついばむという描写を加えています．この厳しい処分を書き加えたわけは，19 世紀にはおとぎ話への教育的期待が高まっていたからだと思われます．人間は昔から現代に至るまで，お話をいろいろに変えながら利用してきたのです．伝統はこのように変化しつつ受け継がれていきます．

・・・

CINDERELLA ACCORDING TO THE GRIMMS
Jacob and Wilhelm Grimm were two German brothers who became famous for their collection of folk tales in early nineteenth century. They **published a version of Cinderella in their 1812 book *Kinder- und Hausmärchen*** (usually translated into English as ***Children's and Household Tales***). This book eventually became an international best-seller and helped establish the foundation for the comparative study of folk tales in Europe. They gave the title of the story in German as "**Ashenputtle**," which translates into English as "**Ash Girl**."

　In the 1812 Grimm version, Cinderella's mother has died and she is mistreated by her stepmother and stepsisters by being forced to do housework and sleep in the kitchen. In compliance with her dead mother's wishes, the girl plants a tree on her mother's grave. Her stepsisters give Cinderella the difficult task of picking lentils out of the hearth, which she accomplishes with the help of talking birds. When the time for the ball comes, Cinderella obtains proper clothing and transportation from the tree, which is presumably the spirit of her dead mother. Cinderella leaves behind a shoe at the ball, and when the king's men come to her house looking for the girl who fits the shoe, her stepsisters cut off pieces of their own feet in order to make it fit. The king is initially fooled, but the stepsisters' deception is called out by the birds, who note that the shoe is bloody and that the brides are false. The birds approve of Cinderella's fit and she marries the prince.

In this version of the story, **Cinderella is a more active heroine** in a number of ways. First, **she obtains magical help from the tree** because she has properly completed her dead mother's wishes; that is, she has ritually cared for the dead. **Her reward is based on her actions**, rather than on her temperament, an emphasis found in other versions of "Cinderella" as well. Second, **Cinderella actually attends the ball twice, and in both accounts successfully escapes from the prince**. Third, **she is not nearly as meek or forgiving** as in the Perrault or Disney versions. Cinderella allows her stepsisters to cut off pieces of their feet without revealing that she is the owner of the shoe. In fact, **in a later Grimm version published in 1857, Cinderella's birds peck out her stepsisters' eyes at her marriage ceremony**, leaving them blind for the rest of their lives. An excerpt from the 1857 story is below.

Cinderella asking tree for help

> On the day that the wedding with the prince was to take place, the two false sisters came to ingratiate themselves and to share in Cinderella's good fortune. When the bridal couple set out for the church, the oldest sister was on the right, the younger on the left. Suddenly the pigeons pecked out one eye from each of them. And as they came back from the church later on the oldest was on the left and the youngest on the right, and the pigeons pecked out the other eye from each sister. Thus they were punished with blindness for the rest of their lives due to their wickedness and malice.
>
> (Grimm and Grimm [1857] 1987)

This change to the story was introduced by the Grimms, who edited and revised many of their tales over time. The fact that the sisters are blinded because of their wickedness reflects **a growing desire over the nineteenth century to use fairy tales for didactic instruction**. It also reflects a growing emphasis on middle-class moral standards that included good manners, obedience, and punishment. This example illustrates how **people have used fairy tales over time** (and, by extension, other traditions) to suit their own immediate needs and circumstances, as well as how **traditions change over time**.

4 シンデレラ・キャット

　グリム童話は19世紀の出版で，ペローのおとぎ話集は17世紀末です．それよりさらに前の17世紀前半にイタリアで出版されているバジーレ作「シンデレラ」の類話「灰かぶり猫」[1]は，他のどれとも異なる魅力を備えています．この物語の主人公はゼゾッラという名の少女で，逆境を自分の判断で乗り越えていきます．継母にいじめられているゼゾッラは，家庭教師にそそのかされて継母を殺します．家庭教師だった女性はゼゾッラの父と結婚し，2番目の継母となりますが，最初の継母よりゼゾッラを邪険に扱い，台所で働かされたゼゾッラは「灰かぶり猫」と呼ばれます．そのあとの冒険は下の英文や物語を読んでいただくとして，ゼゾッラは王に見初められる機会を作りながら3回も姿をくらまし，最後は，逃げる途中で落とした靴をたよりに彼女を探した王の妃となりました．

CINDERELLA CAT

Another, quite interesting version of Cinderella is **an Italian version** that translates into English as "Cinderella Cat." This version is found in **a two volume book called *Il Pentamerone*, which was published between 1634-1636 by Giambattista Basile**. The protagonist's name is **Zezolla** and, unlike Walt Disney's character, **she evidences the ability to think on her feet and work her own way out of difficult situations**.

　In this version of story, Zezolla is mistreated by her father's second wife. At the suggestion of her governess, Zezolla kills the second wife by dropping a

---

[1] バジーレ『ペンタメローネ［五日物語］』杉山洋子・三宅忠明訳，大修館書店（1995）所収

trunk on her neck and convinces her father to marry the governess as a replacement. The father does so and at first the governess treats Zezolla well. Eventually, however, the governess elevates her own daughters and treats Zezolla even worse than the previous wife. Zezolla is assigned to kitchen drudgery and her name is changed to Cinderella Cat. Zezolla eventually obtains a magical tree from the fairies, which she carefully tends. When the tree is grown, a fairy appears to grant Zezolla's wishes. Zezolla wishes to be able to leave the house freely without her sisters knowing.

Over the course of the story, her sisters attend various feast days in fine clothing. Zezolla obtains rich clothing and horses from the tree and attends the feasts unrecognized. The king sees her, falls in love with her, and orders his servants to capture her, but she escapes from his men three times. She leaves a shoe and is eventually discovered by it. She marries the king.

　この物語のヒロイン，ゼゾッラは，とても活発に行動し自らの失敗から学びつつ大人になっていきます．最初は家庭教師の言いなりになって継母を殺してしまいますが，それが失敗だったとわかったあとは，自ら妖精の援助を求め，指示された通りの儀式を行い，彼女を捕らえようとする王の従者から逃げおおせ，義姉たちを見下すばかりか嫉妬のとりこにして玉の輿に乗ったのでした．そのたくましさたるや，ディズニー映画のシンデレラとは比べものになりません．失敗から学び，策略をつかって運を切り開いていくのは，この物語が出版された当時のナポリ人の価値観を表しているのでしょう．主人公にゼゾッラという固有の名前がついているのも，この物語の特徴です．

....

　This version presents **a lively heroine who learns from her mistakes and improves her situation by her own actions**. Zezolla first tries to improve her situation by listening to her teacher and killing her stepmother. Unfortunately, her situation worsens, rather than improves. Zezolla then seeks the help of fairies, performs proper rituals, and improves her situation on her own. She also escapes the king's servants and taunts her sisters, purposefully fanning the flames of their jealousy and illustrating a personality quite different from the meek and sweet Cinderella found in Disney. The excerpt below describes how Zezolla escapes from the king's servant by throwing down money:

> When he [the king] saw Zezolla's extraordinary beauty, he was immediately enchanted, and asked his most trusted servant to get some information about this phenomenon of beauty—who she was and where she lived.
>
> Without a moment's delay the servant went after her; but she, having discovered the ambush, threw out a handful of golden coins that she had obtained from the date tree for that purpose. The servant, when he caught sight of the money, forgot about following the horse, preferring to grease his own palms, while Zezolla dashed back and slipped into the house. (Basile [1634, 1636] 1999: 206)

Zezolla is not a submissive heroine who waits for help; rather, at the beginning of the story Zezolla is a bit naïve. She mistakes an enemy for a friend (the governess) and learns from her mistake. She receives help from the fairies because she has acted appropriately by carefully tending to the tree. She is conniving and able to improve her situation through her own cunning and guile. While these may or may not be qualities that are encouraged today, **they reflect the perspective of Naples, Italy during the seventeenth century and illustrate how folk tales reflect different sets of morals or values**.

5　考　察

　伝統的な文化がそうであるように，シンデレラ物語には幅広い時間と空間にわたってバリエーションが存在します．類話を見極めるには，共通するフォーミュラやモチーフをたどっていけばよいのです．変化にも，他の物語の場合と共通してパターン化した変化を遂げた部分と，ダイナミックに独自な変化を遂げた部分を観察できます．「シンデレラ」は，逆境にある少女が本人の価値を認められて身分の高い人と結婚する話です．そのフォーミュラの中で，物語は，家庭内虐待や希望とサバイバルの物語としてさらに変化していくでしょう．変化の詳細には，その文化に属する人々の価値観やモラルを読み取ることができます．ディズニー映画のおとなしいシンデレラがアメリカの50年代における女性観を反映しているように，です．現代でも「シンデレラ」には，活字になった物語のみならずさまざまな形態のバリエーションが作られ続けています．それがどんな教訓を伝え，価値観を表し，世界観を形作っているのかを研究するのは面白いでしょう．

DISCUSSION

Like all traditional forms of culture, **the story of Cinderella exists in multiple versions and can be found across time and space**. The story of Cinderella is recognizable because it follows **a pattern or formula**, and it has **identifiable motifs** that can be found in other versions of the story. However, **Cinderella also changes, adapts, and continually updates, exhibiting the conservative/dynamic processes found in all forms of folklore and traditional culture**.

Cinderella is an ancient, traditional, and widespread story with many enduring themes. There seems to be nearly universal appeal to the story of a young woman of low status who is treated badly but who is eventually recognized for her worth and rewarded with marriage to nobility. The story also speaks to issues of family abuse, and suggests themes of hope and survival, albeit by various means.

Yet is important not to generalize too widely the specific ideas that the story might represent. **Cinderella teaches important lessons and reflects values but those lessons and values are culturally specific and variable**. The way in which Cinderella is told, what details are emphasized, and how the story is framed are particular to specific times, peoples, and places. The character of Cinderella in the Disney version survives because of her sweet temperament, yet this version reflects a very passive and submissive Cinderella, an idealized vision of femininity specific to the US in the 1950s. Other versions depict a tough and resilient heroine who escapes a bad situation because she does what is right. **By comparing and contrasting different versions, we can learn much about what is enduring and what is particular in any tradition**.

People receive stories in many different forms. Cinderella is popular. The story is told orally, and found in novels, books, plays, operas, symphonies and of course, in film. Cinderella images and toys are marketed to young children, and these toys also reference the story in some way. The stories we tell each other orally, see in films, television, and the mass media, read in newspapers and books, and even the stories that circulate online **all teach lessons, articulate values, and shape our impressions of the world around us**. It is important to pay attention.

6 演 習

下に引用した19世紀ロシア版の「シンデレラ」を読んでください．英語本文で論じたことを参考に，本文で紹介された物語と比べてください．このロシアの物語が「シンデレラ」の類話だといえるのはなぜですか．この話に独特なのはどこでしょうか．ここにはどんな考え方や価値観が表されているでしょうか．文章の中から例を引用し，あなたの考えを証明しながら，意見を交換してください．

ACTIVE LEARNING

Read the nineteenth century Russian version of Cinderella below. Compare and contrast it to the discussion of Cinderella above. How do we know it is another "Cinderella" story? What is unique or different about this version? What ideas or values are given emphasis in this version?

ADDITIONAL READING MATERIAL

"The Golden Slipper"

> An old man and his wife had two daughters. Once the old man went to town and brought a fish for the elder sister and a fish for the younger sister. The elder sister ate her fish, but the younger one went to the well and said: "Little mother fish, what shall I do with you?" "Do not eat me," said the fish, "but put me into the water; I will be useful to you." The maiden dropped the fish into the well and went home.
>
> Now the old woman had a great dislike for her younger daughter. She dressed the elder sister in her best clothes, made ready to take her to mass, and gave the younger one two measures of rye, ordering her to husk it before their return from church.
>
> The young girl went to fetch water; she sat on the edge of the well and wept. The fish swam to the surface and asked her: "Why do you weep, lovely maiden?" "How can I help weeping?" answered the maiden. "My mother has dressed my sister in her best clothes and gone with her to mass, but she left me home and ordered me to husk two measures of rye before her return from church." The fish said: "Weep not; dress and

go to church; the rye will be husked." The maiden dressed and went to mass. Her mother did not recognize her. Toward the end of the mass, the girl went home. Very soon her mother too came home also and said: "Well, you ninny [meaning "silly or dumb"], did you husk the rye?" "I did," the daughter answered. "What a beauty we saw at mass!" her mother went on. "The priest neither chanted nor read, but looked at her all the time—and just look at you, you ninny, see how you're dressed!" "I wasn't there, but I know all about it," answered the maiden. "How could you know?" asked her mother.

The next day the mother dressed her elder daughter in her best clothes, went with her to mass, and left three measures of barley for the younger one, saying: "While I pray to God, you husk the barley." So she went to mass, and her younger daughter went to fetch water at the well. She sat down at the edge and wept. The fish swam to the surface and asked: "Why do you weep, lovely maiden?" "How can I help weeping," the maiden answered. "My mother has dressed my sister in her best clothes and taken her to mass, but she left me at home and ordered me to husk three measures of barley before she returns from church." The fish said: "Weep not. Dress and go to church after her. The barely will be husked."

The maiden dressed, went to church, and began to pray to God. The priest neither chanted nor read, but looked at her all the time. That day the king's son was attending mass; our beautiful maiden pleased him tremendously and he wanted to know whose daughter she was. So he took some pitch and threw it under her golden slipper. The slipper remained when the girl went home. "I will marry her whose slipper this is," said the young prince. Soon the old woman too came home. "What a beauty was there!" she said. "The priest neither chanted nor read, but all the time looked at her—and just look at you, what a tatterdemalion [meaning "ragged person"] you are!"

In the meantime the prince was traveling from one district to another, seeking the maiden who had lost her slipper, but he could not find anyone whom it fitted. He came to the old woman and said: "Call your young daughter hither; I want to see whether the slipper fits her." "My daughter will dirty the slipper," answered the old woman. The maiden came and the king's son tried the slipper on her: it fitted. He married her and they lived happily and prospered. (Afanas'ev [1855–1863] 1945: 44–46)

2章
同時代伝説（都市伝説）——不安を洞察する

Chapter 2
Contemporary Legends: Reflections of Current Anxieties

1 同時代伝説とは

　日本語で「伝説」というと古い言い伝えをイメージしますが，英語の"legend"は「伝説」とはニュアンスが異なります．信じがたいことが事実として起こった，それを伝えるのがレジェンドです．信じがたいことを成し遂げ，人々の語り草になった人物をレジェンドと呼ぶこともあります．昔のことである必要はありません．本書では，レジェンドと同義で「伝説」という言葉を使います．ですので，この章で扱う同時代伝説とは，「信じがたい内容を含み」つつ「事実に基づいているという前提で」広まる話をさしています．

INTRODUCTION
Contemporary legends are supposedly true stories about outrageous, incredible, or extraordinary events that stretch the boundaries of believability. They are often about celebrities, crimes, sex scandals, or horrific events, and they circulate orally, in newspapers, and on the Internet. Contemporary legends are also called "urban legends," even though these stories can be found in both rural and urban settings. They are some of the most common stories in the United States.

　同時代伝説では，通常，大っぴらに話すのがはばかられるようなとんでもない内容に，真実味を加える工夫が施されています．本当にあったことだと信じられてこそ，話が発信するメッセージは力を持つからです．伝え話なのに，なぜ真実味がそれほど大事なのでしょうか．それは同時代伝説が，人々の今の不安や恐怖を反映しており，現実生活に対して何らかの警告を与えようとしているからです．

過去60年間に広まったアメリカの伝説からは，自立したい思春期の子供たちの不安，男女の役割の変化，大企業の力，科学技術の進歩などに対する恐怖を読み取ることができます．

....

Contemporary legends are told as if they were true, despite the outrageous content. They **usually contain a bizarre plot twist**, which is barely believable but also possible (although highly unlikely). Most contemporary legends did not actually happen, while others are highly exaggerated versions of a much smaller event. Contemporary legends seem like they might be true because they contain **narrative devices designed to increase plausibility**. Contemporary legends must be plausible because they contain powerful messages that are more easily accepted if the story is thought to be possibly real.

Just because most legends are not true does not mean they are unimportant. **Contemporary legends reflect social anxieties or fears and contain implicit warnings**. Examples of American social fears over the past sixty years include fear about changing gender roles, fear of teenage autonomy, fear of large corporations, and fear of technology. Contemporary legends that have circulated in different eras reflect these anxieties and contain warnings about these fears. Let's see how this works at different points in US history.

2 車の同時代伝説：思春期の恐怖

第二次世界大戦後のアメリカでは，10代の若者と車とに物語の題材をとった同時代伝説が盛んに語られました．なかでも「フック」(引っかけるカギ状の鎌，針) とタイトルがつけられた話は，10代のカップルが偏執狂に殺されかけた話です．詳しくは英文で読み取ってほしいのですが，10代の男女が車のなかでラジオをかけながらキスをしていて，そのとき，ラジオが性犯罪と強盗で服役中の脱獄囚がその辺りにいることを警告します．脱獄囚には右手がなく，フックが義手の代わりについているというのです．二人は怖くなってすぐにそこを去り，彼が彼女を家に送り届けたとき……．

....

FEARS OF TEENAGE AUTONOMY: CONTEMPORARY LEGENDS ABOUT CARS

Some of the most popular and widespread contemporary legends emerged after the end of the World War II (1945). These contemporary legends focused on teenagers and automobiles. One of the most well-known legends, called "The Hook," tells about a teenage couple in a car who are almost killed by a crazed maniac with a hook for a hand. The version below was printed in the newspaper in a popular advice column in 1960.

> Dear Abby:
> If you are interested in teenagers, you will print this story. I don't know whether it's true or not, but it doesn't matter because it served its purpose for me: A fellow and his date pulled into their favorite "lovers' lane" to listen to the radio and do a little necking. The music was interrupted by an announcer who said there was an escaped convict in the area who had served time for rape and robbery. He was described as having a hook instead of a right hand. The couple became frightened and drove away. When the boy took his girl home, he went around to open the car door for her. Then he saw—a hook on the door handle! I don't think I will ever park to make out as long as I live. I hope this does the same for other kids. (Brunvand 1981: 48-49)

この話では，ラジオで警告のあった危険人物が実はそのときそこにいて，すんでのところで命が助かったのだという点が，一番面白い．しかしまさにその，本当らしく聞こえるけれど現実離れした展開こそ，この話が現実ではなく伝説であるゆえんです．戦後アメリカでは，ガソリン供給が豊富になって車の製造が増大しました．アメリカは世界一の自動車生産国となり，1950年までに59%の家庭が車を所有しています．車は生活に欠かせなくなりました．「フック」の話は，車が10代の若者にそれまでなかった自由を与えたことへの社会的不安を反映しています．車社会によって変化した若者の行動に，警告を発しているのです．

In this contemporary legend, the teenage couple are in their car kissing, or "necking," (an old-fashioned word). They hear a warning on the radio about a dangerous man with a hook for a hand who has escaped from a local prison. Frightened, the couple stops their romantic activities and returns home, only to discover a hook embedded in the car door. The story suggests that the man (a murderer) was just about to open the car door, presumably to harm them, when they drove away. The teenage couple supposedly narrowly escaped with their lives. **The bizarre plot twist in this story is that the couple is almost harmed by the exact same person they heard about on the radio** and that they drove away just before he opened the door. These bizarre plot twists make stories interesting, but they are also good indicators that the story is a contemporary legend. Real life is not as neat and tidy as contemporary legends suggest.

　Legends about teenagers and cars became popular after World War II. During the war Americans were forced to limit their consumption of luxury goods. Car manufacturing stopped in 1942 and did not resume until 1946. After World War II, the United States experienced a period of great prosperity. The US became the world's largest manufacturer of automobiles, and cars played a much larger role in people's lives. Economic prosperity and increased car production contributed to the rise of American "car culture," which is a culture structured around the purchase, use, and symbolism of cars. By 1950, 59% of American households owned a car nationally. Cars began to shape where people lived, shopped, and ate.

　The contemporary legend "The Hook" speaks to social fears about cars and increased teenage freedom. Teenagers with access to cars had more freedom because they could escape watchful parents. Parents worried about dangers such as teenage promiscuity. **This story warns teens about the dangers of being alone in cars without adult supervision. The story is designed to frighten people into changing their behavior by playing on social fears.**

　人を脅かしたり警告を与えたりできる語りには，様式化された工夫が施されています．その一つが，舞台設定の局地化です．事件が実在の特定地域で起こったことにして，恐怖をあおるのです．「フック」の事件話は，ユタ州，カンザス州，ウィスコンシン州，インディアナ州，オレゴン州，テキサス州の各地で起こったこととして流布しているそうです．同時代伝説は，口伝もされますしメディアでも流布します．「フック」は格段に人気があり，小説や映画にもなっています．

Contemporary legends often contain narrative devices designed to increase the plausibility of the story. **A narrative device is a formal feature that serves a particular purpose**. If people think a story is true, they are much more likely to be frightened by it and heed the warning the stories contain. One narrative device designed to increase believability in contemporary legends is **localization**, meaning that when people tell a contemporary legend, they change the location of where the story supposedly happened to make it somewhere nearby. For example, Brunvand (1981:50) reports that when the legend "The Hook" circulated in Utah, Kansas, Wisconsin, Indiana, Oregon, and Texas people changed the story to make it seem like it happened in those places. If an allegedly true scary story happens nearby, it is much more frightening than if it happens far away. This is one way that contemporary legends seem more believable.

Many legends circulate both orally and through the media. "The Hook" is one of the most popular contemporary legends of all time. Versions of this legend can be found in novels, and in films such as *Meatballs* (1979). It especially is popular in horror films such as *Candyman* (1992), *I Know What You Did Last Summer* (1997), and *Urban Legend* (1998).

3 知らずに汚染されることへの恐怖

Many Americans eat fast food in their cars

同時代伝説の多くが、病気や汚染への恐怖を表しています。1960年代には、汚染された食物の摂取を扱った話が多く広まり、71年に記録されたものに、フライドチキンだと思って食べていたのが実はネズミの肉だった、という同時代伝説があります。背景には、生産者や調理者の顔が見えない大工場で用意されたファストフードの流行があり、人々は何を口にしているかわからずに不安だったのです。車社会の加速に並行して、ファストフード店で買った料理を持ち帰って食べる習慣が広まりました。ドライブスルーといって、車から降りずに注文し商品を受け取る窓口をハンバーガー店で見たことのある人もいるでしょう。そうしたオートメーション化した流れに人間の食習慣が影響されたのです。個人

の顔が見えない工場で生産されたものを食べているけれど,それは汚染されているかもしれない,危ないぞ,真実は「暗闇の中」だぞ,という恐怖が人々の心の中に湧き上がってきました.

....

FEAR OF CONTAMINATION

Many contemporary legends reflect fears about disease and contamination. Contemporary legends about people eating contaminated food emerged in the 1960s. One famous story is about a woman who supposedly orders fried chicken and discovers that her piece of fried chicken is actually a rat. This legend was first published in 1971, but probably circulated in oral tradition many years earlier. An example is below.

> Two couples stopped one night … for a fried chicken snack. The husband returned to the car with the chicken. While sitting there in the car eating their chicken, his wife said, "My chicken tastes funny." She continued to eat and continued to complain. After awhile the husband said, "Let me see it." The driver of the car decided to cut the light on and then it was discovered that the woman was eating a rodent, nicely floured and fried crisp. The woman went into shock and was rushed to the hospital….
> (Brunvand 1981: 82)

This legend plays on fears about eating food that is manufactured by large, impersonal corporations. "Carry out" (or fast food) is mass produced food that is designed to be cooked and eaten quickly. Fried chicken is a common example of fast food, and many versions of this legend identify the restaurant as KFC (Kentucky Fried Chicken). **This legend warns that people who eat at fast food restaurants don't know what they are eating**. This is symbolized in many stories by the description that the people eating the food are **"in the dark," a phrase that means a "lack of knowledge"** (Fine 1992). Consumers don't know what goes into the process and preparation of their food and in this story, the victim eats a rat, an animal that symbolizes filth.

Fast food restaurants became more common in the United States during the 1950s and 1960s. **As people increasingly used cars, fast food restaurants emerged that catered to American car culture**. Signs for fast food restaurants were made large enough so that people could see them from car windows, and people took their food order "to go," meaning that they took their food back to their cars. Fast food production became corporatized, and food production became like a factory assembly line. Contemporary legends emerged that played on **people's fears about the consequences of allowing large, impersonal corporations to prepare food by warning about possible food contamination**.

　ネズミの肉の話は，同時に，ジェンダーに関する人々の意識も浮かび上がらせています．伝説の中でネズミの肉を食べるのは，たいていは女性です．これをどう考えればいいのでしょうか．20世紀の前半までは，食事は主婦が家で調理するものでした．ところが戦後，ファストフードが出回るようになり，女性は以前ほど料理をしなくなりました．ですからこの伝説には，生活習慣の変化によって男女の役割分担が変化することへの恐怖や嫌悪が反映していると考えられます．類話の比較は同時代伝説の分析には特に有効で，それはネズミの肉の話にもあてはまります．女性が暗闇で知らずにネズミ肉を食べることや，彼女の息子ぐらいの年齢の若者のアルバイトがファストフード店でわざとネズミを調理したことなどが，いかにも本当らしく語られるとき，既存の男女の役割を逸脱する者への語り手の悪意を読み取ることは容易でしょう．

....

　Another message in this story is about gender. The character who eats the rat is usually a woman. **In many contemporary legends, the characters break a mild taboo or social rule, but suffer severe consequences**. In this case, the woman has chosen to eat out, rather than prepare the meal herself. Before World War II, women prepared the majority of food at home. With the rise of fast food restaurants after World War II, American eating habits began to change. The story implies that rat incident would not have happened if the victim, a woman, had stayed home to cook. **The tale uses fear and disgust to reinforce traditional gender roles in a context of changing social habits**.
　Contemporary legends exist in multiple versions and comparing versions allows scholars to identify important points. The ideas about gender discussed above are evident in other versions of the same story.

> A lady was sitting in her living room watching TV and eating Kentucky Fried Chicken. She bit into it and after a couple of bites, she noticed that it tasted funny, and she turned on the lights and saw that it was a rat she was eating with extra-crispy coating on it. Later I heard a boy that worked at Kentucky Fried Chicken fried it for a prank. I can believe that it would be true. There are crazy people in this world. （Fine 1992: 127）

Like the previous version, this version focuses on a female character who eats her food **in the dark**. It is only after she turns on the lights that she discovers her chicken is actually a rat. And, like all contemporary legends, this version **is told as if the story were true**, an essential quality of legends. The narrator states, "I can believe that it would be true. There are crazy people in this world." These lines make it sound as if there really are teenage boys disguising rats as fried chicken, **increasing the plausibility** of the story and the effectiveness of its gendered message.

> There was this lady and she went to Kentucky Fried Chicken and she went in there and she came out in the dark and it was raining, and she sat in her car eating a bucket of chicken and one of the pieces tasted funny. And she turned on the light in the car and saw a rat. She took it back in there and sued them. （Fine 1992: 130）

登場人物が実在するという前提もまた，話に説得力をつけ加える工夫です．「ある女の人が」とは言わずに，「友達の友達が」のように語るのです．義姉の友人でもいいし，遠い親戚でもよく，旧知ではないが実在していそうな誰かであればよい．それによって物語は真実味を帯び，「事実に基づいているという前提」の伝説となって流布します．

....

Another narrative device contemporary legends use that is designed to convince people that the story is true is to **identify the story character as a real person**. The Kentucky Fried Rat stories above simply describe the character as "a lady," but the presumption is that the character is an actual person. In some legends, the narrator may identify the story character specifically as someone with whom he or she is distantly connected, such as the relative of a friend, or someone another friend knows. Identifying the story character as someone the narrator might know is a rhetorical device designed to fool people into believing the story actually happened. Contemporary legend scholars call this narrative strategy **"friend-of-a-friend"** (abbreviated FOAF for short), because the story character is never an immediate known person to the narrator, but always a person once or twice removed. The "friend-of-a-friend" doesn't literally have to be a friend-of-a-friend; it could be a friend of a sister-in-law, a hairdresser's aunt, or anyone else to whom the narrator seems distantly connected. The main point is that identifying the story character as a "friend-of-a-friend" increases the plausibility of the tale.

4 進歩する科学技術への不安

　アメリカの同時代伝説に読み取れるもう一つのことは，科学技術の進歩に対する不安です．最初に引用するのは，電子レンジが普及し始めた1970年代に流布した話ですが，現在ではもうあまり語られません．びっくりする内容なので，ぜひ英文を読んでくださいね．1996年に記録されたバージョンは，20年間あまりにわたって口伝される間に物語としての形を整え，⑴通常の予想を超えることが起き，驚くべきオチがあり，⑵事実であるかのように語られ，⑶事件が実在の場所で起こったことにされており，⑷同時代の不安を反映し警告を発し，⑸登場人物は行為の代償として，とんでもなく悲劇的な結末に甘んじざるをえない，という同時代伝説の要素が全部含まれています（類話の比較には，それがいつ，どのような状況で，誰によって記録されたのかに注意を払う必要があります．語り手が聞き手を意識して話を変える場合もあるし，伝説を集めた人が中身を変えて記録する場合もあるからです．資料の特性に注意して研究しましょう）．

FEAR OF TECHNOLOGY

Another common fear in the United States is **anxiety about technology**. The contemporary legend below was popular during the 1970s and no longer circulates. It reflects anxiety about microwave ovens! This seems funny today, but in the 1970s people were wary of microwave ovens, which was a new technology. The story below was printed in 1979 as an example of a common story in circulating at that time.

There was an old lady who had been given a microwave oven by her children. After bathing her dog, she put it in the microwave oven to dry it off. Naturally when she opened the door the dog was cooked from the inside out. (Brunvand 1981: 62)

Below is another version, recorded in 1996.

A rich elderly lady from Harrogate was taking her pet poodle for a walk when they were caught in a downpour. Rushing back inside, fretful for her pampered pet, she was desperate to dry him out and warm him up as soon as possible. So she took him straight into the kitchen, opened the door of her daughter's new microwave cooker for the first time, and thrust him in, moving the dial to a moderate setting. She patted his head and carefully closed the door with a click. The old lady was still drying her hair when the cooked dog exploded, ripping the door off the microwave. (Mikkelson 2008a)

Note the narrative devices that identify these stories as a contemporary legend. First, the story is about **a strange or extraordinary occurrence, with a bizarre plot twist** (the pet explodes). Second, the story is **told as if it were true**. Third, in the example above **the story is localized**—it supposedly happened to someone from nearby Harrogate. Fourth, the story **reflects contemporary anxieties and issues a warning**: in this case, it expresses fears about new technology and warns about potential dangers from the little-understood microwaves. Finally, **the characters suffer extreme, tragic consequences as a result of their actions**; the owner's pet explodes as a result of her technological ignorance.

　1970年代を境に，科学技術は私たちの生活を大きく変えました．そして，現在でも人々の不安は絶えることがありません．同時代伝説は，新しく生まれた恐怖や不安を反映し続けます．だからこそ「同時代の」伝説なのです．「トーキング・アンジェラ」をみなさんはご存知でしょうか．大きな目の可愛い猫がプレイヤーに話しかけてくるゲームアプリです．2013年頃，このアプリをめぐって，プレイヤーとなった子供のプライバシーが犯罪目的の情報収集者に流れているという話が広まりました．犯罪を企む情報収集者が，アプリの猫の目を通して子供の様

子を見ているというのです.

....

Technology has changed greatly since the 1970s, but people remain uncomfortable with it. Fear of microwave ovens seems quaint by today's standards, but there are plenty of contemporary legends that play on modern technological fears, such as fear of the Internet. **Contemporary legends get updated over time, reflecting the latest fears and anxieties—this is why they are "contemporary."** The "Talking Angela" contemporary legend below combines anxiety about digital technology with other, newer fears, such as the loss of privacy and fear of strangers.

"Talking Angela" is a real application game program (app) featuring a cute cat that talks to the user, who is often a child. The "Talking Angela" contemporary legend claims that strangers use the app to collect information about the child, and spy on the child through the cat's eyes for immoral purposes. This contemporary legend originated in approximately 2013 and continued to circulate at the time of the publication of this book. The version below was told by a nine-year-old girl named Kika in 2016.

The Talking Angela app has been the topic of contemporary legends

I was in art class when I asked my friend Clara if she had played Talking Angela. Clara told me that there was a little shadow man living inside Talking Angela's eye. The man was standing in a room. She said that somebody she knew had seen it. I felt really uneasy inside my stomach 'cause Talking Angela is really fun, and it was weird for someone to tell you that there was a man living inside her eye. I came home, told my mom, and she looked on Snopes [a website that investigates whether or not urban legends are true] to see if it was true. It turned out that it was a hoax that said there was a pedophile that was taking pictures of children and was stealing them. Even though it was a hoax, I was still scared.

Kika
Personal communication, April 13, 2016.

この伝説を信じなくても，不気味であるのは確かですね．同時代伝説は，仕組みを把握しきれない科学技術に浴していると，よからぬことに巻き込まれるのではないかという現代人の恐怖を刺激し，その話を信じようと信じまいと，自分の行動を抑制するように働きかけています．

　　　　　　　　　　　　　　　　　　　　　　　　　　　　　　　　

　The warning in this legend is clear: be careful of technology, and be careful of strangers who might use technology for reprehensible purposes. The girl Kika says that she knew the story was false, but it frightened her anyway. This is why it is unimportant whether or not legends are true. Contemporary legends **frighten people into changing their behavior,** whether they are true or not and whether or not people actually believe them.

5　考　察

　では，同時代伝説が人々に信じ込ませようとしているのは，何なのでしょうか．もともと，伝説は社会秩序を守るのに役立つ一つの表現形式です．社会の恐怖や不安を基に，現実にありそうでありえないことを述べて，警告を発します．現実と架空のぎりぎりの境界線で話されるため，人々の現実感が揺さぶられます．伝説研究者のリンダ・デイは，伝説がリアリティに対して疑いを呼び起こすので「伝説とは哲学的なものである」としています．伝説は，何が現実なのか，リアリティとはどう実現するのかという問いを私たちに提示する，影響力のある物語なのです．

　　　　　　　　　　　　　　　　　　　　　　　　　　　　　　　　

DISCUSSION
Why do contemporary legends attempt to make people believe them? Primarily, **legends are a form of social control**. By purporting horrific events that seem possible and that are based on social fears and anxieties, contemporary legends warn people of perceived (though not necessarily real) danger and frighten them into changing their behavior as a result. Secondly, legends describe highly unusual events as if they were real and so exist at **the border between fiction and non-fiction**. Legends therefore **challenge our worldview**, meaning they call the boundaries of reality into question. They

compel listeners to ask: Is this extraordinary event possible? Are teenagers safe by themselves? Is mass produced food reliable and appropriate? Is our technology and privacy protected? Linda Dégh, a prominent legend scholar, describes legends as "philosophical" because they **compel the audience to ask questions about the nature of reality**. Legends force people to think about what might be real and what the possibilities of reality are. They are powerful stories.

6 演　習

英文本文の分析を参考にしながら，次の物語を分析してください．どのような語りの工夫や技術が使われていますか．メッセージを読み取り，社会に漂うどんな恐怖が表れているか説明してください．同様な話が日本にあれば，クラスに持ち寄って分析してみましょう．

ACTIVE LEARNING

Analyze the story below, using the discussion above as a model. What narrative devices can you identify that mark this story as a contemporary legend? What messages or social fears does this story reflect? Are there similar stories found in Japan?

ADDITIONAL READING MATERIAL

When I was fifteen or sixteen years old, bouffant hairstyles were very much the rage. It was almost as if it were a contest to see which girl could rat her hair the highest and pour the most spray on it. One day I went to the beauty shop to have my hair done. My hairdresser told me this story, and she swore that it really happened to a friend of her niece's. There was this girl who had ratted her hair so high, and put so much hair spray on it, that she never took it down and combed it out or washed it. One day a spider fell into her hair. When the baby black widow spiders hatched, they bit her scalp and she died. （Mikkelson 2008b）

3章
大災害の脅威──経験を伝える

Chapter 3
Disaster Stories: Narrating Experiences and Morals

1 個人的経験の語り

強烈な経験をしたあと，少し落ち着くと人はそれを語り始めます．「個人的経験の語り」は伝統的な語りとは異なり，決まった物語の出だしや終わり方といった共通のパターンを持たず，個別の経験談は伝承されることもありません．けれども，多くの語りを集めて比べてみると，テーマや価値観が通じ合っていることが読み取れます．なかでも「災害に関する語り」は，人々が不幸な経験から受けたトラウマやその経験の暴力的な様相を描くもので，話のなかに災害に付随して明らかになる社会問題が結晶化して，まざまざと現れます．歴史的な事件や事故，災害があった時，人々は何をどう観察しどのような心持ちで生きたのかを，私たちはこうした語りの研究を通して知ることができるのです．

INTRODUCTION

The most common kind of stories told in the United States are called "**personal experience narratives**." These are stories people tell over and over again about themselves, their families, and their life experiences. Unlike the stories introduced earlier in this book such as fairy tales and legends, the content of personal experience stories is **not traditional**. Each story is unique and the narratives are not usually told by others or passed down through time. Yet despite the fact that each story is unique, researchers can find common themes and social values in personal experience narratives if they analyze large numbers of them.

One dramatic kind of personal experience story is "disaster stories," which are narratives of trauma and violence. These stories emerge in the wake of disasters, such as floods, hurricanes, and earthquakes. People who have experienced a man-made disaster such as war or becoming a refugee, or natural disasters, such as earthquakes or hurricanes, may only tell one or two stories about their experiences, but the stories are important because they **crystalize themes that provide insights into society**. These themes reflect what is important to society at that time. Additionally, personal experience narratives about disaster also contribute to an understanding of important historic events by adding the perspective of ordinary people.

2 ハリケーン・カトリーナ

　ハリケーン・カトリーナは，2005年8月29日にフロリダからテキサスにかけた湾岸地方を襲い，甚大な被害をもたらしました．歴史と文化の都・ニューオーリンズは深刻な洪水に見舞われ，約1,600人が亡くなりました．【カトリーナ物語1】(*Katrina Story #1*: Gutted) では，語り手は，洪水のあとですっかり破壊され泥だらけの自宅へ帰った時のことを物語っています．語り手は，家族とともに「自分たちの家」を回復するのに，2年あまりかかったと言っていますね．他方，ニューオーリンズにはいまだに復興が果たせていない家々が数多く残っています．ハリケーン・カトリーナの襲来からすでに10年以上が経ったにもかかわらず，です．

....

　One important natural disaster in the United States was Hurricane Katrina, one of the deadliest hurricanes ever to have hit the United States. Hurricane Katrina hit the southeast region on August 29, 2005. It damaged many areas along the Gulf Coast from Florida to Texas, and it flooded much of the city of New Orleans, an historically important and culturally diverse city. Approximately 1600 people died in this natural disaster. The personal experience narrative below was told by a person who returned to her home after flooding, only to find it ruined by water damage and mold. Years after Hurricane Katrina, many houses in New Orleans still remain in ruins and uninhabitable.

【カトリーナ物語1】　*KATRINA STORY #1: GUTTED*
"When my family and I came back to the city after evacuating in advance of Hurricane Katrina, we had a home that looked okay on the outside. However, when you opened the door you were hit with the awful odor ....

We had a home, but there was nothing left to save. Everything was gone, we had nothing to salvage, there was mold everywhere. Ceilings had collapsed in three of the four rooms we have. But, this was the house my parents raised us in. We couldn't just leave it. This was home. We got to work. We all helped as much as we could with everything, it took us almost two years to finish with everything but we eventually got back into the familiarity of a home; our home."[1]

Flooding in New Orleans after Hurricane Katrina

Anonymous, "Gutted,"
Hurricane Digital Memory Bank

個人的経験の語りを研究する理由

　こうした個人的経験の物語は，どのような展望を私たちに与えてくれるのでしょうか．政治・軍事・経済などの分野の重要人物が記録される「歴史」に対して，個人の物語は，普通の人々がある重大な出来事をどう経験したかを教えてくれます．ここで大事なのは，物語が「本当のこと」を語っているという前提です．確かに，経験に基づいた話なので事実とも言えそうですが，話には誇張や省略もあるのでありのままの出来事とは限りません．とはいえ，事実の背後にある何らかの真実について語ってはいるでしょう．先ほどの話（"Gutted"）には，深い喪失感が表現されていましたね．喪失感や悲しみや不信といった人間の感情は「歴史的な事実」ではありませんが「本当のこと」ではあるのです．個人的経験の語りを研究するもう一つの重要な理由は，災害によって生じた社会的あるいは文化的な課題を，物語が浮き彫りにしてくれることです．"Gutted"では，「ここは私たちの家だから」と思って家族が結束して働いたことが記されています．話の終わりは，希望と絆の言葉で結ばれていて，それはカトリーナ物語に特徴的です．ところで，個人的経験の話は一人称の語りであることにお気づきでしょうか．とはいえ，これにもバリエーションがあり，「私」が主語の時と「私たち」が主語の時があります．「私たち」が主語の時には，災害がみんなに襲いかかったという気持ちがよく表れます．複数一人称の語りからは，一丸となって協力し復興を果たした人々の姿が浮かび上がるのです．

....

1　The stories in this chapter have been edited lightly for readability.

As you read this story, think about how it **contributes a perspective** that is normally left out of history. Often, history consists of the written records of the elite classes, such as political leaders, military strategists, or the wealthy and powerful. The voices of ordinary people are not included. However, by paying attention to people's personal experience stories as important sources of historical information, scholars can gain insight into how everyday people experienced the event.

The most important aspect of personal experience narratives is that they are **considered to be true** rather than fictional, because they are based on someone's actual life experience. Despite this perception, however, personal experience stories may not be factually accurate. People may exaggerate parts of their stories, or details are forgotten or changed over time. This is why such stories are sometimes overlooked as sources of historical information. Yet the stories may **speak to truths that lie beyond mere facts**. Personal experience stories are considered as "true" by the people who tell them because they reveal a truth or perspective on an event as the person understands it. This personal experience story about Hurricane Katrina, for example, reveals the emotional depth of the disaster. Emotions are important, but they are not always considered as "historical facts." The narrator notes that "everything was gone" and "this was the house my parents raised us in," leaving the reader with a profound sense of loss. Emotions like sadness, loss, and disbelief were common for people who survived Hurricane Katrina and should be included in the historical record.

Personal experience narratives also are important to study because they **highlight important social or cultural themes** that emerge over the course of a disaster. For example, this story emphasizes resilience and the importance of working together as a family to overcome crisis. The storyteller says specifically, "We couldn't just leave it [the house]. This was home. We got to work." The final message is one of hope and togetherness, which is common in Katrina stories.

Many personal experience narratives are **told in the first person**, meaning that the narrator is also the main character. But this characteristic can vary, depending on the purpose of the story. In this example, the speaker talks about her own experiences, but instead of using the first-person "I" or "me" she uses "we." **Using "we" emphasizes the collective dimensions of the disaster** and helps crystalize the themes of collective resilience and family effort.

語りのテーマ

　話の結びに表される，回復，努力，協力といったテーマは，他のカトリーナ物語にも共通します．次の話 "Our Lives Changed Right Before Our Eyes" もそうです．そのとき語り手はまだ 11 歳でした．予報されたハリケーンを避けて海側のシャルメットから内陸のバトンルージュへ避難していた時，ホテルのテレビで，ニューオーリンズとシャルメットが洪水に飲み込まれる様子を見たのです．この話には，前に引用した話にはない別の要素が読み取れます．どんな要素があるのかは，以下に引用する英文の物語を読んでいただいてから説明します．

・・・

　Themes of resilience, hard work, and coming together emerge in other stories about Hurricane Katrina as well. The next story about Hurricane Katrina illustrates some of these same features, as well as additional elements.

【カトリーナ物語 2】　*KATRINA STORY #2: "OUR LIVES CHANGED RIGHT BEFORE OUR EYES"*

　　"... I was just an eleven-year-old boy from Chalmette, Louisiana who, along with fifteen other family members, evacuated to Baton Rouge to escape Hurricane Katrina. As we sat on that hotel bed, my attention was completely centered on the small T.V. that was right in front of me. All I can remember is the videos of helicopters flying over New Orleans and Chalmette showing that the water had reached the rooftops. I can't tell you what anyone else in the room was doing, because I was in shock. Shocked is the only way to describe it. I didn't know what was going to happen next. Were we going to be able to go home? Were we going to live in this hotel forever? I had absolutely no idea; all I knew was my life as I knew it was over...."

　　　　　　　　　　　　　Anonymous, "Our Lives Changed Right Before Our Eyes,"
　　　　　　　　　　　　　　　　　　　　　　　Hurricane Digital Memory Bank

メディアと災害の語り

　この話にも喪失のテーマがあることは明らかです．しかし，語り手が喪失に打ちのめされる過程が，最初に引用した物語 "Gutted" とは異なっています．最初の物語では，話者は洪水で破壊された自宅に衝撃を受けるのですが，2 番目の物語の話者は，洪水が家々の屋根まで達する様子をテレビで見て激しいショック

を受けたと言っています．ここには，災害においてメディアがどういう影響を与えるかが明らかにされています．メディアもまた社会を洞察して表現するという役割を持っています．新聞やテレビ番組などの社会的メディアは，自然災害の時に人々が受け取る情報や感情を左右します．それが個人的経験の語りにも反映されます．2番目の物語では，語り手はテレビ映像から自分の人生が劇的に変わってしまったのだと理解していることがわかります．この話も一人称話者で語られていますが，話者自身と物語の主人公には距離があります．主人公は何も知らない11歳の少年である一方，話者はハリケーンによって多くを失いそのトラウマに悩み，生き延びて今に至った大人です．彼は，自分がかつてどのような人物であり，今はどんな人物になったかを語っているのです．言い換えれば，物語の主人公と話者とのずれにその人のアイデンティティが表れ，物語には話者の個人的な価値観や信念が読み取れます．

....

Just like in the first Katrina story, the theme of loss emerges here too, since the person says, "all I knew was my life as I knew it was over." However, *the way* in which the loss is revealed differs from the first story. In the first story, the person describes her feelings of loss upon seeing her ruined house after she returns to the city. In contrast, this story highlights the **role the media play in disasters**, which is **another insight into society**. Disasters impact many people, draw national and sometimes international attention, and are perceived to have national significance. In the United States and other places, newspapers, television programs, and social media play an important role in shaping public perception of natural disasters, and this role of the media finds its way into personal experience narratives. In this example, the narrator focuses on watching TV and the importance of the images in shaping his understanding: he is "shocked" as he watches videos of the water rising over the rooftops. **The media images lead him to recognize that his life has been irrevocably changed**.

This story is **told in the first person**, which is common for personal experience narratives. This makes personal experience narratives interesting because the teller (or author) is also the main character in the story. **Yet the narrator and the story character are not the same person**. There is a distance between the narrator and the story character that allows the narrator to comment about him/herself as he or she was in the story to make a point. In this story, for example, the narrator refers to himself by saying "I was just an 11-year-old boy." The narrator implies that, before Hurricane Katrina, he was an innocent child. Now, as the person telling the story, he is no longer an innocent 11 year old boy; he has changed. He has suffered trauma; he has lost the life he knew before the disaster; and he is now a survivor. He is a different person than he was before the hurricane. This distinction between the narrator telling the story and the narrator as a story character is an important feature of personal experience narratives because it allows the author to make a point about **individual identity**. People reveal who they used to be and who they are now. Therefore, not only do personal experience narratives reveal **insights into society** but they also reflect the **values and beliefs of the individuals telling them**.

3 2001年同時多発テロ

　2001年の9月11日，テロリスト集団アルカイダは4機の旅客機をハイジャックし，それを武器にしてアメリカ合衆国を攻撃しました．この同時多発テロを9-11（ナイン・イレブン）と呼びます．ハイジャックされた4機のうち2機はニューヨークにあった2棟の世界貿易センタービルに突撃し，美しく金色にそびえ立っていた一双の高層ビルは両方とも火を噴いて崩れ落ちました．もう1機は「ペンタゴン」と呼ばれるアメリカ国防総省の本庁舎に突っ込み，西側を破壊しました．最後の1機はハイジャックされた後に地上に墜落しました．この大惨事の死者は，救援にあたった消防士や警察官を含め約3,000人に上りました．研究者や活動家たちは，事件後に人々の個人的経験の聞き取りを始めました．次に紹介する話は，9月11日の数か月後に記録されています．ここには人々の感情や信念，価値観が表れ，アメリカ社会の様相や課題が洞察できるとともに，アメリカ文化を支える中心軸は何なのかをうかがい知ることができます．ナイン・イレブンの語りから浮かび上がる中心軸の一つは，人々のナショナリズムです．引用例はニューハンプシャーの小学校教諭の語りで，子供達が急に愛国的になったことがわかります．それまでアメリカ合衆国の"Pledge of Allegiance"「忠誠の誓い」をそろって言うときに起立しなかった生徒たちが，9-11を境にすっかり態度を変え，さらに合衆国国歌の"The Star Spangled Banner"（「星条旗」または「星条旗よ，永遠なれ」）を校長先生に申し出て「忠誠の誓い」の前に歌うようになったとあります（6章も参照してください）．

．．．

Another kind of disaster story in the United States is personal experience stories about 9-11. On September 11, 2001 (which makes the date "9-11"), the terrorist group al-Qaeda coordinated a series of attacks in the United States by hijacking commercial airplanes and using them as weapons. One attack targeted the World Trade Center in New York City. This place, made of two towers, symbolized international finance and world markets. Two airplanes were flown into the towers, and the buildings collapsed, killing many people. Another attack targeted the Pentagon building, which is the headquarters of the United States Department of Defense and symbolizes U.S. military power. An airplane was flown into that building as well, collapsing the west side. A fourth airplane also was hijacked, but it crashed in a field. Approximately 3,000 people died during the attacks, including many firefighters and police who were trying to help victims.

Scholars and activists began documenting ordinary people's experiences by asking them to record their personal experience narratives. The stories below were recorded only a few months after Sept. 11, 2001. As personal experience stories, they reflect the feelings, beliefs, and values of the individual speaker, and they provide insights into society by illustrating themes that continue to shape American culture.

Terrorist attack on World Trade Center buildings in New York City

One theme that emerges in 9-11 disaster stories is the **theme of nationalism**. The following 9-11 story was told by an elementary school teacher in the state of New Hampshire. It has a strongly patriotic tone (see Chapter 6 for examples of patriotic songs).

【9-11 物語 1】 *9-11 STORY #1*
Date Collected: December 03, 2001

"What was really striking at school was a lot of times kids would not stand for the Pledge of Allegiance. I know because I have tried to get them to stand. But most of the kids would never say the Pledge out loud. Well, the next day [after 9-11] there wasn't a student that wasn't standing and saying the Pledge of Allegiance. In fact, the student body went to the Principal and asked to sing the Star-Spangled Banner that first morning afterwards. So the Principal announced they were singing the Star-Spangled Banner before the Pledge."

Folk Coll. 26, Box 1, Folder 46,
Fife Folklore Archives, Utah State University

災害に影響される価値観とその語り

　アメリカ合衆国は，同時多発テロ以降，ずっと国家主義的になりました．多くの人々がテロ攻撃を合衆国への脅威と受け止め，これに対する反応として国家への忠誠心を示そうとしたのです．引用した語りには，語り手である教諭自身が9-11以前から愛国的な価値観を持っていたことと，事件以降の生徒の愛国心の高まりに満足していることが読み取れます．少なくとも物語の中では，テロ攻撃をきっかけとして先生と生徒の価値観が一致したということです．

....

　The United States became much more nationalistic as a response to the terrorist attacks. Many people responded to the 9-11 attacks by declaring their loyalty to the country, since they perceived the attacks as a threat to the nation. The rise in nationalism continues to drive US foreign policy years after the attacks. Note how nationalism emerges in this story. The narrator, who is a schoolteacher, begins her personal experience narrative by pointing out the students' lack of willingness to say the Pledge of Allegiance, which is an oath of loyalty to the United States recited in schools. She says "Most of the kids would never say the Pledge out loud," implying that they were not patriotic. However, after the attacks, not only did the students recite the Pledge, but they were willing to sing "The Star-Spangled Banner," which is the title of the national anthem. Her point is that the students were willing to go beyond their normal school requirements for patriotism—they demonstrated super-patriotism after the attacks. In addition, the speaker implicitly demonstrates her own personal patriotic values to the audience by saying "I know because I have tried to get them to stand." She suggests that she has always been patriotic, but that the children were not, in effect demonstrating an aspect of her individual identity and personal values to the audience. Only after the attacks did the children and teacher come together to share this value—if not in reality, at least in her story.

コラム

Pledge of Allegiance
I pledge allegiance to the Flag of the United States of America, and to the Republic for which it stands: one Nation under God, indivisible, With Liberty and Justice for all.

The Star-Spangled Banner By Francis Scott Key, 1814
Oh, say can you see, by the dawn's early light,
What so proudly we hail'd at the twilight's last gleaming,
Whose broad stripes and bright stars thru the perilous fight,
O'er the ramparts we watch'd were so gallantly streaming?
And the rocket's red glare, the bomb bursting in air,
Gave proof through the night that our flag was still there,
Oh, say does that star-spangled banner yet wave
O'er the land of the free and the home of the brave?

4 考　察

　個人的経験の物語から浮かび上がる社会的なテーマは，受け手側の集団的な力の影響を受けています．言わんとすることや，含まれている教訓，ものの見方が，物語を聞いたり読んだりする人たちに受け入れられた場合は，話を聞いた人たちの間に気持ちのつながりが生まれ，その人たちを結びつけます．そしてその物語は繰り返して語られたり，本や雑誌に印刷されたりもします．物語が受け入れられなかった場合は否定的な反応を受け，消えたり，形を変えて語り直されたりします．本書で説明してきたように，9-11 の物語群から浮かび上がるのは「メディアの役割」「ナショナリズム」「恐怖」といったテーマです．9-11 では，「一般の人々の英雄的なところ」のような肯定的なテーマも見られます．こうしたテーマが明らかになる前に，「話の持つ個別の力」（話の内容や語り手の見方や語り方）と「受け手側の集団的な力」（話を聞いた人々［集団］がその話に関心を払うかどうかによって決まる力）が相互に作用しています．ですから，物語は，物語を受け入れる集団（共同体，仲間，何らかの共通性を持つ人々）によってその語りの内容や様式を変化させるものなのです．その意味で，物語は事実に基づいていても事実そのものではなく，事実の単純な報告よりも複層的に現実を映し出すこともあります．「よい話」とは，ある集団の意識的・無意識的な要求を満たすものだといえます．

How do broad social or cultural themes arise in personal experience stories? The themes that emerge in personal experience stories are a combination of individual and collective forces. When personal experience stories are told to other people in particular situations, the **audience evaluates the story** for effectiveness. If the point, moral, or viewpoint of the story is acceptable to the group, the teller receives **positive feedback**. For example, the audience might listen attentively, or ask the narrator to tell the story again, or tell similar stories of their own. Although we don't know specifically how the audience responded to the 9-11 narrative above, we can presume they supported the story in some way. A successful personal experience narrative **promotes bonding among the group**. With positive feedback, the narrator might tell the story again at a future date (or even write it down for publication). However, if the narrator receives **negative feedback**—people act bored, disagree, don't pay attention to the story, or change the subject—the teller will be less likely to tell it again. Or, he or she may reshape the story to reflect different themes that are more acceptable.

Some common themes that arise in American 9-11 stories are the role of the media, nationalism, and fear. Positive themes emerge as well; many 9-11 stories emphasize the heroism of everyday people. These themes were shaped socially and define what constitutes a successful 9-11 personal experience story. However, it is important to note that since personal experience stories reflect both individual and group values, different communities and groups have different requirements for what makes a successful personal experience story. Not all personal experience stories are the same. 9-11 stories reflect a particular set of national ideas and values, but stories emerging in smaller communities will reflect different ones. Stories told by New Yorkers about the difficulties of living in New York City, for example, must include humor in order to be considered as successful personal experience stories (Cody 2005). Figuring out what the requirements are in a particular community—that is, "what makes a good story"—is a common way to conduct research.

5 演習

次の物語を読み，議論してください．社会の本質を洞察したテーマやそれぞれの語り手のアイデンティティを指摘し，物語のどの部分を根拠に，あなたがそう考えたのかを説明してください．

....

ACTIVE LEARNING

Analyze the stories below, using the discussion above as a model. Can you identify themes that provide insights into society? What points do the speakers make about themselves and their individual identities?

ADDITIONAL READING MATERIAL: 9-11 STORIES

The woman who told this story watched the attacks on the World Trade Center in New York on television from her home in the state of Utah. It was recorded by a college student for a class project on 9-11 stories.

Date Collected: October, 2001

"I had just sent my son off to school and sometimes when I do that, I like to turn on the news and see what's going on in the world. I don't do that very often. I turned on the news and it was showing pictures of the towers at that time. Both towers had been burning; they believed that the airplanes had flown into the towers and it was a terrorist attack. I thought, "Wow! I don't believe this!" So, as I was watching, the first tower collapsed live. I just couldn't believe it was happening. And then I called my husband and told him what had happened. Then I went back to the television and yes, it did interrupt my day. I sat there and watched it because it was so unreal. I couldn't believe it was really happening, that those buildings would fall like that and that somebody could do that."

Folk Coll. 26, Box 1, Folder 4,
Fife Folklore Archives, Utah State University

The story below was told by a man who worked as a police officer at the Pentagon. It was recorded by a college student for a class project on 9-11 stories.

Date Collected: December, 2001

"I had to take the day off for my son because it affected him more than it affected me. My son is ten years old and they had to write about it [the 9/11 attack] in school. He wrote something that really touched me. I was asleep and my wife brought it to my attention. It said that the world is coming to an end and he's going to lose his mom and daddy at home because of what's been going on. He's thinking that there's going to be an attack at home. That really got my attention."

Folk Coll. 26, Box 1, Folder 1
Fife Folklore Archives, Utah State University

The story below is also told by a police officer at the Pentagon. It was recorded by a college student for a class project on 9-11 stories.

"I'm a police officer at the Pentagon, [and] part of the Emergency Services Tactical Unit …. [On] the morning of September 11, my initial duties were to go down to the health clinic …. There was a big commotion in the lobby. [I] went out to the lobby, watched the TV about the two aircraft hitting in New York. Upon seeing the second plane hit, I drove to Federal Office Building #2 …. I was getting out of the truck, telling one of the canine officers [a policeman who uses a dog] what I had just witnessed on TV. At that point, a plane streaked over our heads and sounded like a missile. The first thing I yelled was, "Incoming!" A second later was a sonic boom and breaking glass everywhere. I grabbed a medical bag and jumped back in the truck, went down toward the Pentagon Heliport area. One of my supervisors … [was] running into the building. It was my responsibility is to make sure that our people are okay, so I ran after him. And all of the sudden, we were in the middle of it."

Folk Coll. 26, Box 1, Folder 19
Fife Folklore Archives, Utah State University

第Ⅱ部
歌
——価値観の反映として

Part II
Songs and Singing

4章
仕事の歌――働く辛さと生きる喜び

Chapter 4
Work Songs: Expressing Hardship, Lifting Spirits

1 仕事の歌

　働く時に歌う歌や仕事に直接関係する歌を「ワークソング」といいます．古い歌は肉体を使って働く仕事に特徴的なもので，集団作業のタイミングを合わせたり身体の動きのリズムを保ったりするのに役立ちました．船乗り，カウボーイ，木こり，露天商，鉄道工夫など，さまざまな職種の人が自分たちの仕事の歌を持っていました．現代では動力が人力から機械力に変わったので肉体労働者の数が圧倒的に減り，仕事の歌も様変わりしました．働くときに歌う歌に代わり，人々は自分の仕事についての歌を作っています．英文で引用したのは，イギリスの医学生グループが創作した歌で「麻酔医の讃美歌」という題です．ワークソングは時代に合わせて生まれているのです．ワークソングを研究すると，人々が自分自身や現状をどう思っているか，自分にとっての仕事の意味をどう考えているかが見えてきます．ワークソングは娯楽であり，感情のはけ口であり，不満や抵抗の表現です．困難な労働に従事しながらも，気分を持ち直して幸福を感じるため一瞬の喜びを与えてくれるものでもあります．

INTRODUCTION

Work songs are songs that people sing to accompany work. Traditional work songs, which are no longer commonly found, helped accomplish hard, physical labor by coordinating movements of the body. They aided workers by timing the rhythm of the work correctly. Such **work songs were found among people who worked on boats along waterways, as well as among cowboys, loggers, vendors, and railroad workers**. They were tools for getting work done.

　The nature of work has changed over time. More people work in offices and with computers than in the past. Singing songs to coordinate physical labor is unnecessary in this modern environment. Instead, people may compose and sing songs about work. Doctors, for example, may upload songs they have written onto the Internet for other people to enjoy. The following verse is from a song called "The Anesthetists Hymn" and was written by a medical singing group (former British medical students) called the Amateur Transplants.

> Everybody wonders what anesthetists do
> while the patient is asleep.
> Everybody wonders what we do for three hours
> while that machine goes beep.

This song suggests that people don't understand the job of anesthesiologists. It is funny to people undergoing medical training and can be considered an example of **the evolution of the work song**.

Examining work songs of both the past and present offers insights into how people view themselves, their conditions, and their relation to work. Work songs help pass the time, express emotions, and voice protest. Importantly, singing songs can lift the spirits by bringing momentary joy or happiness into difficult situations.

2 受刑囚の歌

　受刑囚の歌は「チェイン・ギャング・ソング」とも呼ばれ，19世紀から20世紀にかけて懲役刑に服したアフリカ系アメリカ人（黒人）の歌をさします．かつてアメリカでは，受刑囚が強制的に重労働をさせられていました．労働環境はきわめて悪く，多くの人が服役中に死亡しました．刑務所の環境は改善されていきましたが，南部では1970年代まで受刑囚の強制労働は続きました．逃亡を防ぐために囚人たちは数人が足を鎖でつながれていて，労働中も鎖を引きずっていなければならなかったので，鎖でひとまとまりにされた集団をチェイン・ギャングとよび，こうした人々の歌を「チェイン・ギャング・ソング」というのです．

PRISON SONGS

Prison songs, or "chain-gang songs," are a type of work song sung primarily by African American prisoners between the late nineteenth and mid twentieth centuries. **Prisons in the southern United States used to force prisoners to work**. African American convicts and others were leased to private companies in order to earn money for the prison. Prisoners were forced to do hard labor such as logging, mining, or working on railroads. They also worked on prisons that functioned as large plantations. Prisoners picked cotton, harvested, and hoed fields. Conditions were terrible. The prisoners frequently were not properly fed or clothed, and they often died. Although prison conditions slowly improved over the course of the twentieth century, the practice of forcing prisoners to work continued up through the 1970s in the south.

刑務所での歌にはいくつか機能がありました。その一つは、作業のリズムやペースを整えることです。斧やツルハシを集団で振り上げたり振り下ろしたりする時、次に引用するような歌を歌ったのです。こうした刑務所の歌の多くは、コール・アンド・レスポンスのスタイルでできています。コール・アンド・レスポンスは黒人の歌に特徴的な歌唱スタイルで、リーダーがソロで１フレーズを歌うと、残りの人たちがソロの掛け声に応えるように次のフレーズを歌って返す、ソロとの掛け合いです。リーダーが歌う間にみんなは息をついで斧を振り上げ、自分が歌う時、声を出しながら息も吐き出して斧を振り下ろすのです。

．．

Prison work songs performed a number of functions. **One important function was to coordinate the physical movements of the men as they worked.** Prisoners worked in a group, and the rhythm of the song set the pace of the work. A group of men chopping wood together, for example, might swing their axes downward on one beat of a song they were singing, and upward on the second beat. It worked like this:

        [up]   [down]   [up]   [down]
You better watch my timber/ Let your hammer ring
        [up]   [down]   [up]   [down]
Cause there won't be no more jackin'/ Let your hammer ring

                              (Afro-American Work Songs, 1966)

The rhythm of the song coordinated the men's movements and set the speed of the work.

Many prison work songs were structured in **a solo/chorus, or call-and-response**, style. One person was the song leader. The other men sang the chorus or responded to the singer. The lead singer was important. He had to pace the song so that everyone could keep up with the work. If the leader sang too fast, the men would be unable to work the long hours. If the leader sang too slowly, the prisoners would be punished for not working hard enough. The lead singer also had to know many songs, and to improvise verses as needed.

　受刑囚は，さまざまな感情を歌に表現しました．以下，最初の引用では，刑務所に来なければならなくなったことを嘆く気持ちが表されていますし，その次に引用した歌詞では，刑務所の外の普通の生活に強く憧れているのがわかります．さらにその後二つ引用したように，刑務所で自分たちを監督する看守に対する反感，嫌悪をあからさまにするもの，労働させられて水ももらえないような待遇の酷さを訴えるものもあります（受刑者たちが歌いながら働いている様子は，インターネットで見ることができます：Folksongstreams.net "Afro-American Work Songs in the Texas Prison"）．

....

Prison work songs expressed a range of emotions. The song below was recorded in a prison on Texas in 1966. The singer **expresses regret** for his situation ("don't want to come to this place again") and ("makin' us wish we'd a stayed at home"). Note that the song follows the call and response style. After the lead singer sings his line, the rest of the group sings the chorus (Yeah, yeah, yeah, yeah) in response.

> Six long years I've been in the pen [prison]/ *Yeah, yeah, yeah, yeah*
> Don't want to come to this place again/ *Yeah, yeah, yeah, yeah*
>
> Captain and the boss is drivin' us on/ *Yeah, yeah, yeah, yeah*
> Makin' us wish we'd a-stayed at home/ *Yeah, yeah, yeah, yeah*

A different verse in the same song **expresses longing** for life outside the prison and a desire to settle down.

> Gonna settle down for the rest of my life/ *Yeah, yeah, yeah, yeah*
> Get myself a job and get myself a wife/ *Yeah, yeah, yeah, yeah*

Some prison songs were forms of protest. Prisoners subtly voiced complaints or even make fun of their overseers. In the lyrics below, the singer comments on the fact that the guard is not working.

> I see the captain sittin' in the shade/ *Yeah, yeah, yeah, yeah*
> He don't do nothin' but a he get paid/ *Yeah, yeah, yeah, yeah*
> (*Afro-American Work Songs* 1966)

Another example of protest is below. This song verse comments on the fact that the boy who brings water to the prisoners is late. The prisoners are thirsty and in the song they wonder whether he has drowned. By suggesting the water boy perhaps has drowned, the thirsty singers protest against how long it is taking to get some water.

> Did you hear 'bout that water boy gettin' drownded [drowned]
> Did you hear 'bout that water boy gettin' drownded
> In Mobile Bay, Lawdy, Mobile Bay? (Lomax 1997)

刑務所の歌の内容は確かに重いのですが，歌が受刑者たちの一時的な救いになっていたことは間違いないでしょう．服役囚の待遇改善に伴い，20世紀後半にはこれらの歌はその一次的な機能をほぼ失い，現場で歌われることはなくなりましたが，ブルースなど他の音楽ジャンルに源流として伝統を留めています．かつての刑務所での労働と歌の記録資料は，私たちが過去から学ぶために重要です．

....

Although lyrics to prison songs were often sad and regretful, **the act of singing was a way to uplift the spirits**, another important function of prison songs. Singing songs passed the time, made difficult work easier, eased the mind, and expressed deep emotions felt by the men. Singing made people feel better, at least temporarily.

Prison songs are no longer sung because **the context in which they were used has changed**. Prisons in the United States no longer force prisoners to work. As conditions for prisoners has slowly improved, **prison work songs are no longer needed or useful**. However, remnants of prison songs can be found in other kinds of music, such as the blues. Today, **historic recordings of old prison songs serve as important reminders of the injustices of the past and the resiliency of the people who survived**.

3 軍人の歌

兵士にも仕事の歌はあります．「ミリタリー・カデンス」と呼ばれます．兵士たちが合唱して呼びかけをするような歌で，足並みをそろえて行進するときに歌われます．有名な「ダックワース・チャント」はコール・アンド・レスポンスのスタイルをとり，全国の基地に何百というバリエーションがあるそうです．

MILITARY CADENCES

Another type of work song is **a military cadence**. Military cadences (or "calls") are songs or chants sung by people in the military. Like prison songs, military cadences function to coordinate movements of the body, and they are often sung in a call-and-response style. **Military cadences frequently are used when soldiers march together in step**. The soldiers must coordinate their movements exactly. Cadences are a singing tool to help the soldiers accomplish the marching.

The American military uses chants and calls to help soldiers march in time together

The most well-known military cadence is called the "Duckworth Chant." It is sung in a call-and-response style. The leader sings the first part of the line; the men respond in the second part of the line.

Sound off! / *1-2* / Sound off! / *3-4*
Cadence call / *1-2 ... 3-4!*

When soldiers sing this cadence, they march more easily. This cadence is found throughout the US military. It has hundreds of different variations.

ミリタリー・カデンスに圧倒的に多いテーマは家（ホーム）です．「ジョディ」という登場人物が出てきます．いつも家にいるジョディは，服務で家を留守にしている兵士の妻や恋人を奪ってしまうのです．歌詞には皮肉なユーモアや諦めが聞こえます．軍隊に属しながら家に帰りたいと熱望する兵士の本心を，ジョディという不道徳で自由な架空人物が具現化しています（ここで紹介した歌が聞けるサイトは，本書のホームページからリンクできます）．

....

One dominant theme of military cadences is home, represented by a stock character named "Jody." Instead of fighting like a soldier, **Jody stays at home and steals the soldiers' wives and girlfriends**. Jody makes the soldier think about home and what might be happening there. In the call below, Jody provides "company" for the soldier's girlfriend while the soldier is away, meaning that Jody is now the girlfriend's new lover.

> Your baby was lonely, as lonely could be / *Til Jody provided the company*
> Ain't it great to have a pal / *Who works so hard just to keep up morale*
> Sound off! / *1-2* / Sound off! / *3-4*
> Cadence count! / *1,2,3,4,1,2 ... 3,4!*

The lines "Ain't it great to have a pal/ Who works so hard just to keep up moral" are ironic. Jody is not a "pal," (meaning "friend"), but a threat. Below is another example of a Jody call.

> Ain't no use in callin' home/ *Jody's on your telephone.*   (Burns 2012: 79)

Richard Allen Burns (2012) suggests that Jody calls may be a form of protest. **They subtly express resentment against military authority and represent a desire to return home**.

ミリタリー・カデンスのもう一つの特徴は，性差別的な歌詞です．少し以前ま

で，軍隊は男性だけの組織でした．女性のいない軍隊では，男性中心主義や肉体的に強い男をめでる価値観があり，それは依然として根強く残っています．軍隊で歌われる歌詞では女性がしばしば物体として扱われ，たとえば女がレンガで男がレンガを積む職人だったりするのです．このような人格無視の扱いは，やはり女性がいなかった航海の現場，船乗りたちの歌にも見られる傾向です．肉体の強い男をよしとする価値観と並行し，暴力的な表象もミリタリー・カデンスには頻繁に使われます．性的表現と暴力表象が組み合わされるのも一つの特徴です．

....

Another dominant quality found in military cadences is sexism. Women are not traditionally part of military culture. **Military culture is hyper-masculine, meaning that traditional masculine qualities are over-emphasized.** Soldiers are expected to be tough, not to show emotion, to embrace violence, and to kill people if required. Homosexuality is despised, and likely to incite anger. Women frequently are viewed as sex objects. Similar themes can be found in the work songs of other organizations where women are not present, such as in the sea shanties of sailors and boatmen. As an example, the call below is a play on words. Women are "bricks" and the soldier is a bricklayer, or mason—an occupation that works with bricks.

Well I wish all the ladies/ were bricks in a pile
And I was a mason/ I'd lay 'em all in style.　　　　　(Trnka 1995: 233)

Some military cadences are graphically violent. These songs speak directly about shooting and killing people. Many calls conflate sex and violence, depicting violence as something that should be done for pleasure. Other cadences suggest that weapons bring soldiers the same happiness as women. The song below conflates sex and violence. It is found throughout the military:

This is my rifle/ this is my gun
This is for killing/ this is for fun.

あらゆるサブカルチャーがそうであるように，ミリタリー・カデンスも時代の流れとともに変化するでしょう．近年では女性も軍隊に加わるようになり，兵士の歌が今後どのように変化するかは興味深く観察していきたいところですね．

As with any subculture, American military culture has changed and evolved over time. Today there are many more women serving in the military than in the past. The military is less tolerant of graphic and obscene songs than it once was, although many such calls still circulate out of the earshot of authorities. The diversification of the military will influence what kinds of songs survive and which ones will pass into history.

4 子守の歌

赤ちゃんの世話は，昔は女性の仕事と決まっていて，女性も歌いながら働いたに違いないのですが，家庭内の仕事でありしかも女性の歌なので重要視されることなく，時代の流れとともにほとんどが失われてしまいました．そのために研究が進んでいません．アメリカでは，母親たちはいろいろな歌を子守唄（赤ちゃんを寝かしつける時の歌）代わりに使っていたという研究があります．

LULLABIES

Lullabies are songs that women traditionally sing to babies to make them fall asleep. Lullabies often are not considered as work songs because work songs typically are associated with the hard, physical labor done by men. Taking care of newborn babies is also exhausting, physical labor, but **the work songs that women sing as they accomplish domestic tasks have largely gone unnoticed or have been considered as unimportant**. Therefore, the study of American lullaby traditions is not well developed. American mothers may use any song they want to sing their babies to sleep; Bess Lomax Hawes (1974) for example, recalled that she used a church hymn as a lullaby. The tradition of singing lullabies is world-wide and the origins of many American lullabies likely are rooted in Europe.

子守唄も身体のリズムに合わせて歌われ，赤ちゃんと母親の両方を静める役目を果たします．ワーナーの研究によれば，曲調は哀愁を帯びている場合が多いそうです．歌詞もよく読むと，どきっとしたりぞっとしたりするような内容が少な

くありません。死のイメージもよく出てくるのです。引用の歌詞を見てください。

....

Like the prison songs and military cadences discussed above, **lullabies help accomplish work because they are associated with rhythms of the body. The songs soothe both the baby and the singer**. Lullabies accompany particular body rhythms such as rocking, walking, or swaying. The tunes of lullabies also are designed to calm both the baby and the mother or caregiver. Maria Warner (1998) notes that the mood is melancholy. The song is in a minor key, a tonality that evokes feelings of sadness or pathos.

Mothers around the world sing lullabies to soothe children to sleep

In contrast to the restful nature of the tune and lulling body rhythms, **the lyrics to many lullabies evoke upsetting or distressing imagery**. The most well-known lullaby in the United States is called "Rock-a-Bye Baby." The words to this song are below.【子守歌1】

> Rock a bye baby/in the treetop
> When the wind blows/the cradle will rock
> When the bough breaks/the cradle will fall
> And down will come baby/cradle and all.

This lullaby describes a baby rocking gently to sleep in the branch of a tree. At the end of the song, the tree branch breaks, and the baby falls out of the tree, presumably to its death. **Images of death are quite common in lullabies**. The lullaby below also is commonly sung in the US and contains upsetting imagery and themes of death.

> 【子守歌2】 *"All the Pretty Little Horses"*
> Hush-a-bye, don't you cry/ go to sleep you little baby
> When you wake you shall have/ all the pretty little horses
> Blacks and bays, dapples and grays/ coach and six-a little horses
> Hush-a-bye, don't you cry/ go to sleep you little baby
> Way down yonder in the meadow/ lays a poor little lambie

The birds and the butterflies/ peckin' out his eyes
The poor little thing cries "Mammy."

In this song, the singer promises the baby beautiful horses if the baby goes to sleep. By the end of the song, however, the baby is alone in a meadow and insects have pecked out his eyes.

　子守唄に，なぜこうした歌詞がつくのでしょうか．赤ん坊を世話する母親の不安を表すとか，死を持ち出すことで厄払いしているのだとか，説は複数あります．子守りという重労働に耐えかねた母親の抵抗の表れとも聞くことができます．最後に引用したとても有名な子守唄では，次々に示されるプレゼントがどれも見かけ倒しの価値のないものだとわかるのですが，最後には，歌いかけられている赤ちゃんには揺るぎない価値があるとされて，赤ちゃんが唯一の大事なものだという特別な気持ちや希望が伝わってきます．

....

Why do lullabies contain such images? This is a difficult question to answer. Some scholars suggest that themes of death represent **the mother's resentments or anxieties** about the difficulties of having to take care of a newborn. Others, such as Maria Warner (1998), have suggested that evoking death in lullabies is a way of warding it off, somewhat like **a blessing disguised as a curse**. Such themes may also express a mother's grief or be a way of acknowledging that the world is filled with danger for the newborn. **The words may also be a form of protest** against the exhaustion a mother feels from having to take care of a newborn without the baby actually understanding it.

　Not all American lullabies evoke disquieting images. The song below, for example, retains the melancholy tone typical of American lullabies but promises the baby riches.

【子守歌 3】 *"Hush Little Baby"*
Hush little baby/don't say a word
Momma's gonna buy you a mockingbird
If that mockingbird don't sing
Momma's gonna buy you a diamond ring

If that diamond bring turns brass
Momma's gonna buy you a looking glass
If that looking glass gets broke
Mamma's gonna buy you a billygoat
If that billygoat won't pull
Momma's gonna buy you a cart and bull.
If that cart and bull turn over
Momma's gonna buy you a dog named Rover.
If that dog named Rover won't bark
Momma's gonna buy you a horse and cart.
If that horse and cart fall down
You'll still be the sweetest little baby in town.

This song promises the baby riches, but also acknowledges that riches are often not what they appear. A diamond ring, for example, might turn brass (that is, not be made of gold), a mirror might break, and useful farm animals such as goats and bulls might fail. This lullaby is hopeful, however, since the message is that **no matter what becomes of material things, the baby is still sweet and loveable**.

5 考 察

　仕事の歌は，人間と仕事との関係についてさまざまなことを教えてくれます．まず，歌は身体を規則的に動かしてする仕事には欠かせない道具でした．そして，歌詞はあらゆるレベルの感情を表現しています．多くの場合そうした感情表現は，苦しみや悲しみや悔しさの訴えですが，一方で，歌が人に活力を与えてもくれました．このような歌の機能は，厳しい肉体労働や軍隊での労働現場における歌にもあてはまるし，子守唄のような家庭内労働の歌にもあてはまります．人はいつも，いろいろなことを感じ自分を励ましつつ，一生懸命働いてきたのですね．

DISCUSSION

Work songs offer insights into relationships between people and work. First, **work songs are tools** that help people coordinate movements of the body with the task at hand. Elements of rhythm such as the beat, meter, and tempo help determine the pace of work, when to move, and in what order. Body and voice join together in an intricate web of interrelationship. Second, the lyrics to **work songs express a range of emotions**. Many work songs express feelings of sadness, hardship, homesickness, or resignation. Work songs may also be subversive, allowing workers to protest their conditions in veiled ways. Yet while many songs are sad or nostalgic, **singing songs can uplift the spirit**. People sing at work to move work along, pass the time, ease their burden, and forget their cares. While the song may be sad, singing can even bring pleasure or happiness to the worker. These functions are also true for lullabies. Lullabies join bodily movement and voice together when a mother rocks her baby, and lullabies express a range of emotions, from sadness to joy.

6　演　習

日本にも仕事の歌はありますね．以下の分類で探し，特徴を探ってみましょう．
(1) 身体を使って働き，リズムやペースを合わせるのに役立つ歌
(2) 虐げられた環境で働く人々が，苦しみや抵抗，喜びや望みを歌詞ににじませている歌
(3) 軍隊のように規律に厳しい場所で働く人々が，自ら作って集団で歌う歌
(4) 日本の子守唄のうち，子守として雇われていた人々（多くは貧しい家庭の少年少女）が作って歌ったと思われる子守唄

....

ACTIVE LEARNING

There are many types of work songs in Japan. Collect and analyze songs according to the categories below.

Songs by people who work in heavy physical labor, and which are sung to keep the pace and rhythm of the work;

Songs that express feelings of bitterness or protest, and songs that might function to uplift the spirit of people who feel downhearted;

Songs that are made and sung by groups of people who work in strictly ruled organizations, such as the military;

Japanese traditional lullabies, made and sung mainly by young nurses from poor families who are hired by affluent families.

5章
ヒーロー・バラッド──本音の価値観

Chapter 5
American Hero Ballads: What Do People Value?

1 ブリテン島周辺地域のバラッドとその広がり

　「バラッド」とは，物語を楽曲に合わせて歌う芸能です．ブリテン島周辺地域に12世紀頃発生したといわれ，古くは口承されて今に伝わります．17,18世紀には新しい歌が楽譜とともに印刷されて広まり「ブロードサイド・バラッド」と呼ばれました．1曲売りの楽譜ですが美しい挿絵のある表紙をつけたものも多く，データベースで見ることができます．そうして広まった歌は，移民とともに大西洋を渡って，アメリカ大陸へ伝わりました．アイルランドやスコットランドの人々は，北米のアパラチア地方に多く移民したので，合衆国南部の北東にあたる広い地域には伝統的なバラッドがたくさん残っています．とはいえバラッドは全米各地にあり，ヒスパニック系の人々が多いテキサスとメキシコの国境付近ではスペイン語のバラッドが数多くあります．

INTRODUCTION

A ballad is a song that tells a story, and hero ballads tell stories about heroes. Ballads are a European song form that date to about the twelfth century. **They primarily stem from the British Isles**, which is made up of countries such as Ireland, Scotland, and England. **Some traditional ballads are passed down orally**, meaning that people learned them from others, rather than in school or from books. Other ballads, called **broadside ballads, are printed and circulated on paper**, and were popular in England between the seventeenth and nineteenth centuries.

　Ballads can be found in the United States because many people from Ireland, Scotland, and England immigrated to the US in the eighteenth and nineteenth centuries, bringing ballads and ballad-composing traditions with them. Irish and Scottish people settled in Appalachia, a region that stretches from the northern part of southern states such as Mississippi, Alabama, and Georgia through western Pennsylvania. This region is famous for its knowledge of old ballads, since so many settlers there came from the British Isles. However, ballads and ballad traditions can be found throughout the United States, including in Texas among cowboys, in the north among shipworkers and riverboatsmen, and among Spanish-speaking people along the Texas/Mexico borderlands.

ヒーロー・バラッド

　バラッドは，大事な出来事を物語にして記憶・記録していくのに役立ちました．現代の新聞やニュースレポートのように，人々に事件を伝えました．一方，昔のバラッドが今でも愛されているわけは，歌が文化の中で重要なことを伝えているからです．たとえばこの章で扱うヒーロー・バラッドには，ヒーローとして愛される人にはどういう要素があるのかというアメリカ人の価値観を読み取ることができます．権力や圧力への抵抗心，強靭さと狡猾さ，大胆さと勇気，そして意外にも，社会的な弱者であること．またヒーロー・バラッドは，労働者と資本家側の対立や法律に逆らわざるを得ない人々の緊張などといった，現代に通ずる問題にも歌い及んでいるのです．

....

　As noted above, the main purpose of ballads is to tell a story, and so **ballads recount important events**. Some scholars even characterize ballads as being similar to newspapers. Before people had access to newspapers and the mass media, people sometimes spread news about events by composing and singing ballads. **The songs circulated quickly and people learned about the events because they had heard the ballad, much like people get their news from newspapers today**.

　Some ballads remain popular today even though they recount events of long ago. This is because they still speak to **issues or ideas that remain important to American culture**. Hero ballads, for example, reveal qualities that Americans still think are important for heroes. These include **defiance against authority, strength, cunning, daring, or extreme bravery**, and surprisingly, **a position of weakness**. Hero ballads also speak to broader themes that still influence American life, such as **tensions between labor and management and between law and disobedience**.

2 ジョン・ヘンリーの歌

　アメリカで一番有名なヒーロー・バラッドは「ジョン・ヘンリー」です．インターネットでもいろいろなパフォーマンスでこの歌を聞くことができます．ジョン・ヘンリーは19世紀に実在したアメリカの黒人で，鑿（のみ）と重いハンマーを使って岩に穴を開ける重労働に従事していました．こうした仕事をする人を，「スチール・ドライバー」と呼び，ジョン・ヘンリーは強靱（きょうじん）で有能なスチール・ドライバーだったのです．彼は鉄道会社に雇われてトンネルを掘っていたのですが，蒸気ドリルが発明され，この機械とジョン・ヘンリーのどちらが速く深く穴を掘れるか競争するということになりました．誇り高く頑強なジョン・ヘンリーは見事蒸気ドリルに勝つのですが，過労で心臓が止まり，死んでしまいます．

....

HERO BALLADS: JOHN HENRY

The most well-known hero ballad in the United States is called *John Henry*. **John Henry is the name of an African American man who worked driving steel on the railroads as they were being built during the nineteenth century.** A "steel driver" drives holes into rock by hitting metal spikes with a large, heavy hammer. John Henry supposedly was the best steel driver around and was admired by everyone for his great strength. According to the ballad, one day someone from the railroad company came to the workers with a steam drill, boasting that the machine could drive steel better than any of the workers. A steam drill is powered by steam and drills holes mechanically. John Henry, who was a proud man, challenged the machine to a competition to see which one of them could accomplish the most work. The contest was exciting, pitting man against machine. John Henry won the contest, but his heart stopped from the exertion, and he died.

John Henry with hammer

危険な鉄道工事

　日本でもそうでしたが，19世紀のアメリカでも，国力を増強させるのに鉄道建設は大事な役目を果たしました．その建設労働者に黒人がたくさん雇われたの

です．またジャガイモの飢饉で苦しみアメリカに移民したアイルランド人も，鉄道建設を支えました．刑務所に入れられた囚人たちも，こうした過酷な重労働の現場で強制労働をさせられたのでした．貧しく，教育も十分には受けられず，社会的に弱い立場にあるこうした人々を鉄道会社は利用して，奴隷のように働かせつつ危険な鉄道建設を推し進めました．ジョン・ヘンリーのバラッドで彼が掘っていたと歌われているビックベンド・トンネルは，困難をきわめた危険な現場として知られています．人々は，「ジョン」というどこにでもいる名前の労働者をヒーローとし，その最期を歌語りすることで，理不尽な鉄道会社のやり方を表現したのですね．ジョン・ヘンリーは，この世に誕生するなり次のように予告したと歌詞にあります．「ハンマーが僕の死を呼んでくる」．

....

The building of the railroads is an important part of American history. Railroads were built throughout the nineteenth century and into the twentieth. John Henry worked for the Chesapeake and Ohio railroad company, called the "C&O" for short, which was founded in 1869. Its railroad lines reached from Virginia to Ohio. An important part of its business was transporting coal from coal mining areas such as West Virginia to commercial hubs in Ohio. **After the American Civil War (see discussion below), which ended in 1865, the C&O and other railroads hired freed African American slaves as workers**. They also hired many Irish immigrants, who came to the United States in order to flee poverty and famine in Ireland. Some people think John Henry might have been a freed slave. It also is possible that John Henry was a convict who had been leased by a prison to do railroad work (see Chapter 4).

Railroad companies notoriously exploited their workers. The freed blacks, Irish, and others who worked on the railroads were mostly poor, uneducated, and had little political power. **Conditions were terrible. Workers were poorly paid and the work itself was dangerous**. Thousands of people died from cave-ins, dust inhalation, and exhaustion. Convicts who were sentenced to work on the railroads could expect to live about three years; about ten percent died within four months. Tradition has it that John Henry was working on a tunnel called the "Big Bend Tunnel" in West Virginia when he challenged the steam drill to a contest, although historians disagree about whether or not this is correct. The Big Bend Tunnel was very difficult to build; it took 1000 men three years to finish and many people died working on it. **Whether or not the Big Bend Tunnel is actually the tunnel John Henry worked on, it represents the exploitative nature of the railroad industry and the terrible conditions of railroad workers**. This association of death and railroad work is noted in the verse below. John Henry is a baby, and he makes a prophetic statement about his own future death as a railroad worker.

> John Henry was a little baby/ Sitting on his papa's knee
> He picked up a hammer and little piece of steel
> Said "Hammer's gonna be the death of me, Lord, Lord
> Hammer's gonna be the death of me."

ジョン・ヘンリー・バラッドのテーマ

　人間と機械の微妙な関係は，ジョン・ヘンリー・バラッドのテーマの一つです．アメリカでは1820年から70年にわたり産業革命が起こり，仕事の多くが人の手から機械に移っていきました．ジョン・ヘンリーは機械との勝負を持ちかけられて，プライドを持って戦いました．彼の勝利は，機械に仕事を奪われて行く人々が機械に勝ちたいという願いを表していますし，彼の死は世の中が変化していく現実を表しています．歌詞にそのことを読み取りましょう．機械に肩入れする現場監督が，ジョン・ヘンリーがハンマーを振るう音に怯える様子も，アメリカに独特のユーモアと誇張を使って見事に表現されています．

∙∙

　One main theme of the ballad "John Henry" is the ambivalent relationship between men and machines. John Henry is a powerful, strong man and a hard worker. He is a leader, the best steel driver, and admired by other men. However, his existence is threatened by the steam drill, which claims to be able to accomplish more work, and presumably for cheaper. **This tension between manual labor and mechanized machine characterizes the Industrial Age, the period between 1820 and 1870 when production in the United States came to be dominated by machines and factories, rather than by hand**. The railroads were essential to the Industrial Age because they expanded transportation and increased trade. In the verses below, John Henry's boss, the "captain," brags that his steam drill machine is going to "whop that steel on down," meaning that it can hammer steel more effectively than a worker.

> The captain said to John Henry/ "Gonna bring that steam drill 'round
> Gonna bring that steam drill out on the job
> Gonna whop that steel on down, Lord, Lord
> Gonna whop that steel on down."

The captain essentially is saying that he doesn't need his workers anymore. He now has a new mechanized invention that can do the job.
John Henry is a strong and proud man who defends his rights as a worker. He illustrates heroic qualities of grit, determination, and standing up for himself.

> John Henry told his captain/ "A man ain't nothing but a man
> But before I let your steam drill beat me down
> I'd die with a hammer in my hand, Lord, Lord
> I'd die with a hammer in my hand."

John Henry acknowledges that he is a man and not a machine, but says that he'd rather die than be beat by a machine. He challenges the machine to a race to prove his worth.

As the competition ensues, it becomes clear that John Henry is winning. In fact, John Henry works so hard and drills so deep the Captain is afraid that the tunnel they are working on might cave in.

> John Henry's captain said to him
> "I believe these mountains are caving in."
> John Henry said to his captain: "Oh, Lord!"
> "That's my hammer you hear in the wind."

John Henry tells the captain the tunnel is not caving in, but it is the sound of wind from his hammer. In addition to grit and determination, **Americans admire swagger**; here, John Henry is bragging to his captain about how quickly he can work.

　労働者と会社（資本家側）との緊張も，ジョン・ヘンリー・バラッドの重要なテーマです．ジョン・ヘンリーのように，仲間には一目置かれているものの社会

的に差別されていたり負ける立場にある人のことを「アンダードッグ」といいます．アメリカ人は，アンダードッグを応援するのが好きなのです．アンダードッグは，アメリカン・ヒーローの典型です．日本でも「判官びいき」といって，兄の源頼朝に追い詰められた弱い立場の義経（源九郎義経判官）を応援する気持ちに由来する言葉がありますね．義経と弁慶の話は，能や歌舞伎，義太夫やおとぎ話とさまざまに再創作され伝えられてきていますが，同様に，ジョン・ヘンリーについてもバラッドだけではなく三文小説やディズニーをはじめとする数々の映画が創作され，1996年には切手の図柄にもなりました．

....

A final important theme in the ballad about John Henry is the tension between workers and corporations. John Henry is a hero, but also an underdog. An underdog is a person or character who is admired but has little status and is less powerful than his opponents. Americans like to root for underdogs, but they are expected to lose. John Henry is strong and prideful, but he has little social or political power, and is forced to work for a powerful and uncaring corporation. Incredibly, John Henry beats the steam drill in a demonstration of physical prowess, but he dies in the end because he has worked too hard.

> Now the man that invented the steam drill/ Thought he was mighty fine
> But John Henry made fifteen feet
> The steam drill only made nine, Lord, Lord
> The steam drill only made nine.

> John Henry hammered in the mountains/ His hammer was striking fire
> But he worked so hard, he broke his poor heart
> He laid down his hammer and he died, Lord, Lord
> He laid down his hammer and he died.

Although the song "John Henry" recounts events that happened in the nineteenth century, the ballad remains important to Americans. **John Henry is a typical American hero**. He is strong, masculine, and stands up for himself against powerful corporate interests, such as the railroad. **He is also an underdog**, a politically powerless worker whose only strength is physical. He faces and triumphs over incredible odds, but his victory over the steam drill ultimately costs him his life. **This tension between men and machines and between workers and corporations continued to resonate with American audiences throughout the twentieth century**. John Henry was made into a novel in 1934 by author Roark Bradford, and several other novels about John Henry have been published as well. Walt Disney has made several animated short films about John Henry. There is a festival in West Virginia, where the event supposedly took place, called "John Henry Days," and in 1996 the United States postal service issued a commemorative stamp with John Henry's picture on it illustrating his status as national folk hero. Perhaps most appropriately, there even is a comic book hero named "Steel" that is based on John Henry.

3 アウトロー，ジェシー・ジェイムズのバラッド

　無法者（犯罪者）たちもまた，ヒーローとしてバラッドに歌われました．無法者にもアンダードッグと同じヒーローの性質がそなわっています．すなわち，社会的には弱い立場にありながら，権力に大胆に歯向うところです．無法者を歌ったものを，アウトロー・バラッドといいます．19世紀から今日まで歌われ，人気を保っているのが，ジェシー・ジェイムズのバラッドです．ジェシーは，実際には人殺しもする危険な盗賊でしたが，歌詞ではフィクション化されており，金持ちからうばった金を貧しい人に与えたとあります．経済的強者や権力に痛手を負わせるジェシーは，死後，神話的な西部のヒーローとなったのでした．

OUTLAW BALLADS: THE BALLAD OF JESSE JAMES
Another type of hero ballad is the outlaw ballad. An outlaw ballad is a ballad about a criminal or fugitive who becomes a hero. **Outlaws become folk heroes when they display similar characteristics to an underdog: that is, despite their position of weakness, they defy authority and are unusually brave or daring**. Like underdogs, outlaw-heroes often lose in the end. Outlaw heroes are also violent figures, but their violence usually is justified in the name of some presumably larger cause or moral attitude.

　One outlaw ballad that has remained popular over time is the *Ballad of Jesse James*. Jesse James was a bank robber and murderer who lived between 1847–1883. Tradition says that Jesse James was a robber who stole from the rich and gave to the poor, but this is not true. The reality is that Jesse James was a dangerous man who stole money for his own gain. However, during his lifetime he became well known for his bold exploits and defiance of authority, and he was both feared and admired by the public. **After his death, James was immortalized in a ballad, and his story has entered the mythology associated with the American West** (see below).

Portrait of Jesse James

　ジェシー・ジェイムズは 1847 年にミズーリ州に生まれ，奴隷制度の存続をめぐって国内を二分した南北戦争（1861-1865）で，南軍兵士として戦いました．彼はここで殺人や略奪を覚え，戦後は兄のフランクとともに凶悪な強盗集団を組織しました．どんな犯罪を犯したかは，英文に書いてありますよ．

Jesse James was born in the state of Missouri in 1847. He fought as a guerilla soldier on the Confederate side during the American Civil War. The Civil War, which occurred between 1861-1865, was a brutal war fought primarily over the issue of slavery. It pitted the northern states against the southern ones. The southern states, known as "Confederates," were pro-slavery and wanted to secede from the US. The northern states, known as the "Union," wanted to abolish slavery and keep the country from splitting apart. Many atrocities were committed on both sides, and it was during the Civil War that Jesse James learned to kill.

　After the Civil War, Jesse James and his brother Frank turned to a life of crime. They mainly stole money by robbing banks, trains, and stagecoaches in states such as Iowa, Texas, Kansas, and West Virginia, and they often killed people during their robberies. The two brothers, who eventually formed the James-Younger gang, became notorious for their daring and outrageous exploits. For example, they derailed a train in Iowa, meaning they forced a train off of its tracks in order to rob it. They also raided a fair in Kansas in front of a large crowd. Additionally, the James brothers are associated with the first daylight robbery in US history, which occurred in 1866 and in which $57,000.00 was taken, although historians disagree about whether or not they were really involved.

人々の受け止め方を表現するバラッド

　バラッドは歴史的な事件について歌っていますが，事実ではなくその事件を人々がどう受け止めたかを表現しています．次に引用した歌詞を丁寧に読んでみましょう．ジェシーは，苦しむ者に同情を惜しまないヒーローとして描かれています．そうした描写によって，彼はアウトロー・ヒーローの枠（フレーム）に収まることになりました．バラッドは歴史の記録ともいえる一方で，作詞家がより面白い話にしようとしたり，自らの安全を守るために事実を曲げて書いている部分も少なからずあることを忘れてはなりません．

．．．

Although ballads record historical events, they are not necessarily historically accurate. Rather, they reflect the public's perception of events. For example, some verses of the *Ballad of Jesse James* suggest that Jesse James had a kind heart, was intelligent, and cared about people.

> Jesse James was a lad that killed many a man
> He robbed the Danville train
> He stole from the rich and he gave to the poor
> He'd a hand, a heart, and a brain.

In this verse, James is set up as a figure who cares about the poor, because he "stole from the rich and he gave to the poor." In the example below, James is portrayed as a "friend to the poor" and as a person who couldn't bear to see another person in pain.

> Jesse was a man, a friend to the poor
> He couldn't see a brother suffer pain
> And with his brother Frank he robbed the Springfield bank
> And he stopped the Glendale train.

Setting up Jesse James as someone who cares about others allows the audience to admire James's exploits and frames him as an outlaw-hero. His supposed kind heart and the idea that he stole from the rich and gave to the poor (although he did not) provides a moral justification for stealing money and killing people, even if it is not supported by historical evidence.

The verses above also commemorate James's deeds. **Memorializing history is an important function of ballads**, and this is why they are sometimes compared to newspapers. For example, the line "He robbed the Danville train" refers to a train that James robbed, although scholars debate whether "Danville" refers to Danville, Kentucky or is a euphemism for another location. **Sometimes ballad composers changed some of the details of the story to make it more compelling or to protect themselves**. This is why ballads are historical but not entirely accurate. The line "And with his brother Frank, he robbed the Springfield bank" commemorates robberies committed by the James' brothers.

アウトロー・ヒーローの条件

　ジェシーは，ロバート・フォードという自分の手下に殺害されました．フォードは身代金目当てに親分を裏切ったのです．この事実は，ジェシー・ジェイムズがアウトロー・ヒーローになる重要な要素です．敵に負けて殺されたのではないため彼の強さは不滅となり，裏切り者ロバート・フォードを悪とすればジェシー・ジェイムズは正義の側に回るからです．12章に詳しく述べるように，アメリカ西部（歴史的には，中西部を含む）は法的秩序がない暴力的な場所，自分の力に頼って生きなければならない場所として，アメリカ文化の中でロマンチックに脚色されていきました．ジェシー・ジェイムズは，その西部を代表するヒーローの代表です．名だたるミュージシャンたちがジェシーのバラッドをカバーし，2016年までに41本ものジェシー・ジェイムズの映画が作られています．

．．

Jesse James was shot in the head by a man named Robert Ford, who was a member of James's own gang. Ford killed James on April 03, 1883, in order to collect reward money. Jesse James was 34 years old. This act is also commemorated in the ballad.

> Then on a Saturday night, Jesse was at home
> Just talking with his family brave
> When Robert Ford came along like a thief in the night
> And laid poor Jesse in his grave.

Now, the people held their breath when they heard of Jesse's death
They wondered how he came to die
It was one of his own gang called little Robert Ford
And he shot Jesse James on the sly.

The fact that Jesse James was killed by one of his own gang also is part of why he became a folk hero. **Folk heroes often experience betrayal by people they know**. In the ballad, Ford is considered to be a traitor and a coward. The fact that Ford was a member of James's own gang fits into a larger cultural pattern of folk heroism and helped propel Jesse James into the status of folk hero.

The story of Jesse James has become part of the mythology of the American West. The "West" in the United States loosely refers to the expansive western region of the United States (see Chapter 12). Historically this region was sparsely populated, with vast amounts of land between towns and cities. Law and order were not well established, particularly during the nineteenth century, and so **the "West" is associated with lawlessness, danger, and violence**. Today, the American public imagines the West as a place where people carved out a living on their own, and where individualism and freedom were paramount. **The James-Younger gang looted areas in parts of the Old West, and so their exploits of recklessness, defiance, boldness, violence, and disregard for authority fit neatly into romantic ideas about the West**. It is perhaps for these reasons that the *Ballad of Jesse James* has been recorded by many famous artists, including Woody Guthrie, Pete Seeger, the Pogues, Van Morrison, and many others. Additionally, the story of Jesse James has been told in more than 41 films, a testimony to the enduring popularity of this outlaw-hero in American culture.

4 考　察

　ヒーロー物語を歌うバラッドには，人々の価値観や道徳観，美徳観が表れます．弱い立場の人間が活躍するのを喜び，特に権力に対する抵抗を喝采します．ジョン・ヘンリーのように人種や貧困による差別を受けた者，ジェシー・ジェイムズのように時代に翻弄され犯罪者となった者．バラッドの中のジョン・ヘンリーは，肉体労働者の職場を奪う機械文明の圧力に抵抗し，ジェシー・ジェイムズは民衆

を守らないで強者の味方となっている警察権力に楯突きました．それが事実でなかったとしても，歌詞に表現される抵抗心を人々は賞賛するのです．現在でも，ヒーロー・バラッドの伝統は日々新たに創造されつつあります．たとえば，「ナルココリード」と呼ばれる，麻薬密売人をヒーローとするスペイン語のバラッドが，アメリカのラジオで人気になっています．メキシコとの国境地帯が舞台です．これについては，ウェブで詳しくみてくださいね．

....

DISCUSSION
Ballads are songs that tell a story, and ballads about heroes that have endured through time reveal important qualities and values. First, Americans like to root for underdogs. Underdogs are heroes who are in a position of lesser power against their opponent. **People are glad when a weaker hero wins, because it upsets the status quo**. Second, as underdogs, **American heroes tend to defy authority**. John Henry stood up against a powerful corporation, while Jesse James rebelled against established law and order. Finally, **American heroes embody moral virtue in some way**. John Henry was virtuous because he refused to be beaten by a machine; by winning the competition against the steam drill, he stood up for the rights of workers everywhere. The real Jesse James was not morally virtuous. He was a notorious outlaw who committed robberies, killed people, and defied authorities. However, because the public admired him for his daring, bravado and rebelliousness, which are other qualities ascribed to American folk heroes, he is given the virtuous qualities of generosity and kindness toward the poor in the ballad. **This tradition of celebrating outlaw heroes in ballads continues even today** with new ballads that celebrate modern outlaws, such as drug-runners. These Spanish-language ballads, called *narcocorridos*, even have become popular on the radio. Like other ballads, they report events, and commemorate the exploits of people involved in the drug trade. They are **a modern form of outlaw hero ballads** and can be placed alongside the older ones **to illustrate the continued importance of these songs**.

5　演　習

(1) 新しい歌で，物語を伝えるものを知っていますか．「新しい」とは，英語であれば作詞家のわかる歌，日本語であれば明治時代以降にできた歌，を目安としてください．
(2) その歌は，歴史的事件や事実をもとにしていますか，それとも架空の物語の歌でしょうか．
(3) 人間，生活，社会などを考える上で示唆的なテーマや問題点を，その歌から読み取り話し合ってください．
(4) どの人の立場でその歌は作られ，どのような人々の思いや価値観を代弁していると考えますか．そう考えた理由も含めて説明してください．
(5) あなたが普段楽しんでいるような現代の歌についても，(1)から(4)の質問を考えてみましょう．現代の歌は，物語歌（バラッド）が多いと思いますか，それとも感情や印象的な描写を中心にしていると思いますか．

ACTIVE LEARNING

Can you think of an example of a modern song that tells a story?
Is the story based on historical events or invented?
What overarching themes or issues emerge?
What perspective or point of view does the song represent?
Do modern songs usually tell stories or do they evoke feelings and images?

6章
アメリカ人の愛唱歌——生活に大事なこと

Chapter 6
Best-Known Songs: What Is Important in Life?

1 国籍で愛唱歌は決まらない

　この章では，多数のアメリカ人が知っていていっしょに歌うような歌を扱います．でも実際は，アメリカ人なら誰でも知っている歌というのはないでしょう．アメリカの国土は広大である上に，移民を積極的に受け入れて国力を増してきたという歴史的背景から，日本に比べてはるかに多様な人々が住んでいるからです．人々が愛する歌というのは，国籍（シティズンシップ）や国民としての自覚（ナショナル・アイデンティティ）で決まるものではありません．むしろ，その人の暮らす地域，民族性，宗教，年齢などといった多様な要素に左右されます．また，広く知られ人々がともに歌いたくなる歌は，何かしら役に立つ性質を持っています．そのことを見ていきましょう．

INTRODUCTION

This chapter is about the songs that Americans may know and sing together in groups. As noted throughout this book, the United States is a very large and diverse country. Although Americans sing songs, there are probably no songs that all Americans know. **The songs most people know and sing likely are associated more with other factors than nationality, such as the region in which people live, ethnicity, religion, age, or some other identity factor**. Therefore, while the songs discussed below are widespread, it is important to remember that they only represent a tiny fraction of what people sing, and that the selection inevitably does not represent many groups of people or singing contexts.

　Group singing in the US occurs on particular occasions. People may sing to themselves individually any time they choose, but singing together with other people occurs at specific times and in specific places. **Many best-known songs are functional** (see Chapter 4). **That is, rather than having a symbolic meaning, they are used to mark events, create group cohesiveness, to entertain, or for some other purpose.**

2 お祝いの歌，祭日の歌

「ハッピー・バースディ」の歌はみなさんもご存知ですよね．家族やお友達が，あなたのために歌ってくれたら嬉しいですね．こうした歌は，お祝いを特別なものにする役目を果たします．ケーキに歳の数だけロウソクを立てて，揺れる灯火のもとでみんなは「ハッピー・バースディ」を歌ってあなたの幸せを祈ってくれます．それからあなたがロウソクの火を一度に吹き消すことができたなら，みんなの祈りが通じて，あなたはまた一年幸せでいられるでしょう．

....

SONGS FOR CELEBRATIONS AND HOLIDAYS

Some of the best-known songs in the United States are sung only at certain times of the year, such as birthday or holidays. **Such songs serve the important purpose of marking out an event as special**. One special occasion that people sing is on birthdays. Birthdays commonly are celebrated with a cake. People place lighted candles on the cake, with each candle representing one year of age. (However, after a certain age, people stop putting on candles, since there is no room left on the cake!) After the candles on the cake are lit, people sing the "Happy Birthday" song, which goes like this:

    Happy birthday to you/ Happy birthday to you
    Happy birthday dear ___ (insert name of person having birthday)
    Happy birthday to you.

Singing "Happy Birthday to You"

Singing the birthday song is the most important way of wishing someone happy birthday (see Chapter 13). After the song is over, the "birthday person" blows out all of the candles on the cake and makes a wish. If he or she blows out all of the candles in one breath, the wish supposedly comes true.

祭日にも人々は歌いますね．クリスマスはその代表でしょうか．クリスマスは，救世主イエスの生誕を祝うキリスト教徒のお祭りですが，同時に，買い物をしたりご馳走を食べたりして家族や友人と冬を楽しく過ごす，非宗教的な休暇の期間でもあります．アメリカ人のなかにはキリスト教徒でない人が多数いて，クリスマスをそれぞれの宗教や文化に沿った冬の祭りとして祝います．

....

Holidays are another time that people sing songs. Many people sing songs at Christmas, and there are a lot of very well-known songs (called "carols") associated with this holiday. **Christmas is both a religious and secular holiday**. It is a religious holiday because it celebrates the birth of Christ, the founder of Christianity. It is a secular holiday because it is a time for shopping, exchanging gifts, and being together with family and friends to celebrate the cold winter weather. **It is important to remember that not all Americans are Christians** (there are many Jews, Muslims, Hindus, Buddhists, atheists, neo-pagans, and other religions in the United States) and members of these religions may not celebrate Christmas. Conversely, **people who are not religious or who practice other religions may celebrate Christmas since Christmas is not just a religious holiday but also a seasonal, winter celebration**.

クリスマスキャロル

　クリスマスキャロルは，冬の休暇がきた喜びや平安の気持ちをわき起こします．何人かのグループで家々の玄関先に立ち，クリスマスキャロルを歌う習慣を「キャロリング」といいます．自分の家の前に歌声が聞こえると，人々は玄関を開けて歓迎します．キャロリングの歌い手たちから，歌の贈り物を受けとるのです．こうして歌が人々の心を結びつけるのですね．クリスマスキャロルには宗教的な歌もそうでない歌もあります．「ジングル・ベル」は雪と冬を愛でて昔の生活を懐かしく思わせてくれる歌（宗教的でない歌），「サイレント・ナイト」は救い主イエスの誕生を祝う静かで神聖な歌（宗教的な歌）です．

....

During the Christmas season, which begins in December, people decorate their houses with Christmas trees, hang stockings, and put up brightly colored lights. They also socialize with friends and family, and bake sweets. **Christmas carols, which help mark the holiday season**, may be sung in church, at parties, or during an activity known as "caroling." Christmas caroling entails going out with a group of people to sing outside, in front of other people's houses. The person inside the house hears the caroling, opens the door to listen, and is given the gift of a song. After caroling, the group may return home to drink hot chocolate, cider, hot buttered rum, or some other kind of hot drink. **Christmas caroling brings people together.**

Some famous Christmas carols celebrate snow and winter, such as the chorus to the song "Jingle Bells":

Jingle bells/ Jingle bells/ Jingle all the way
Oh what fun it is to ride/ In a one horse open sleigh!

A sleigh is an old-fashioned snow carriage pulled by horses. As the horses pull the sleigh across the snow, the bells make a pleasant jingling sound. It is a Christmas image that **evokes nostalgia for a less complicated way of life**.

Other Christmas carols remind people of the religious aspects of Christmas. One of the most well-known religious Christmas carols is called "Silent Night." It begins:

Silent night/ Holy night
All is calm/ All is bright

The image in this carol is of stillness, quiet, and waiting on the night preceding the birth of Christ.

ハヌカの歌

　キリスト教以外の例をあげましょう．ユダヤ教の冬の祭りはハヌカといいます．ハヌカは「光の祝祭」として知られます．12月25日から8日間にわたり，9本枝の飾り燭台にロウソクを灯し続けるからです．ここに紹介するハヌカの歌はよく知られた歌で，ユダヤ人の子供もユダヤ人でない子供も歌います．粘土で作ったよ，と歌われている「ドレイドル」は四角い独楽です．

Hanukkah is Jewish holiday that occurs during the Christmas season. Although Hanukkah is less important than other Jewish holidays, it is widely celebrated in the United States as an alternative to Christmas. Hanukkah is known as **the "Festival of Lights,"** and is celebrated for eight days with an exchange of gifts and the lighting of a menorah, a candelabrum with nine branches. One of the most well-known Hanukkah songs is a children's song, known and sung by Jewish and non-Jewish people alike.

I have a little dreidel/ I made it out of clay
And when it's dry and ready/ O dreidel I shall play.

The term "dreidel" refers to a four-sided wooden top, which is a toy that children play with during Hanukkah.

3 愛国的な歌

　アメリカでは，自分が「アメリカ人だ」と表現したい時，強く意識したい時に歌う歌があります．スポーツのイベントや学校で，また独立記念日の７月４日に歌われるものなどがあります．愛国的な歌の代表はアメリカ合衆国国歌，"The Star Spangled Banner"「星条旗」でしょう（3章に歌詞があります）．フランシス・スコット・キーの作詞で，1812年米英戦争での戦闘の翌朝，勇壮にはためく国旗を歌ったものです．ただ，歌うのがとても難しいので一般にはあまり歌われません．それに比べ，ウッディ・ガスリー作詞作曲の"This Land is Your Land"「これは君の土地（わが祖国）」は，歌いやすく親しみやすい愛唱歌として知られます．西のカリフォルニアから東のニューヨーク，北西部に広がるレッドウッドの大森林から南のメキシコ湾岸まで，広大な合衆国はそっくりあなた方のものなんだよと歌っています．確かにこの歌は国土に対する愛を感じさせるので，今では愛国的な歌の代表となっていますが，ガスリーはむしろ国の体制を批判する抵抗歌（プロテスト・ソング）として作詞したのでした．この国の土地は，そこで働くすべての人々のものであって，資本家や大地主や政治家たちのものではないのだと訴えているのです．

PATRIOTIC SONGS

Patriotic songs emphasize love or loyalty to the nation. **People sing patriotic songs to demonstrate their personal patriotism, and they are used to represent an occasion as "American."** For example, patriotic songs are commonly sung at sporting events, in schools, and on the 4th of July, which is national Independence Day, all of which are considered appropriate contexts for expressing patriotism. Sporting events commonly are patriotic because sports have a militaristic tone to them and competing teams symbolically are at war with each other. Schools, which are run by the government, also emphasize patriotism. Finally, Independence Day is the day that the United States declared its independence from the British Empire in 1776. Patriotic songs may be sung at other times as well.

The most common patriotic song is "The Star-Spangled Banner," which is the national anthem (see Chapter 3 for lyrics). **The words of the lyrics refer to seeing the American flag ("broad stripes and bright stars") in the dawn after a battle with the British in 1812**, an image that symbolizes the endurance of the United States against conflict. Unfortunately, this song is quite difficult to sing because some notes are too high for most people to reach. Therefore, while most Americans know this song, they often leave the actual singing of it to professional singers.

Another very well-known patriotic song is called "This Land Is Your Land." The chorus goes like this:

> This land is your land/ This land is my land
> From California/ To the New York island
> From the Redwood forest/ To the Gulf Stream waters
> This land was made for you and me.

This song was composed by folk singer Woody Guthrie in 1940. **The chorus signifies the noble idea that the United States belongs to all of its people.** California, for example, is on the west coast of the country, while New York is on the east coast. The song says that all of the land from California to New York belongs to everybody ("you and me"). This idea is repeated again with the reference to the Redwood forest, which is a large, expansive forest in California. The "Gulf Stream waters" refers to the southern region of the US, and the idea is that all the land between belongs to the people. Interestingly, although "This Land is Your Land' is considered a patriotic song today, Woody Guthrie originally composed it as a protest song. **He felt that too much of the United States was closed off to the common people and reserved for the rich and powerful. However, not many Americans know the original, subversive intent of this song**.

スポーツイベントでの歌

　スポーツのイベントで歌われる歌は，愛国的になることがよくあります．スポーツの試合は勝負を争うので，軍隊のように戦闘的な雰囲気と味方に肩入れする愛国的な姿勢が歌に表れます．最も有名なのは"Take Me out to the Ball Game"「野球に連れてって」という歌で，試合の7回表終了時に観客全員が立ち上がって身体を伸ばし，これを勇ましく歌って一息いれる習慣があります．

SPORTING EVENTS

Some songs are associated with sports. One of the most well-known sports songs is "Take Me out to the Ball Game," which is sung at baseball games. **This song is usually sung during the seventh inning as a way for people to take a break from the game**. The break is called the "seventh inning stretch." People stand, stretch, take a break from the long game, and sing the song.

Baseball player leading fans to sing "Take Me out to the Ballgame"

> Take me out to the ball game/ Take me out with the crowd
> Buy me some peanuts and Cracker Jack/ I don't care if I ever come back
> 'Cause it's root, root, root for the home team
> If they don't win it's a shame
> 'Cause it's 1-2-3 strikes you're out/ At the old ball game!

The song is sung in an energetic manner. Cracker Jack is a snack made up of peanuts and popcorn that are coated in caramel and molasses. Both peanuts and Cracker Jack are common, old-fashioned snack foods associated with baseball games.

ロックンロールの曲もスポーツイベントで歌われます．イギリス出身のロックバンド「クイーン」が 1977 年にリリースしたヒット曲 "We Will Rock You" は，足を踏み鳴らしたり手をたたいたりしながら，味方のチームを強く鼓舞するように歌われます．また，同じくクイーンの "We Are the Champions" (1977) は，勝っているチームが気勢をあげ負けている相手チームをおとしめるように歌われます．このほかに，各地のスポーツチームが応援歌をもっていて，応援歌を歌うとファンは活気づき選手の意気が上がります．

....

Some rock and roll songs are connected with sporting events. The rock group Queen, for example, had a popular hit called "We Will Rock You" that was released in 1977. The chorus to this song, which is accompanied by vigorous stomping and the clapping of hands, has become very popular to sing at all types of sporting events as a **way to rouse team and audience members**.

> We will, we will, rock you! Rock you!
> We will, we will rock you! Rock you!

Another Queen song called "We Are the Champions," also released in 1977, has become common for fans of the winning team to sing to fans of the losing team. Most people don't know the verses, but people **sing the chorus as a way to celebrate their victory and humiliate their opponents. All songs function in the same way: to pep up the fans, boost morale, and give energy to the players.**

> We are the champions — my friends
> And we'll keep on fighting/ Till the end
> We are the champions/ We are the champions/ No time for losers
> 'Cause we are the champions of the world.

4 宗教歌と黒人霊歌

　人々がいっしょに歌う機会が最も多いのは教会です．アメリカ合衆国の約76％が何らかの信仰をもっており，70％がキリスト教徒，6％はそれ以外の宗教の信者であるという調査結果があります（Pew Research Centerによる）．宗教団体によって讃美歌は異なりますが，宗教の違いを越えて愛されているものに"Amazing Grace"「アメイジング・グレイス」（1799）があります．信仰が弱く迷った魂を神が見つけて，救ったことを歌っています．讃美歌は信仰を明らかにするもので，それを聞いた人々が神様に気づき信者になって連帯する役目を果たします．キリスト教以外の宗教の歌では，たとえば，日本からアメリカへ移住した人たちや布教に渡った開教師（仏教の伝道師，宣教師のこと）が建設した浄土真宗本願寺派のお寺（Buddhist Churches of America）で歌われている，英語の「讃仏歌」があります．「黒人霊歌」は，奴隷制時代の黒人の歌をルーツとしていますが，現在では人種に関わらず歌われています．なかでも"Swing Low Sweet Chariot"「降りてきて，やさしい馬車よ」は，代表的な黒人霊歌です．歌詞にある"home"は天国のことで，天国から遣わされる馬車に乗って神の国へ行きたいと言っているのですが，同時に，奴隷制度のない自由な土地へ逃げて行きたいという気持ちを表現してもいるといわれています．「降りてきて，やさしい馬車よ」を録音した多くの歌手の中には，ポール・ロブソンやニナ・シモンなど世界的に有名な歌手も少なくありません．

....

RELIGIOUS SONGS AND SPIRITUALS

One of the most common places that people sing together in groups is in church. Songs sung in church are called "hymns." According to the Pew Research Center, approximately 76% of the US population identifies with some kind of religion. Of this number, approximately 70% identify as Christian, and about 6% identify as non-Christian. Many religions and denominations have specific songs associated with them, so it is difficult to identify common religious songs that most Americans sing because the religious landscape is so diverse. One hymn, however, that is sung by many different religions is called "Amazing Grace," which was written in 1779.

　　Amazing Grace, how sweet the sound
　　That saved a wretch like me

I once was lost
But now am found/ Was blind, but now, I see.

This Christian hymn refers the idea of being saved by God. Christian hymns frequently use the metaphor of being "lost" and "found." Being "lost" refers to an unhappy state of being prior to knowing God, and being "found" means the happiness experienced afterward, when one has come to know God better. **The purpose of hymns is to express spiritual ideas, help people find God, and come together as a group.**

Spirituals are a broad and popular category of religious songs associated with African American enslavement. Many spirituals today are sung by both African Americans and Anglo Americans. One of the best known spirituals is called "Swing Low Sweet Chariot."

Swing low, sweet chariot/ Coming for to carry me home
Swing low, sweet chariot/ Coming for to carry me home.

I looked over Jordan, what do I see/ Coming for to carry me home
A band of angels coming after me/ Coming for to carry me home.

The history and meanings of this song have been debated extensively. From a religious perspective, **the term "home" in the song refers to heaven**. Heaven is the Christian idea about what happens to people after death. Many people think they will go to live with God in a place called "heaven" and be happy. However, **because this song is associated with slavery, some scholars have argued that "Swing Low Sweet Chariot" also is about the escape of people from slavery into freedom. The idea of freedom from slavery and spiritual freedom are mixed together in many African American spirituals**. "Swing Low Sweet Chariot" is one of the most popular spirituals of all time. It has been recorded by many famous African American artists, including Paul Robeson and Nina Simone.

子供の歌

　子供たちはみんなでいっしょに歌うのが好きです．2，3歳で覚える子供の歌を "nursery songs" といい，人々は大人になってもそれを忘れずにいて，機会があれば子供たちと歌います．日本で，「マザー・グース」として知られるイギ

リスの伝承歌の多くがこれにあたります。マザー・グースではありませんが，アメリカ民謡の "Row, Row, Row, Your Boat" は日本でもよく知られた歌ですね。最後の一節 "Life is but a dream"（人生は，ただ，夢だから）というのは，仏教的な無常観にも通じる気がします。歌う楽しさや生きる喜びを伝えるこうした歌に，ふと大人の哲学や現実への洞察がすべりこんでいるのは珍しいことではありません。"Mary Had a Little Lamb"（「メリーさんの羊」）は，楽譜の読み方を習ったりする時によく使われるので，日本の子供もよく知っている歌でしょう。"London Bridge is Falling Down"（「ロンドン橋」）は，テムズ川にかかるロンドン橋が落ちるよという内容で，この歌の最初の印刷記録は17世紀に遡ります。遊び歌になっていて，向かい合った二人の子供が頭上で手をつないで「橋」をつくった下を，子供たちは歌いながら順番にくぐっていきます。そして，最後の "My fair lady!" という歌詞のところで手をつないでできていた「橋」がどさっと落ちて，ちょうどそこを通っていた子供をつかまえます。あなたもこうして遊んだ思い出がありますか．

....

CHILDREN'S SONGS

Children regularly sing songs together. Children sing songs at school, while they are playing, and with friends and family. **Children learn songs called "nursery songs"** (songs for babies) as early as two or three years of age. As they grow up, children stop singing these songs, but **many people remember them their whole lives**. They may even sing them again when their own children are little. One common example of a nursery song is:

Row, row, row, your boat/ Gently down the stream
Merrily, merrily, merrily, merrily/ Life is but a dream.

There is not much meaning to this song beyond the image of a boat floating down a stream（see Chapter 13）. **The song is used primarily to teach children how to sing and to amuse them**. Another, similar example is:

Mary had a little lamb/ Little lamb, little lamb
Mary had a little lamb/ Its fleece was white as snow.

This song also does not have a lot of symbolic meaning. **It is used to keep children entertained, or to teach them to sing, or read music during** music lessons.

Many children's songs are associated with games, such as the song "London Bridge."

> London bridge is falling down/ Falling down/ Falling down
> London bridge is falling down/ My fair lady!

The words to this song refer to a bridge in London, England that crosses the Thames River. This nursery song was first recorded during the seventeenth century. During this song, children stand opposite each other holding hands with their arms in the air so that their arms form a "bridge." Other children go underneath the "bridge." At the end of the song, the children forming the bridge drop their arms and catch one of the children. **The main function of this song is to organize the game and tell children when to drop their arms**. It makes the game more fun.

5 考　　察

　愛唱歌についていちばんの特徴を指摘するとしたら，それは「機能性や実用性がある」ということです．誕生日の歌はパーティをにぎやかにし，スポーツイベントでの歌はチームやファンを活気づけます．愛国的な歌は祖国を慕う気持ちを強め団結を促しますし，子供の歌は歌う楽しみを教え音楽学習にも用いられ，遊びにも欠かせません．宗教歌の歌詞は特に深い意味をもち，それでもやはり第一には，教会で共に歌い他人や神とのつながりを感じるという大事な機能を果たしています．多くの人に愛され続けている歌は，よりよい日常を送るために役に立つのだといえます．

DISCUSSION

What can be said of best-known songs? Primarily, **many American best-known songs are functional**. They serve a practical, rather than symbolic purpose. The "Happy Birthday" song, for example, is a way to wish someone "happy birthday" and liven up the party, while songs at sporting events energize fans and relieve boredom. Patriotic songs evoke feelings of love for country and mark an event as being "American," and children's nursery songs often have either an educational value, such as teaching them to sing or read music, or an entertainment value because they are associated with games. Some songs, particularly those associated with religious contexts, do have deeper or more symbolic meanings because they address metaphysical issues. However, **the evocation of deeper meanings appears to be of secondary importance for best-known songs in many contexts. Rather, best-known songs tend to serve immediate, practical purposes**.

6 演 習

日本でよく知られている歌は何でしょうか．その歌について，次の問いを追求，考察し，研究発表してください．
(1) どのような人々が，どのような時期に，どのような場面や状況でそれを歌いますか．それぞれについて証拠となる情報を収集し，まとめてください．
(2) その歌が果たす役割を分析してください．歌った人や歌われた場面や，歌の現場にいた人々に，その歌がどのような効果を及ぼすかを考えましょう．

ACTIVE LEARNING

What are some of the best known or best loved songs in Japan?
In what contexts are they sung?
What are some of the functions of these songs? That is, what do they accomplish?

第Ⅲ部
モンスター・幽霊・ファンタジー
　　　　　──想像力と文化

Part III
Monsters, Ghosts, Fantasy

7章
怪物の伝承——環境と創造

Chapter 7
Monsters: Landscape and the Creation of Culture

1 大自然に住むモンスターたち

　不思議な生き物，モンスター．北米大陸の大自然は，巨大な怪物たちの住まう場所です．アメリカ合衆国は広大な土地ながら3億を超える人口のほとんどが都市に集中しているので，国土には利用されていない土地が茫漠と広がっています．容易にたどり着けない大森林，険しい山々，奥地の湖や河川，限りない平原や砂漠などを，人々ははるか遠くに感じ，そこに巨大なモンスターが住んでいると考えました．未知で神秘な自然に対して湧き上がってくる畏怖や恐怖の感情を，モンスターは体現しています．中でもよく知られているのが「ビッグフット」と湖のモンスターたちです．彼らは過去の遺産や単なるファンタジーではありません．現在でもその存在を信じる人々がいるのです．

INTRODUCTION

The term "monster" in English refers to a creature of unusual size, an unknown species, or a creature with unusual powers. Often monsters have all of these qualities. Monsters have an essential strangeness to them, meaning that **people cannot fully understand them. Monsters usually live in remote areas that are unfamiliar or scary to people**.

　In the nineteenth century, the territory of what eventually became the United States was very remote. People thought that different kinds of monsters existed there. Many places were completely unknown except to Native American groups. People could travel for weeks without seeing a village or a town. Nature was scary and threatening. Since people didn't know the landscape very well, they imagined that monsters inhabited the land.

　The mainland territory of US today is approximately 8,080,464.3 km^2,

("Contiguous United States," *Wikipedia*), which is slightly smaller than China. The landscape has been explored thoroughly. Nature is less threatening and so people believe in fewer monsters than they did in the past. But the United States is still empty and remote compared to China. China has almost 1.4 billion people, while the United States only has about 325 million people. There are still large, remote portions of the US where there are no people, only mountains, rocks, desert, trees or animals. In such places, nature can still be a little threatening.

Some remote places in the United States are still associated with monsters. The most famous monsters are Bigfoot and lake monsters. Bigfoot lives in the forest. Lake monsters live in mountain lakes or sometimes rivers or the ocean. These places have been explored and mapped, but they **symbolize inaccessible, unknown places**. Bigfoot and lake monsters represent old ideas about monsters and landscapes that have survived into modern times.

2　森のモンスター，ビッグフット

　ビッグフットは大きな猿のような生き物で，森に住み，足跡を残すので「ビッグフット」と呼ばれています．怪力のモンスターですが，あまり恐ろしくありません．説明を読んでみてください，なんだか可笑しい怪物です．恥ずかしがり屋で，逃げる時に叫び声をあげたりする．家畜がいなくなるとビッグフットが盗んだといわれたり，動物の大きな糞もビッグフットのせいにされたり．こんな怪物が実在するのかあるいはただの想像なのか，まだ確かめられてはいませんが，ビッグフットが現れたという話は現在でも聞くそうです．特別な匂い，甲高い叫び声，いつも逃げてしまう，というのがビッグフットの特徴です．

....

BIGFOOT

Bigfoot is a large, brown, hairy, smelly monster that lives in the forest. Another name for Bigfoot is Sasquatch. It looks like a very big ape. It reminds people of a human being, but it is not human. It is called Bigfoot because it leaves large footprints in the dirt. Bigfoot is very shy. It does not harm people. It is scared of people and people are scared of Bigfoot. It just runs away, or sometimes it screams. Bigfoot can throw very large objects, like rocks; some stories say that Bigfoot throws objects weighing as much as 700 pounds (317 kilos). Animals, such as horses, are frightened of Bigfoot. Bigfoot also leaves a bad smell. Sometimes people accuse Bigfoot of stealing animals from traps for food, or they blame Bigfoot when they find the remains of a large animal in the woods.

Bigfoot is interesting because it is a mystery. What is it? Some people think that Bigfoot is imaginary, while other people think that Bigfoot might be real. Bigfoot's existence has never been proven, but there many reports of Bigfoot sightings. Bigfoot reports are short stories that people tell about strange things in the woods that might be Bigfoot. Below is an example of a story about a Bigfoot sighting. It contains many familiar Bigfoot motifs. **A "motif" is a story element or narrative unit that appears in different stories** (see Chapter 1). Common motifs in this story include a strange smell, a scream, and Bigfoot running away. The people are frightened and confused about their experience, but they are not harmed.

【伝承1】 Date collected: 1999
My dad's friend Allen Fife was camping in northern California with another friend. They were sleeping out on cots. Late in the night he had to go to the bathroom. As he was standing there, he saw a huge shadow. He went to get his lantern to see what it was. The creature started running up an embankment. When Allen got his lantern the creature must have gotten scared, because it let out a high pitched scream. This woke up the other guy who was scared to death. They were both terrified of what they had seen and heard. When they had their things together the creature was gone, but they could smell a strong odor that it had left. They were so scared that they would not go to the same camping place again. They have never even gone back to the area where this happened.
Folk Coll 8a Group 7: SNL Box 12, Folder 14, L2.5.4.1.52
Fife Folklore Archives, Utah State University

大自然との接点に現れるビッグフット

　ビッグフットが現れるのは北カリフォルニアの森です．北カリフォルニアには，1万6,000平方キロにも及ぶ大森林に，高さが9メートルで幹の周りが76メートルもあるような大木が立ち並んでいます．かつて，夢がかなう土地と信じられたカリフォルニアの神秘な自然の中に，ビッグフットは住んでいます．休暇をア

ウトドアで過ごすのが好きなアメリカ人が，キャンプやハイキングなどで非日常の自然空間に触れた時，ビッグフットは現れるようですね。

・・

Another important motif of this story is that the sighting occurred in California. **Bigfoot sightings commonly occur in Northern California**, where there are very large forests. Forests in northern California can range up to 16513 km^2 and some trees can grow to more than 9 meters in diameter and 76 meters tall. It is exactly the kind of large, isolated landscape that breeds stories about monsters. **California also is a place in the American imagination where dreams supposedly come true**. Historically, people moved to California to build a better life and to escape the past. It is not surprising that the thick forests of California are thought to have a Bigfoot. For Americans, **California is a place where anything is possible**.

A final motif in the story is that the people were camping when they saw Bigfoot. **Bigfoot stories frequently are associated with camping, hunting, hiking or other outdoor activities**. Camping means to live outside for a short period of time in the forest or desert. People cook, eat, and sleep outside while they are camping. Some people also hunt while camping. Americans love nature and outdoor activities. They like to camp because it is an activity that brings them closer to nature. They also feel awe and sometimes even fear when they visit, hike, camp, and hunt in remote landscapes.

People's feelings about Bigfoot reflect their feelings about nature. Just as Americans love and admire nature, they also love and admire Bigfoot. Most people don't really believe that Bigfoot exists, but people embrace the idea of a large, mysterious creature that can't be found. They have affection for Bigfoot because Bigfoot survives in a modern world. And, just as nature can sometimes be threatening, actually seeing Bigfoot is a frightening experience, as it was for the people in the story. The appeal of Bigfoot is that civilized people sometimes might catch a glimpse of something completely wild, uncivilized, and unknown.

ビッグフットの歴史

ビッグフットがいつから，どのように語り始められたのかはわかっていません。第二次世界大戦後に知られるようになり，60年代，70年代にはビッグフット探しが人気になりました。ビッグフットは，ヒマラヤの伝説の生き物イエティのア

メリカ版だという人もいれば，アメリカ先住民（ネイティヴ・アメリカン）の伝説に基づいているという人もいます．また，カリフォルニアの木こりたちが言い伝えた話だという学説を出した研究者（Joshua Buhs）もいます．カリフォルニアの森は深く，木こりの集団は森の中で長期間にわたって野営（キャンプ）しながら伐採にあたるため，夜や休憩時間に物語をし合って楽しんだのです．木こりたちの見たという不思議で巨大な足跡が，本当なのか嘘なのか，あるいは，だますために誰かがわざと跡を付けたのか，いまでもわからないのだそうです．

....

HISTORY

No one knows how the idea of Bigfoot started. Many societies believe in wild, primitive humans or human-like creatures that live on the edge of civilization. In the United States, this idea became popular after World War II. **Searching for Bigfoot was a popular activity in the 1960s and 1970s**. Some scholars think that the idea of Bigfoot came from the Himalayas. The Himalayas have a monster called a *yeti*, or "abominable snowman" in English. The *yeti* is a large, hairy creature that allegedly lives in remote parts of the Himalayas. Reports from the Himalayas introduced the *yeti* to the English-speaking world in the early twentieth century. **The American Bigfoot could be an American variation of the Himalayan *yeti*. Other people, including various Native American tribes, think that Bigfoot is an idea that came from Native Americans**. The term "Sasquatch," for example, is a name for Bigfoot derived from a term for a wildman from First Nation (Native American) peoples in British Columbia, Canada. And, one scholar named **Joshua Buhs (2009) traces the idea of Bigfoot itself as being invented in California among loggers in 1958** (a logger is a person who cuts down trees in the forest for a living). It is important to note that loggers have a long tradition of telling stories and playing pranks. Buhs writes that a logger named Jerry Crew "noticed a few footprints in the leveled earth but thought nothing of them until he climbed onto his tractor and looked down upon them. The prints were big and manlike. They pressed deeply into the earth" (2009:68). When Jerry Crew told other people about the footprints, "they had their own gossip about giant, humanlike tracks to pass on" (Buhs 2009:68). **The men traded stories about strange events in the camp**. They found vandalized equipment, dogs were missing, and they saw mysterious, large tracks. People wondered whether or not the tracks were a joke or whether they were real and they began to call the creature Bigfoot.

ビッグフットを楽しむ

　ビッグフットを信じない人たちは，「ビッグフット」という伝説をフィクションとして使っていろいろないたずらをします．写真やビデオの加工でビッグフットがいた「証拠」を作り，インターネット上にあげたりして楽しむのです（13章も参照してください）．だまそうとしているわけではありません．ただ人を笑わせたいから，面白いからやっているのです．日本にも同じような生き物がいますか．「さだこ」や「つちのこ」でしょうか．どこがビッグフットと共通していてどこが違うでしょうね．

．．

PLAYING WITH BIGFOOT

Americans have conflicting beliefs about their monsters. On the one hand, most Americans don't believe monsters are real. They think monsters are imaginary, or are lies, jokes, or tricks. One the other hand, Americans are curious about their monsters and feel affection for them. They wonder if, in spite of everything, monsters might exist. Americans also are a little bit afraid of their monsters. **American monsters therefore hover between an alarming creature and an affectionate joke**.

　Americans express these conflicting ideas by playing with their monsters (Dorson 1982). This playful attitude is a unique way of interacting with monsters. One way in which Americans play with Bigfoot is through pictures and videos. There many photographs and videos of Bigfoot on the Internet. Some of the pictures and videos are serious. People take a picture of something strange in the woods, and post it to the Internet asking other people whether or not the picture might be Bigfoot. People comment on the pictures and videos. They give their opinion about whether or not the picture is really Bigfoot. The Internet allows people to debate the question of whether or not Bigfoot is real.

　Many other pictures and videos of Bigfoot are fake. Some are fake but pretend to be real in order to trick people. People dress up as Bigfoot and get others to film them in the woods. They post the video as a "real" Bigfoot sighting and try to fool other people into thinking it is true. Other videos also are fake, but they do not try to fool people. They are just funny. It is obvious that the producers are having fun. They make Bigfoot into a joke to make people laugh. For example, a person might dress up as Bigfoot and then do regular, everyday activities such as drinking a soda, going to work, or taking a nap. Both kinds of pictures and videos, the serious ones and the fake ones, reinforce the conflicting ideas that Bigfoot is a joke or for fun but maybe also real.

観光の目玉として

ビッグフットに限らず、モンスターをビジネスチャンスに変える人々もいます。なかでも一番お金を稼ぐのは、ビッグフットを目玉にした観光です（アメリカ人が、ビッグフットについてどれほど噂しあい、冗談を楽しむかを示しているサイトの情報は本書の専用サイト（p.viii 参照）にあります）。

....

MONSTERS AS A RESOURCE FOR TOURISM

Another way that Americans play with their monsters is by using them to sell products. People use the image of Bigfoot for commercial purposes. Bigfoot is used to sell beer, tools, T-shirts, coffee mugs, postcards, stuffed animals, clothing, electronics, food, and almost any other item you can think of. The main way Bigfoot is used for commercial purposes is for tourism. **Tourism sells the ideas associated with a place or a landscape**. Tourism encourages people to visit a place because it is somehow special. When tourists visit, they spend their money in restaurants, hotels, and on souvenirs. Americans use Bigfoot to attract tourists to places that Bigfoot supposedly lives, which is another way in which Bigfoot is connected to landscape.

The most well-known example of Bigfoot tourism is in the small town of Willow Creek, California. Willow Creek has a long (although contested) history of Bigfoot sightings. The most famous video of Bigfoot was shot nearby, in 1967. That video supposedly shows a female Bigfoot turning to the camera. People have debated since 1967 about whether or not the video is real. Willow Creek capitalized on Bigfoot's popularity by adopting Bigfoot as its mascot in order to attract tourists.

Bigfoot beer, an example of Bigfoot marketing

3 湖のモンスターたち

　水に関わるモンスターは，多くは森林の湖に現れ「水の馬」と呼ばれます．まれに河川や海に現れる時もあり，海のモンスターは「海の大蛇」と呼ばれます．姿は龍や恐竜のようでも，性質はビッグフット同様に恥ずかしがり屋で，人を害することもなければ人に捕まることもありません．モンスターのいる湖には，大事な特徴があります．寒い地方の深い湖，暗くて神秘的な湖，湖底に洞窟があること，湖底に自然の地下道があって他の湖とつながっていると信じられていること，の4つです．そして，人々はモンスターを信じていない時でもモンスターと特別な関わり方をします．モンスターをご当地名物にする，愛情を感じてニックネームで呼んだりすることなどです．そのようなモンスターとの結びつきは一体，何を意味するのでしょうか．

....

LAKE MONSTERS

　Another common monster is the lake monster. **Lake monsters live in mountain lakes, although they also less commonly live in rivers or the ocean**. Lake monsters sometimes also are called "water horses." If they live in the ocean, they are called "sea serpents." They are large and look a little bit like a dragon or a dinosaur. Lake monsters have many similarities to Bigfoot. They are shy, they do not usually harm people, and they are have never been proven to exist. They have no special powers. The most remarkable aspect of lake monsters is simply that they are sometimes seen by people but cannot be caught.

　Lake monsters need special landscapes in order to make their homes. First, lakes containing lake monsters are unusually cold and deep. People often joke that the lake is "bottomless." Identifying a lake as "bottomless" doesn't mean that people really believe the lake doesn't have a bottom. It means that the lake is very deep and no one knows exactly how deep it is. Second, lakes containing lake monsters are dark and mysterious. Sometimes there are rumors that the lake is sentient, meaning it can think and act on its own in mysterious ways. Third, lakes with lake monsters are often thought to contain underwater caves or caverns where the monster can hide. This is why lake monsters are difficult to find. Finally, the lake sometimes is thought to have underwater tunnels that connect that lake to other lakes in the region

Lake monster sculpture created in ice and snow

(Meurger 1989). Such lakes allow lake monsters to remain remote and inaccessible to people.

Most people don't really believe in lake monsters. But people like to think about the possibility of their existence, like they do with Bigfoot. Most American lake monsters are associated with particular towns or villages near the lake. People who live in villages or towns near lakes containing lake monsters are proud of their lake monster. People often feel protective toward their local lake monster, and they also feel affection. A lake monster gives a town or village a unique identity, adds mystery to the local landscape, and attracts tourists. In this way, **towns or villages and lake monsters form a close bond, which is another way in which American monsters are connected to landscape**.

One way people express pride in their lake monster (and their town) is to give the monster a nickname. **Nicknames make the lake monster more personal** and help people express affection. For example, the most famous American lake monster supposedly lives in Lake Champlain, Vermont. The monster's name is "Champ," which is derived from the name of the lake. Other examples of lake monsters with nicknames include "Sharlie," which is the name of a monster that supposedly lives in Payette Lake, Idaho; "Old Greeny," a monster that lives in Cayuga Lake, New York; "Tessie" of Lake Tahoe, California; and "Peppie" of Lake Pepin, Minnesota. Think about how these names sound in English. They sound friendly, not threatening. They also sound diminutive, meaning to "size down." Americans name huge lake monsters with names that suggest "littleness" and "affection." These nicknames suggest the monster is not scary, but rather a beloved member of the community. They also suggest that Americans don't take their lake monsters too seriously.

曖昧な存在のスリル

アメリカのモンスターは，日本の妖怪（河童などを想像してください）の大型版のようなところがあります．そのモンスターについての「伝説」と呼べるほどのストーリーがあるわけではなく，現れたかどうか，それが本当にモンスターだったかどうかだけが問題なのです．変なものを見たけど，目の錯覚かな，酔ってい

たのかな，でもひょっとしたら湖のモンスターだったかもしれないよね，と話したりする（そして，ゾッとする）．そういうふうに文化が生まれる母体は人間の心理の多面性や現実の曖昧性なのだと説明する研究者もいます．

・・・

AMBIVALENCE

Like Bigfoot, **there are no complicated, long stories about lake monsters**. There are only stories of sightings. People see something strange in the lake, and then they talk to other people afterwards about what they saw. Very few people who see something unusual in a lake identify what they saw as a lake monster. Other people would think they were crazy! People usually explain the strangeness as some kind of large fish, ducks, a submerged log, or the wind moving the water in unusual ways. It is also common for people to dismiss their sighting by saying they were drunk. These are all traditional explanations for what lake monsters might really be. Only after people give a traditional explanation for what they saw will they say something like "or maybe it was a lake monster" as a kind of joke. **Scholars identify this attitude as "ambivalence," meaning to have mixed feelings or contradictory ideas**.

Americans play with lake monsters, just like they do with Bigfoot. There are fewer videos and pictures of lake monsters than of Bigfoot, but many people use their local lake monster as a way to joke with people. In the example below, one person explains how he used a local lake monster to scare a group of teenagers for fun.

【伝承 2】 "The kids were from Indiana. They were probably 13, 14, 15 years old teenagers. I told them about Sharlie and they asked me, 'do you go swimming'? I told them I wasn't going swimming. I kept a straight face [because I was kidding]. It's something for the locals to play with if you find somebody fairly gullible .... I mean, there's no doubt in my mind that something's out there—I personally think it's a sturgeon [a large fish]. But it's fun." (Retold for readability.)

Interview with author, McCall, Idaho, 7 January 2001.

曖昧な現実に揺れる人間の感情をちょっといじって楽しむ伝統が，アメリカに

はあります．他言を信じやすい人や子供に「シャーリー（アイダホ州のペイエット湖に住むというモンスター）がいるよ」とジョークをしかけるのがその例です．ジョークとは，一部の人には見え透いていて悪意のない嘘のことで，上に引用した【伝承2】の例では，話し手はシャーリーが架空の存在だとわかっているのに警告を発するような，相手を怖がらせる顔をするのです．この深い湖にモンスターがいるんだよという素振りが，一方で，現実に大きな魚がいるかもしれないという実際の注意喚起とバランスをとるので，レイク・モンスターという曖昧な存在がスリルを生みます．モンスター伝承はそうして楽しまれ，語り継がれてきたのです．

....

This quotation illustrates not only how Americans use their monsters as jokes, but also how **people tack back and forth between seriousness and light-heartedness when thinking about monsters**. In the first couple of sentences, the speaker explains that he told a group of teenagers about the lake monster in order to trick them, as a joke. **Tricking or fooling people by using monsters is a common American tradition**. The speaker says that it is fun to fool others if you can find people who are "gullible," which means people who are "easily fooled." At the same time, the speaker says he really believes there is something living in the lake. He thinks it is a sturgeon, which is a large fish. This statement is not for fun. It is much more serious because it opens up the possibility that there really is something in the lake. The final sentence sums up his story by saying "it's fun." Taken together, all of these statements illustrate ambivalence, how **Americans tack back and forth between taking their monsters seriously and using them as jokes**.

4 考 察

　アメリカ人は（どこの文化の人々も，ですが）自然に対して複雑な向き合い方をしてきました．自然は脅威であり人間が征服したり手なずけたりしなければならないものである反面，美しく，深い感動をもたらすものです．アメリカ人は積極的にキャンプやハイキングなどの活動で自然と触れ合い，自然を愛する心を育んでいます．畏怖を感じさせつつ身近でもある自然を体現するのが，大自然に住むと言われるモンスターたちです．自然の神秘や脅威を身に引き寄せて親しみ，

遊ぼうとするアメリカの人々．こうしたアメリカ文化の様子を，日本人が自然とどう向き合うか，超自然の生き物たちどう関わるかという様子と，比べてみるのは面白いのではないでしょうか．

....

DISCUSSION
Americans historically have a complex relationship with the natural landscape, which continues to be reflected in their attitudes towards monsters. On the one hand, Americans viewed—and continue to view—**nature as threatening, intimidating, or as something to be conquered or subdued**. This attitude was particularly prevalent when the territory of the United States was unknown, and still being explored and mapped. On the other hand, Americans also appreciate **the beauty and wonder of nature**. They enjoy the relatively open, sparsely populated, and expansive landscapes of the US. Many people participate in outdoor activities such as camping, hiking, and hunting that bring them closer to nature.

These attitudes towards nature are reflected in the attitudes people have towards monsters, which symbolize unknown, remote landscapes. On one hand, monsters are treated as potentially serious or threatening, particularly when a sighting occurs. On the other hand, monsters more commonly are treated as something more familiar. They are a joke, something to be played with, or they are used for commercial purposes.

This combination of seriousness and familiarity makes monsters useful for tourism. People use monsters to attract outsiders to a place by promoting that location as special. Landscapes that contain monsters are mysterious and incite curiosity. But tourism also promotes fun and enjoyment. Having a playful, familiar attitude towards monsters communicates to people that, although the landscape may be special or mysterious, it also is not too serious or threatening; it is meant for fun.

5 演 習

下のビッグフット物語を読んでください．本文で紹介された話と比較し，共通点と相違点を話し合ってください．この物語に読み取れるモチーフは何でしょう．

ACTIVE LEARNING

Please read the sample story below. What similarities and differences do you see when compared to the Bigfoot stories presented earlier in the chapter? Can you identify any motifs?

ADDITIONAL READING MATERIAL

Date collected: 1983

We were headed out toward Arbon, Idaho to see some friends. It was almost sunset and the sun was in my eyes. We had just passed [a location] when something ran across the road in front of the car. I slammed on the brakes. It looked like a big man. I got out of the car and the thing was running up the mountainside. It was going faster than a horse could have climbed. It was at least nine feet tall, maybe a little more. We couldn't find any solid footprints, just some in the dust and they were at least twice as big as my foot. The animal itself was kind of a dark, rusty brown. ... The only thing it could have been was a Bigfoot.

Folk Coll 8, Box 20, 83-009
Fife Folklore Archives, Utah State University

8章
幽霊話——社会問題と幽霊

Chapter 8
Ghosts: Social Issues

1 幽霊は何をか語る

　近代になって建国されたアメリカ合衆国にも,幽霊はいます.幽霊は死者のエッセンス，または精神であり，生き残った人と死者が何らかの関わりを持ちたい時に現れます．肉体はなく，透明でふわりと飛んだり物を通り抜けたりすることもあれば，まったく見えずに音やすすり泣きや叫び声や，勝手に動く物体などがある時に，幽霊がいるとわかることもあります．幽霊が現れるには理由があり，死に方や埋葬のされ方といった本人の死の事情に関わること，生者への警告や庇護といった生の世界へのはたらきかけ，真実の暴露ややり残したことへの執着といった本人が生きていた時の事情に関わることなど，さまざまです．7章で述べたモンスターの場合と同様に，アメリカ人は幽霊を信じるとも信じないともつかない態度をとっています．そして2章で述べたヒーローと同様に，実在するのかどうかということよりは，幽霊話から何がわかるのかということが重要です．幽霊は，社会で大っぴらに話されないことを物語るからです．

INTRODUCTION

One popular figure in the American imagination is a ghost. **A ghost is the spirit or essence of a person who has died, which has returned from the dead to interact with the living**. People usually are afraid of ghosts and their appearance is thought to be unnatural or a problem. Ghosts may hurt people, but other times they are harmless. Some ghosts may even be helpful.

　Ghosts mostly appear in human form (although sometimes they appear as animals), but they are immaterial, meaning that **they don't have a solid body**. The body usually is portrayed as transparent and colorless. Ghosts supposedly can pass through walls and other solid objects. Ghosts stereotypically may float in the air, fly, or hover above the ground, and they can vanish at will. Some ghosts are completely invisible. They make their presence known to humans through noises, wailing, screams, or by moving objects.

Ghosts traditionally appear for particular reasons. One common reason for ghosts to appear is that the person has died a violent, unnatural death, such as a murder or terrible accident. Some ghosts appear because the person did not receive proper burial. **Ghosts also appear to warn people, give important information, or speak hidden truths**. Ghosts may guard money, or return to interact with the living because of unfinished business, such as the payment of debt.

Americans have an ambivalent relationship to ghosts, much like they do with monsters (see Chapter 7). Americans may say that they do not believe in ghosts, yet many people also readily acknowledge that they have seen a ghost, or experienced something they considered "ghostly." Ghosts also are a popular topic for literature, films, television shows, and even forms of tourism. What is interesting about ghosts is not whether or not they are real, but what they represent (see Chapter 2). Ghosts are mysterious and symbolize areas of life that are complex and ambiguous. **Ghosts frequently speak to difficult issues, making manifest what society would prefer to remain hidden**. Let's look at a few examples.

2 幽霊のいる場所

幽霊は場所に「憑く」と信じられています．墓場など死者に関わりのある場所，橋や川，トンネル，森などといった人間の生活空間の境界となる場所，船，列車，車など移動する乗り物などが，幽霊の憑く場所です．現代では携帯電話やインターネットにも幽霊が憑きます．

LOCATING GHOSTS

Ghosts can appear anywhere but individual ghosts usually are associated with particular locations. **Places containing ghosts are considered to be "haunted."** Large, old buildings, such as mansions, theaters, and student dormitories commonly are thought to be haunted. Popular outdoor locations for ghosts include cemeteries, bridges, tunnels, rivers, and the forest. Ghosts may inhabit trains, cars, ships, boats, and other forms of transportation. They also haunt communication technologies such as cell phones and the Internet.

スリーピー・ホロウの伝説：暴力的な死の現場

　最もよく知られているのが，ワシントン・アービング（1783-1759）の「スリーピー・ホロウの伝説」（1820）です．アメリカ独立戦争で戦死した「頭のない騎手」がときには失った頭を探し，ときには頭を手に持って自分の死に場所に現れます．暴力的に殺された人が幽霊になる例です．作品からの引用文では，幽霊のことを"troubled spirits"「悩める魂」と呼んでいます．「スリーピー・ホロウの伝説」は，10章で述べるハロウィンの時に語られる人気の幽霊話で，ミュージカルなどに脚色され，1949年にはディズニー映画にもなりました．

....

　One of the most famous literary examples of a ghost is a short story called **"The Legend of Sleepy Hollow" by Washington Irving**. This story was first published in 1820 and is an important piece of early American literature. In this story, the ghost is described as a "headless horseman," that is, a person on horseback who is missing his head. The ghost is of a soldier who died during the Revolutionary War, which was the war during which the United States gained its independence from England, between 1775–1783. The Headless Horseman haunts the location of his death, sometimes looking for his missing head, and sometimes carrying it. This story exemplifies how some ghosts are thought to be people who died violent deaths. The excerpt below describes the location where the headless horseman commonly is sighted in the story.

> The sequestered situation of this church seems always to have made it a favorite haunt of troubled spirits. It stands on a knoll, surrounded by locust-trees and lofty elms, from among which its decent, whitewashed walls shine modestly forth.... To look upon its grass-grown yard, where the sunbeams seem to sleep so quietly, one would think that there at least the dead might rest in peace. On one side of the church extends a wide woody dell, along which raves a large brook among broken rocks and trunks of fallen trees. Over a deep black part of the stream, not far from the church, was formerly thrown a wooden bridge; the road that led to it,

and the bridge itself, were thickly shaded by overhanging trees, which cast a gloom about it, even in the daytime; but occasioned a fearful darkness at night. Such was one of the favorite haunts of the Headless Horseman, and the place where he was most frequently encountered.

"The Legend of Sleepy Hollow" is one of the most popular ghost stories in American literature. It is a favorite story to read or tell at Halloween (see Chapter 10) and has been adapted into many formats, including musical scores, theater, opera, and radio drama, and film, notably a 1949 Walt Disney cartoon.

上に引用した一節には，橋のある川のそばにひっそりと建っている教会の墓地に幽霊が出るとあります．そこは境界域です．川や橋は二つの場所の間に，墓地は生と死の間にあります．文明と手つかずの自然の間にあるのが森です．幽霊は，生者と死者の間の存在で，そのような境界域に現れるのです．

....

The passage above describes a secluded church with an adjacent cemetery and nearby bridge and river where the ghost often is found. **Haunted locations, such as the bridge in this passage, are "liminal," meaning "between."** Liminal places have an indeterminate status, meaning that people don't spend much time there but rather use them to pass through from one place to the next. Bridges and tunnels, for example, connect one piece of land to another, while cemeteries are liminal because they are a crossroads between the living and the dead. Forests also may contain ghosts, since they are between civilization and wilderness. Such places are appropriate for ghosts because ghosts themselves are liminal figures. They are remnants of people who have died, not living and not quite dead.

建物の中の境界的な場所

幽霊は建物にも憑きます．日本でいう「お化け屋敷」ですが，アメリカの場合は19世紀に多く建設されたヴィクトリア朝風のお屋敷が舞台になります．建物の中で幽霊が現れるのは，屋根裏部屋や地下室などのように日常的に使われない部屋，バスルームのように一時的にしか使わない場所，階段のような境界的な場所などです．

Another common place for ghosts is old buildings. Ghosts may haunt any kind of building, but the most iconic type is a large, old mansion with different floors and many rooms. **Such houses are called "haunted houses."** Although the idea of houses containing ghosts is quite ancient, the origins of the typical American haunted house can be traced to the Romantic literary period of 18th and 19th century Europe, especially England (Goldstein, Grider, and Thomas 2007). In the United States, haunted houses commonly are imagined as old, unkempt Victorian houses (a style of house built in the late nineteenth century) that once belonged to wealthy people but that have now fallen into disrepair.

A typical haunted house with ghosts

The most common household areas for ghosts to haunt are the attic, which is the upper portion of a house where no one lives, the basement, which is the bottom portion of the house that frequently is underground, the bathroom, and the stairs. Like brooks, bridges, and tunnels, these locations are "liminal." They are not places where people spend the majority of their time, but rather **are places understood as private and temporary (the bathroom), transitional (the staircase), or somewhat off-limits (the attic and basement).**

3 幽霊とジェンダー

　幽霊に肉体はないものの，ジェンダーに関する文化的な側面が幽霊話に読み取れることがあります．多くの場合，男性の暴力で命を落とした女性が幽霊となって現れます．ニューヨークの大学生が語る「エリザベス」は，そうした幽霊です．これも暴力的な死に方をしなければならなかった人の幽霊ですが，エリザベスは，男性の暴力にさらされる女性を守ります．ここでは，男性は暴力的で女性は被害者であり，女性の本来的な性質は他人を気遣い世話をやくことだという，文化内に共有されたジェンダー観が読み取れます．そしてまた，暴力によって命を落とした人の幽霊が暴力被害者を守るという話の中に，社会でおおっぴらに語ることのできない性暴力などの深い影がうかがえ，救いを求める多くの人の声を察することができるのです．

GHOSTS AND GENDER

Although ghosts don't have solid bodies, they can **reveal cultural ideas about gender** (Goldstein, Thomas and Grider 2007; Tucker, 2007). Stories about ghosts both reinforce and subvert traditional gender roles. One common type of ghost story is about women who suffer abuse from men in life and become ghosts after death. The story below, told by a college student at a university in New York in 2003, is one such example. This story is about a ghost that haunts a student dormitory. Students call her "Elizabeth."

> There was this girl who lived on the fourth floor of this dorm building named "Cheney." I'm not sure what her name was, but I think it was Elizabeth …. Anyway, I did hear that she was murdered by her boyfriend on that floor. This happened, I think in 70s or maybe the early 80s. So after the girl's death, they put up a painting on the fourth floor to honor her, like some sort of tribute. Ever since, students have said that they see an appearance of a female ghost with the arms stretching out. You get a weird vibe when you see it … [S]ome years later, another girl who was drunk as anything [meaning she was very drunk] fell over the same stairs as Elizabeth, but she survived! Makes you wonder if Elizabeth was protecting her, doesn't it? (Tucker 2007: 148)

Like "The Legend of Sleepy Hollow," this story associates a ghost with violent death: the violent death is presumed to be the reason the ghost exists. This story, however, also **reinforces cultural ideas about gender for both men and women** in several ways. First, it portrays a helpless female victim who dies at the hands of a violent male. **Traditional ideas about women include the notion that they are helpless and easily victimized** or endangered. Second, the story **associates men with violence**. Although most men are not violent, cultural ideas about masculinity link masculinity to violence. Finally, the story reinforces **the cultural notion that women are caring and nurturing**. As a ghost, Elizabeth protects the drunk female student from falling to her death.

Most importantly, however, this story communicates about situations of danger and abuse. **Ghosts often are thought to help, warn, or protect**

people in some way. By telling students the story of Elizabeth and her sad fate, this ghost story speaks to difficult issues that are not easily or straightforwardly addressed in society.

Other ghost stories subvert conventional ideas about gender. One of the most well-known and widespread ghost stories in the southwestern portion of the United States is "La Llorona," which is a Spanish name that literally means "the crier" or is loosely translated as "weeping woman." The southwestern portion of the United States has a large Latino population, meaning people of Mexican decent. La Llorona is a ghostly figure from Mexico and is found in the ghost stories of nearby regions.

A typical American ghost

There are many different versions of La Llorona. The oldest and most common version is that La Llorona was a Native American woman living in Mexico who became the mistress to a Spanish conquistador named Cortéz. Cortéz eventually abandoned her and in her grief, she drowned her children. After death, she became "La Llorona," and now haunts the water's edge, crying and looking for her children.

Not all versions of this story identify La Llorona as an indigenous Mexican woman. La Llorona shifts according to the people who talk about her; she is perceived in many different ways. In the story below, for example, La Llorona **subverts conventional gender expectations**. In this version of the story, La Llorona has children, but no husband and so **defies conventional social norms that presume women with children must be married**. She also is depicted as wanting to be free from her motherly duties in order to be with her lover. **She chooses her own happiness over her family obligations, which subverts common expectation that women should be motherly, self-sacrificing, and put the needs of others above their own**.

> There was a young and very beautiful woman who had three children. She used to be married, or she was single, I don't know which but she had no husband. One day she killed all of her children. You see she didn't know what to do, she had a lover—you know how it is—and she wanted to go with him and she didn't know what to do, so she killed them all.

One of them she smothered with a pillow and one she threw out the window and one she drowned in the river, she had three children and that was how she did it .... She wanted the children back and she would go down to the river, she was always by the river, and she would cry out, *Ay, mis niños*, [oh, my children] and weep and cry. (Jones 1986: 202)

This story reinforces traditional gender values as well. La Llorona is punished for desiring her freedom; she regrets the murder and is doomed to spend eternity as a ghost, searching for children that she shall never find.

4 幽霊，民族，人種

　アメリカの幽霊の多くは，抑圧された少数民族や人種差別の犠牲者です．合衆国南部に多く残る幽霊は奴隷制時代の黒人たちですし，アメリカ先住民（ネイティヴ・アメリカン，インディアン）の幽霊も多いです．数多くの話が伝わるラ・ジョローナは，メキシコからきた先住民の女性幽霊です．幽霊たちを通して，アメリカ社会が抱える困難に読者は気づくでしょう．幽霊は，アメリカが無言で抱えている罪悪感や不安，語られてこなかった悲惨な歴史を後世の人々に暗示し，語りかけているのです．

GHOSTS, ETHNICITY, AND RACE

Some ghost stories identify the ghost as belonging to a specific race or ethnic group. Stories from the American south, a former slave-owning region, may identify ghosts as being the ghosts of former Black slaves. Native Americans also are popular ghostly figures. As noted above, for example, many versions of La Llorona identify her as Native American woman from Mexico.

　Ghost stories in which the ghost is a member of an oppressed minority speak to complex issues of race and power, illustrating again that **ghosts may speak about, warn, or represent difficult social issues**. Many scholars have interpreted **these types of ghost stories as expressions national guilt and anxiety, or as a way to "speak" about tragic, and often little-known histories**. Stories about ghosts of former slaves, for example, remind people that the history of the United States is haunted by slavery and that racism remains a part of culture today.

ビラヴド:幽霊が告発する奴隷制の悪

　ノーベル賞作家トニ・モリスン（1931-）の小説『ビラヴド』は，幽霊をモチーフにして奴隷制時代の悲劇を描いた名作です．奴隷であったセサは白人の主人から逃亡しますが，ひと月後に発見されて捕らえられた時，子供たちが奴隷にされるよりはと，2歳の娘を殺してしまいます．そして，この娘の幽霊がその後の彼女の人生を支配していきます．娘の幽霊は，セサの深い罪の意識の表れです．引用は，セサの家に幽霊が憑いていると述べるくだりです．『ビラヴド』は，奴隷制が社会全体にいかに深い傷を残したか，個々人を根底から破壊する誤った制度であったということを，「幽霊」を圧倒的な存在感で描きながら，えぐるように表現した優れた小説です．日本語の翻訳も出版されていますし，英語でもぜひ読んでください．

....

　One of the most well-known ghosts in literature that symbolizes the tragedy of slavery is found in Toni Morrison's book, *Beloved*. *Beloved* was published in 1987 and is considered by many authors and critics to be one of the best novels of the twentieth century. The book is about a slave named Sethe, who manages to escape her white owners. After spending a month in freedom, she is caught. Sethe decides to murder her children rather than have them captured and returned to a life of slavery. She kills her two-year old daughter, who later returns to haunt her. In the excerpt below, the ghost is a baby who haunts the house in which Sethe lives. The baby ghost has chased away Sethe's sons by breaking mirrors and making ghostly handprints in a cake. It also throws food. The ghost represents Sethe's guilt over the murder of her child and "speaks" symbolically to the indescribable horrors that slavery engenders.

　124 [the house address] was spiteful. Full of baby's venom. The women in the house knew it and so did the children. For years each put up with the spite in his own way, but by 1873 Sethe and her daughter Denver were its only victims. The grandmother, Baby Suggs, was dead, and the sons, Howard and Buglar, had run away by the time they were thirteen years old—as soon as merely looking in a mirror shattered it (that was the signal for Buglar); as soon as two tiny hand prints appeared in the cake (that was it for Howard). Neither boy waited to see more; another kettleful of chickpeas smoking in a heap on the floor; soda crackers crum-

bled and strewn in a line next to the doorsill.　　　　（Morrison 1997: 3）

ラローリー屋敷の幽霊：史実と幽霊

　ルイジアナ州のニューオーリンズに伝わるラローリー屋敷の幽霊話は特に有名です．11 章で述べたように，ニューオーリンズは奴隷貿易の中心地でした．ラローリー屋敷は，かつてデルフィン・ラローリーの夫が所有していたもので，女主人のマダム・ラローリーは奴隷に対する残酷な扱いで知られていました．1834 年，ラローリーの家が火事になったとき消火を手伝った消防隊や近所の人は，台所や屋根裏部屋で鎖につながれた奴隷を何人も発見しました．彼らは飢えており身体の一部を切断されるなどの激しい虐待を受けていました．この家で，多数の奴隷が虐待の末に殺されていたのです．ラローリー屋敷にまつわる幽霊話の多くは口伝えで広まっています．実際にあった事件から 200 年を経た現在でも幽霊が出るといわれるラローリー屋敷は，閉じ込められた歴史を幽霊や幽霊話が暴露すること，後世の人々に警告を発している証拠ともなっています．現在，ラローリー屋敷は観光名所としても知られています．

　　　　　　　　‥‥‥‥‥‥‥‥‥‥‥‥‥‥‥‥‥‥‥‥‥‥‥‥‥‥‥

　Other ghost stories connected to slavery can be found in New Orleans, an historic city in Louisiana that was a center of slave trade in the eighteenth and nineteenth centuries. The most famous ghosts are associated with **the Lalaurie house, which is reputed to be haunted**. "Lalaurie" is the surname of the people who owned the house in early nineteenth century and who became notorious for their abominable treatment of slaves (de Caro 2015). The most common ghosts in this house are the ghost of a small slave child who is seen running along the roof and falling to her death, and the ghost of a large black man bound in chains. Although most stories about the Lalaurie house apparently are told orally, below are a few published examples. The first was originally published in 1920.

　　"[a] resident saw a large black man wrapped in chains on the main stairs .... The chained man disappeared on the last step."
　　　　　　　　　　　　　　　　　　　　　　　　　　　（de Caro 2015: 28）

A more sensationalist and touristic account from 1946 writes about

　　horrible noises of heavy bodies being dragged across floors; of chandeliers falling with a crash of glass and metal; of terrified Negro chatter from the dark and deserted kitchens; of shrieks from the courtyard; of wails and prayers and poundings under the floors; of mad jibberings from the empty garret; of a murderous whip flailing the air in awful rhythm.

(de Caro 2015: 29)

The ghost stories told about the Lalaurie house are associated with actual historical events related to slavery. The wife of the house owner, Delphine Lalaurie, had a reputation for badly mistreating her slaves. She had been fined for her mistreatment by officials, and even had her slaves taken away because of her severe abuse of them. In 1834, the Lalaurie house caught fire. When firemen and citizens came to help, they found slaves chained in the kitchen and the attic, where they had been starved and mutilated. They also found slaves with iron collars on their necks and chains on their feet, and who were permanently crippled from their severe treatment. Many of the slaves later died, Delphine Lalaurie left the country, a mob vandalized the house, and it was abandoned (de Caro 2015). Clearly, the ghosts associated with the Lalaurie house are reminders of the inhumane treatment and suffering that the slaves of this house endured. **That such stories continue to be told nearly two hundred years later is a powerful testament to how ghosts and ghost stories function to warn, inform, and "speak" about difficult, sometimes horrific issues in public ways**.

アメリカ先住民と幽霊

　アメリカ先住民は，先史時代からアメリカ大陸に住んでいた人々で，ヨーロッパ人のアメリカ大陸移住によって危機的な被害を長期にわたって受け続けなければなりませんでした．アメリカ合衆国政府は彼らの土地を奪い，条約を反故にし，戦いを仕掛け，虐殺し，多数の異なる部族の違いや先祖伝来の土地を無視して強制移住をさせました．さらに先住民は，こうした苦難に加えて感染病や飢餓にも耐えなければならなかったのです．当然のことながら，先住民の幽霊話が多く伝えられました．以下に，Haskell Indian Nations University（ハスケル先住民族大学）に伝わる話を引用しています．ハスケル大学の前身は，南北戦争（1861-1865）後に先住民の子供たちを強制的に親から引き離して全寮制で収容した学校です．この学校では先住民の生徒に英語を強制し，彼らの母語を禁じました．そして，自由に親元へ帰ることもできない厳しい環境のもとで，多くの子供が命を落としました．2006年に聞き取りで記録された引用の幽霊話は，文学

になった話のように鬼気迫るものではありませんが，先住民の子供たちがこの学校で耐えた不当で過酷な扱いを，確かに告発しています．現れた幽霊の顔にあるいくつものアザは天然痘を患ったしるしです．ヨーロッパ人の移住によってアメリカ大陸に持ち込まれたこの感染症で，実に多数の先住民が死んだのでした．

....

Stories about Native American ghosts also speak to past atrocities. Most people know that the United States government treated Native Americans harshly in the past, but they may not know specific historical facts. **Sadly, the history of relations between the US government and various Native American groups is littered with stolen lands, broken treaties, war, massacres, disease, famine, and forced removal from homes, families, and tribal lands. It is not surprising, therefore, that stories about Native American ghosts exist**.

The ghost story below was told at Haskell Indian Nations University, a former Indian boarding school. The US government established Indian boarding schools after the Civil War to forcibly educate Native American children in order to acculturate them into mainstream society. Many children were forcibly taken from their homes. They weren't allowed to speak their language, or sometimes even return home to see their families. Conditions were very harsh at the Indian boarding schools and many children, including babies, died. The story below describes a personal encounter with a Native American ghost by a staff member at Haskell Nations Indian University. It was recorded in 2006.

> This one week I was there by myself. This happened when we had a snowfall around 3:00 in the morning. I heard the handicapped door pop open. When I heard the door pop open, I felt a chill come down my spine. That never happened before. I walked up to the door and looked outside. When I stepped back, I saw that on the upper right-hand corner of the door there was a face: the right side of a human face. You could see the crow's feet, the pock marks on the face. You could see the chapped lips of this face on the door.　　　　　　　　　　　(Tucker 2007: 163-64)

This ghost story is not as dramatic or horrifying as literary ghost stories. The narrator feels strange ("a chill down my spine") and sees a mysterious face in the door. The narrator interprets the face as the ghost of an old Indian man who had suffered greatly. The pockmarks on the face are evidence of his suffering. These pockmarks are smallpox scars, a disease that was imported from Europe and from which thousands of Native Americans died. Therefore, **even less dramatic ghost stories such as this one can speak to and remind contemporary listeners of the injustices of the past**.

5 考　察

　幽霊は生者と死者の境界にいて，境界的な場所に憑き，現れます．生者が幽霊を恐れるわけは，一つに，幽霊が未解決の問題を告発するからです．一方，幽霊は生者に見えない真実を暗示することもあります．幽霊の実体のなさは，生や社会のつかみどころのなさと呼応しているようでもあり，幽霊が何かをはっきり説明し尽くすことはできません．もし説明し尽くしてその神秘が失われたら，それはもう幽霊ではないのでしょうから．

DISCUSSION

Ghosts are liminal beings that exist between the living and the dead. They are found in liminal locations, such as hallways and stairs, or on bridges and tunnels, as well as other places. People are afraid of ghosts, and **ghosts frequently exist because there is a problem or some unfinished business**. In the examples found in this chapter, the "unfinished business" is a large social problem or issue that remains unresolved, such as the abuse of women or unresolved histories of oppression.

　　It is important to remember, however, that not all ghosts symbolize difficult issues so concretely. Ghosts are puzzling. As liminal beings, they are difficult to pin down. **They offer glimpses of alternative truths, suggesting that reality is larger and more complex than mere surface details.** Like shadows, **ghosts and the alternative truths and realities they represent are difficult to capture and easily elude our grasp**. Ghosts are mysterious things.

6 演 習

　日本で伝承されたり噂が広まったりする幽霊やそれに類した超自然的な生物から，私たちはどのようなメッセージを読み取ることができるのでしょうか．アメリカの場合のように，人種，民族，ジェンダーなどが重要な問題としてまず浮かび上がるでしょうか．あるいは別の問題でしょうか．そこに読み取れる問題は，日本という国や日本に暮らす人の歴史とどう関わりがあるのでしょう．資料を集め，分析した結果の考察を話し合ってください．

ACTIVE LEARNING

What might supernatural figures in Japan mean or represent?
Why do they exist?
Are there issues of race, ethnicity, and gender that arise, or are the issues and ideas quite different?
In what ways do these ideas tie to the history of Japan?

9章
子どもの遊びと文化——未来を創造する

Chapter 9
Children's Traditions: Creating the Future through Play

1 遊びはなぜ大切か

　子供たちは遊びの天才です．子供は遊びから人生に必要な多くを学びます．逆にいえば，遊びを観察すると子供の世界が見えます．子供の遊びには，社会問題や大人の価値基準が驚くほど深く取り込まれています．同時に，子供は遊びを通して意思伝達をし，自我を成長させます．有名な文化人類学者のグレゴリー・ベントンによれば，遊びの要素を含んだ行為はその行為自体が持つ目的とは異なる目的を持っていて，本当の目的はコミュニケーションにあるといいます．すなわち，ある行為の本来的な目的と遊びとして行為されるときの目的が矛盾していて，ある行為を通してメッセージを発信する側（遊びを仕掛ける側）とそれを理解して受け取る側（受け入れて遊びに乗る側）のコミュニケーションを成立させるものが，遊びだというのです．動物がお互いに，噛み付くようなふりをして遊んでいるのを，あなたは見たことがあるでしょう．動物はそのとき，攻撃しているわけではなく「自分はあなたにとって安全だ，信頼できる仲間だ」「一緒にいて嬉しい，気分がいい」というような受容的な気持ちを，〈軽く〉噛み付くという〈遊びの〉攻撃を通して相手に伝えているのです．そんなふうに，遊びは洗練されたコミュニケーション手段だと，ベントンは言ったのです．

　子供は遊びの中で自分の考えや行為，行動様式を試します．「ずるをする」といったような行動をとれば，結果的には得をするどころか友人から責められたり居心地の悪い思いをするということを，経験を通して知ります．遊びの時間は「本当ではない，真面目ではない」ので，そこで自分の行動を実験してみながら，よいことと悪いこととを学びつつ，大人になった時，社会でどう生きていくかを探るのです．子供たちの遊びと遊ぶ子供たちとを文化研究の視点で観察すると，大人の社会の既存価値観や言語以外の補助的コミュニケーションのさまざまな方法を読み取ることができます．また，未来の社会にどのような文化が継承され，あるいは新たに創造されるのかをある程度推測することさえできるのです．

INTRODUCTION
All humans play, but children are the very best at it. They are the world's experts at playing and if allowed, children spend most of their free time at play. Adults rarely think about what children's play means because adults often presume that play is unimportant. **But children's play reveals much about children's worlds**. Play is an imaginative, child-centered realm where anything can happen. Children create a world that they control and in this world **children deal with surprisingly adult ideas, issues, and themes**.

WHAT IS PLAY?
Play is a sophisticated form of communication. The most important idea about play is that during play, actions do not count. A famous theorist named Gregory Bateson (1972) described play as "paradoxical," meaning that it is self-contradictory. Bateson said that playful actions don't mean the same thing that those actions normally do when people are not playing. His classic example is animals at play. When animals play, they sometimes nip each other. A nip is very similar to a bite; both involve teeth and flesh. The nip in play, however, is not serious, whereas a bite is intended to harm. How can animals tell the difference between a playful nip and a bite meant to harm? Animals communicate that the nip is not a threat, despite its similarities to a bite. The nip represents the bite, but means something else, something playful. This is why **play is a sophisticated form of communication**. When animals and people play, they communicate that their actions should not be taken seriously. This negation is why play is considered to be "paradoxical."

WHY IS PLAY IMPORTANT?
Because playful actions should not be taken as "real," **play is an important area for experimentation**. In play, people experiment with ideas, actions, and behaviors with immunity that otherwise might have serious consequences. For example, a child who decides to cheat while playing with friends is not kicked out of his friend group forever; rather, his friends may simply call him a "cheater" (a person who cheats) and continue playing (Knapp and Knapp

1978). Meanwhile, the child has experimented with the idea of cheating. This makes play a perfect realm for children to research uncomfortable, forbidden, or mysterious aspects of life that they may not fully understand. **Play provides a safe environment to investigate serious ideas in a way that "doesn't count"** because behaviors, actions, and words done within play are not taken seriously.

2 遊びが伝える男女の立場

　子供たちにとって，将来に待ち構えている恋やセックス，男女別に規定される社会的役割は，本当のところを知りたいのになかなか教えてもらえない不可思議な領域といっていいでしょう．ところが，特に伝承の遊びには，隠された秘密の一端を遠回しに明かしてくれるものが多々あります．たとえば，主に女の子がする【縄跳びの歌】には，「シンデレラが王子様にキスされて，蛇にキスしてしまったシンデレラはお医者へ行った」という内容の歌があり，キスから発展したロマンスの結果が「ミステイク」と「医者」（妊娠）につながるという警告になっています．もちろん子供たちは，ただ楽しく歌いながら縄跳びするだけなのですが．漫画『スヌーピー』をもとにした【手遊び歌】では，チャーリー・ブラウンはペパーミント・パティを選ばないで，別な女の子に「エル・オー・ヴィ・イー」(L-O-V-E) と言ってキスします．子どもはこうした歌を歌いながら手をたたいて遊んでいるうちに，男の子が選ぶ女の子はどんな子か，選ばないのはどんな子かという保守的な価値観を学習し，「選ぶ」のは男子であり，告白するのも男子であり，キスするのもまた男子からであるという，性別に左右された定型の行動様式を知らされていきます．以下の英文では，それぞれの遊び歌を詳しく分析していますので，ゆっくり読んでみてください（ペパーミント・パティの歌は，本書のホームページからアクセスして聞くことができます）．

・・

GENDER ROLES IN HANDCLAPS

One serious issue that children investigate during play is gender roles. Issues related to growing up, such as puberty, sex, parenthood, and the social roles of men and women are part of the mysterious world of adults. Children use play to explore these baffling and sometimes forbidden subjects.

　Topics related to gender are prevalent in handclapping and jump rope rhymes, which are popular with girls. Handclaps are a game where two or more girls get together to clap out complex patterns with each other. The clapping patterns are usually accompanied by a song, chant, or rhyme. Jumping rope is a game where children jump over a rope that is being turned by others who hold onto its end. The children jumping rope often chant rhymes or sing songs, while the slapping sound of the turning rope provides the beat or percussion.

縄跳び歌・手遊び歌 【遊び 1】

The lyrics to handclap and jump-rope rhymes frequently concern domesticity, boyfriends, and motherhood, as well as references to sex and pregnancy. **There often is a strong emphasis on traditional roles for women**. The most famous jump rope rhyme in English is this one:

> Cinderella/ Dressed in 'yella [yellow]/ Went upstairs to kiss a fella [fellow] Made a mistake/ Kissed a snake/ How many doctors did it take?
> (1, 2, 3 ...) [girl counts the number of times she can jump rope until she misses. It is then the next girl's turn].

Scholars agree that this rhyme contains veiled references to sex and pregnancy. The girl, Cinderella, is the name of a popular princess from European folklore (see Chapter 1). In the rhyme, she is clearly interested in boys, since she decides to kiss "a fella" (a boy). Unfortunately, her decision leads to a mistake, and by the end of the rhyme Cinderella needs to go to the doctor. Most scholars interpret Cinderella's visit to the doctor as an indication of pregnancy. They believe the rhyme is a veiled reference to sexual activity.

How does such a rhyme create a future for girls? Girls who jump rope to this rhyme are not actively thinking about pregnancy. They are thinking about jumping rope, having fun, and impressing their friends. The rhyme is catchy, easy to remember, and fun to recite. However, **this rhyme also puts a vague idea in girls' heads** that they might need to go to a doctor if they kiss boys. In the rhyme, the girl did not kiss a boy, but kissed a snake instead. The rhyme substitutes kissing a snake for sexual activity. The girls don't think about it as they jump rope, but the idea is there nonetheless. **Play is a safe arena to explore serious thoughts at a silly, childish level**.

Another well-known handclap rhyme is this one:

My name is Peppermint Patty,/ I live in Cincinnati,
With a freckle on my nose/ And eighteen toes,
And this is how my story goes:
One day as I was walkin',/ I saw my boyfriend talkin'
To a pretty little girl/ With strawberry curls
And this is what he said to her.
I L-O-V-E, love you,/ I K-I-S-S, kiss you,
I K-I-S-S, kiss you/ On your F-A-C-E,/ Face face face.

This rhyme is clearly influenced by the popular comic strip series "Peanuts" and closely mirrors the personality of the characters. Peppermint Patty is a tomboy who is in love with Charlie Brown. Unfortunately, Charlie Brown never notices Peppermint Patty. He is in love with the "little red-haired girl," presumably the same "pretty little girl/with strawberry curls" found in the rhyme. Note the references to attraction between boys and girls, kissing, and an emphasis on being pretty as a requirement to attract a boy. Children explore ideas about gender through their play. **This rhyme reinforces traditional ideas about gender**, such as an emphasis on prettiness for girls.

伝承遊び歌の価値観

　縄跳び歌や手遊び歌などの伝承遊び歌は，性的役割について，年月にさらされた大衆の保守的な価値観を表現しています．しかしだからといって，子供たちがそれをそのまま学び人生で採用するというわけではありません．彼らは，世界が歌詞よりもっと複雑であることを，自らの環境と日々の生活の中で感じています．大事なのは，すでに認められてきた価値基準が何なのかを遊びから感じ取り，そこから自分の行き先を自ら選択していくようになることです．出発点に，親や先生など特定の個人の価値観ではない，年月にさらされた大衆の価値観が加わることが，子供の判断力に客観性をつけ加えると考えられます．

・・

In general, **the rhymes that accompany jumping rope and handclap games portray very traditional gender roles**. Many rhymes focus on boy-girl relationships and matters of love. In the rhymes, girls attract boys by being pretty. No jump rope or handclap rhymes suggest that boys might be attracted to girls who are smart, funny, or good at sports. If the character in the rhyme envisions a future, it is as wife and mother, or occasionally as a teacher. There are no known rhymes that talk about a girls' future as an astronaut or as president of the United States.

It is important to note that **just because young girls recite these rhymes as they play does not mean that they will embrace the traditional gender roles found in them**. The world is much more complex than that. Parents, culture, the environment, teachers, peers and many other elements influence children. However, it is true that girls learn gender roles from somewhere, and **one important source are the traditional rhymes that are passed from girl to girl on the playground**.

3 ルールを守る，ルールを作る

　楽しく遊ぶためには，みんなで共同してルールを守らねばならないと子供たちはよく理解しています．【鬼ごっこ】や【隠れんぼ】は，「規則の遵守」「反則と罰則」を子供が経験し，楽しむ遊びです．鬼ごっこはどの文化にもありますが，単純な遊びだけにバリエーションも多いです．アメリカの「スタチューズ（銅像）」という鬼ごっこは，日本の「ダルマさんが転んだ」に似ています．英文の説明をご参照ください．このゲームではタグ付けされた（印をつけられた，つまり「鬼」になった）人は it と呼ばれます．人間でない「もの」になったその人に，みんなの動きを止める力が与えられるというルールです．その他のルールは，以前に遊んだときと同じでもいいし遊ぶ仲間で新たに決めてもいいのです．ゲームのルールが与えられるのではなく子供がルールを主体的に決めて，うまくいけばそのまま遊び，うまくいかなければルールを変えて遊ぶことができる．そのように，プレーヤー自身がルールの決定者になれるという点が，野球やバスケットボールのようなスポーツのゲームと遊びのゲームが異なるところです．あなたが子供の時に楽しんだ鬼ごっこは，どんなルールでしたか．

Children playing tag

MAKING RULES AND BREAKING RULES IN TAG
Children experiment with rules during play. Traditional hiding and chasing games are useful in this regard. Examples of traditional hiding and chasing games include tag and hide-and-go-seek. Tag is a game found across

the world where children chase each other. There are many variations. Once a person is caught (or "tagged"), they have to chase the other children. Hide-and-go-seek is also well known. In this game, some children hide until they are found by the person who is seeking, which in English is called the "it."

鬼ごっこ・隠れんぼ【遊び 2】

The excerpt below from the novel *Dandelion Wine* by Ray Bradbury describes a group of boys playing "Statues," which is a variation of the game of tag. In this game, the children run, and when the "it" calls "statues!" the children must freeze like statues.

> "It was seven o'clock, supper over, and the boys gathering one by one from the sound of their house doors slammed and their parents crying to them not to slam the doors. Douglas and Tom and Charlie and John stood among half a dozen others and it was time for hide-and-seek and Statues.
> "Just one game," said John. "Then I got to go home. The train leaves at nine. Who's going to be 'it'?"
> "Me," said Douglas.
> "That the first time I ever heard of anybody volunteering to be 'it,'" said Tom.
> Douglas looked at John for a long moment. "Start running," he cried.
> The boys scattered, yelling. John backed away, then turned and began to lope. Douglas counted slowly. He let them run far, spread out, separate each to his own small world. When they had go their momentum up and were almost out of sight he took a deep breath.
> "Statues!"
> Everyone froze. (Bradbury 1946 [2009]: 121)

Both tag and hide-and-go-seek are passed down through tradition. The rules are not written down, which means that the games can be played in many different ways. **Traditional games give children power to decide for themselves how the game will be governed**. Everyone must decide what the rules are and how the game will be played. In the passage above, for example, the children must decide who will be "it" (the person who chases after the others). Douglas volunteers to be "it" and the game begins. This kind of decision-making power is typical of traditional games. Each time they play a game, children make decisions such as who will be "it," how players will be tagged, how long a person should be "it," and what the physical boundaries of the playing arena are. This decision-making power is very different from when children play formally organized sports, such as school soccer or baseball teams. In those situations, the rules usually are decided and enforced by adults.

遊びのルール作り

　子供は，自分に都合よく遊びのルールを曲げたりごまかしたりします．先に引用したレイ・ブラッドベリの小説『たんぽぽのお酒』では，it になったダグラスは，引越しして行くジョンを引き止めたいばっかりに，3時間「凍る（固まる）」というルールをジョンに押し付けます．子供はそんなふうに，規則をどこまで曲げられるのか，自分の思うようにしてそれが公正なのかズルとされるのか，どんな結果が導かれるのかを試してみるのです．遊び相手の頭の良し悪しを測り，どこまでいけるか観察するのです．その結果，ルールを曲げる子がずるいとかそのほうがいいとか，子供たちは議論しケンカするかもしれません．しかしその経験を通じて，法則を定め運用する技術を彼らは学び始めます．「真面目でない，本当でない」遊びの時間のルール作りは，未来の世の中を動かすルール作りにつながっているのです．

....

Children frequently test the limits of the rules they have set by cheating or bending the rules in their favor. In Bradbury's book *Dandelion Wine*, Douglas uses the rules of the game to prevent his friend John from going home. Douglas is upset because John is about to move away with his family. The two friends won't see each other again. In the passage below, John is a "statue" in the game and is supposed to remain frozen.

"John now," said Douglas, "don't you move so much as an eyelash. I absolutely command you to stay here and not move at all for the next three hours!"
"Doug ..."
John's lips moved.
"Freeze!" said Douglas.
John went back to looking at the sky, but he was not smiling now.
"I got to go," he whispered.

"Not a muscle, it's the game!" (Bradbury 1946 [2009]: 122)

Here, Douglas is exploiting the game in his favor. According to the rules, John must do as Douglas says. John needs to go home. Douglas doesn't want him to and so Douglas has "frozen" him, telling John he can't move for three hours. Douglas is testing the limits of the rules of the game to see whether or not he can force John to stay.

Such behavior is common in traditional games where the rules are negotiable. **Children set the rules, test the limits of those rules, and observe the consequences of their actions. In doing so, they explore morality**. They experiment with questions such as: What can I get away with? Will people get mad? Will I feel guilty? How much is too much? **Children also test their own cleverness and the cleverness of their friends when they bend the rules of the game**. Who is paying attention? Will anyone notice? Because play is by definition a realm in which actions "don't count," children are able to explore questions of cheating and playing fairly without severe consequences.

What kind of future is created when children make rules and then test those rules? No child ruins his or her future by bending rules while playing with friends. No one will be expelled from school for pushing the limits of a game of tag. But **the child has experimented with serious, moral issues, and better understands the consequences of his or her behavior**.

4 自分を鍛える遊び

異界との交信を試す遊び，経験がありますか．【ブラディ・メアリ（血みどろのメアリ）】はその一つです．デーモンや幽霊，妖怪の類の異界の生き物は，魔法を使ったり人知を超えた力を持ち，科学の知識や自然の法則で説明がつかないことをします．子供は，そうした生き物が本当にいるのかどうか知りたくてたまらないのです．「ブラディ・メアリ」という遊びでは，10歳から15歳くらいの子供たちが灯りを消したバスルーム（シャワーや浴槽とトイレと洗面台がある部屋）に入り，ブラディ・メアリという名の恐ろしいあの世の女を呼び出します．そしてどうなるか……．それはどうぞ英文を読んでください．

EXPERIMENTING WITH THE SUPERNATURAL
Children experiment with the supernatural during play. The term "supernatural" refers to powers that are beyond the laws of science and nature. The supernatural is associated with magic and powerful, unexplained forces. It also is associated with demons, ghosts, and other mysterious creatures (see Chapter 8). Children are usually quite curious about the supernatural and, like most people, wonder whether or not it actually exists. Luckily, there are a number of traditional games designed to provide children with concrete experiments to satisfy their curiosity as they navigate their own interpretations and understandings.

Looking for Bloody Mary in a bathroom mirror is an old children's game. What will she do?

One popular game that plays with the supernatural in the United States is called "Bloody Mary." Other names for this game include "Mary Whales" and "Mary Worth." Bloody Mary is the name of a mysterious, frightening woman who appears in a bathroom mirror when she is summoned. She is a bathroom ghost, occupying the liminal space of the bathroom (see Chapter 8). "Bloody Mary" is played in a group, usually by children between the ages of about 10 to 15. To play the game, a group of children go into a bathroom and shut off the lights so that the room is very dark. Together, they chant "Bloody Mary" several times. Exactly how many times one is supposed to say her name varies. Some children say her name only three times, but others say it many more. After the chant is finished, the children quickly turn on the light. Bloody Mary is supposed to appear in the mirror. Some children think that they see her, but most don't. A debate then ensues about whether or not Bloody Mary appeared and what might be done differently next time to make the game work better.

血みどろのメアリ【遊び3】

「ブラディ・メアリ」のゲームをする時、子供たちはわざと自分を危険にさらして楽しんでいます。血だらけのメアリは子供を襲って殺すと言われているのに、

そのメアリをわざわざ呼び出そうとするのですから．もちろんメアリに殺された子供はいません．でも，子供の想像力の中にメアリは存在するし，本当に子供を殺すかもしれないと思えるのです．そうして彼らは，自分の勇気や覚悟の強さを試験にかけます．バスルームという安全な場所ではありますが，友達と一緒に怖さに勝てるかどうかを試しています．それから，このゲームで子供たちは，自分の能力を試してもいます．いつも大人の力に負けてしまう子供たちでも，あの世のものを呼び出せるなら大人よりすごいではありませんか．だから，「ブラディ・メアリ」をするのは，大人への反抗でもあります．プロテスタント系のキリスト教を文化の基盤とする国であるアメリカ合衆国には，異界の生き物をまったく認めない，あるいは悪と結びつけて厳しく排除する大人も少なくありません．そうした環境でも子供たちは，未知の世界に自分をさらす遊びをして「危険」を乗り越えます．それは，人生で次々に立ち向かわねばならない未知の経験を切り抜ける練習でもあり，空想で自分を鍛える創造性豊かな行為なのです．

....

What ideas are children are experimenting with when they play this game? First, **children experiment with danger, or at least the *idea* of danger**. Bloody Mary is clearly a dangerous and frightening figure to children. According the game, her image—should it actually appear in the mirror—is terrifying. Children expect her to be bloody, or that her eyes will be gouged out. In some versions of the game, Bloody Mary is supposed to attack the children, scratch them, or even kill them. No child has ever been killed playing this game, so the game is not actually dangerous. But children don't seem to know or care about this kind of adult fact. **They use their imagination to create a fantasy world in which the possibility exists that they might be killed by a ghost in a mirror that they have summoned themselves**. They play with the idea of danger in the safe environment of the bathroom.

Children also test their own courage and bravery when they play this game. Do they have the courage to enter a dark bathroom and chant magical words? What will they do if Bloody Mary actually appears? Will they survive her wrath? At the end of the game, when the lights are turned on and no one has been harmed, the children feel they have overcome a great test or obstacle. They have conquered fear and proved their worthiness to themselves and their friends. **Their own imagination and the safe environment of the bathroom provide the materials through which they**

prove their worth.

Additionally, **children experiment with power when playing Bloody Mary**. Children are a group with very little power. Children's lives are generally controlled by adults and so children are interested in various forms of power. Playing Bloody Mary allows children to test whether or not they have the power to conjure up a strange and alarming being. Most children find that they can't summon Bloody Mary successfully, but the game provides them the opportunity to experiment with power, even if the experiment ultimately fails. It also satisfies their curiosity about the supernatural, at least temporarily.

Finally, **playing Bloody Mary allows children to be a little bit rebellious**. Playing with the supernatural is a somewhat controversial behavior. Some adults in the United States don't believe in the supernatural and dismiss it entirely. Others associate the supernatural with evil. Therefore, playing with the supernatural allows children to taste something forbidden, but in a safe manner and with few consequences.

What future is being created when children play Bloody Mary? In this temporary, self-created world, children play with danger, test the limits of their bravery, experiment with power, satisfy their curiosity about the supernatural, and experiment with rebellion. However these important issues play out in their future lives, it will not be the first time that they are experienced by children who have played this game.

5 考　察

　遊びは，コミュニケーションの洗練された方法です．実際に行動したり行為したりするのに，「本当でない」という前提に守られているので逸脱や失敗も重大に取り上げられることなく，子供は遊びの中でいろいろな社会的実験（遊び空間での遊びの「社会」ですが）を試みることができます．彼らは遊びを通して既存の価値観を感じ取り，社会的な規則との付き合い方を実験し，未知の危険や恐怖に立ち向かう訓練を積みます．「本当だけれど，本当でない」遊びの時間と空間は，人間の発達には欠かせないものなのです．

DISCUSSION
Play is a paradoxical, sophisticated form of communication where actions and behaviors are not taken seriously. This paradox allows children to experiment with serious questions and issues in play in a harmless, non-serious way. **During play, children are exposed to conventional ideas and values** as shown in the jump rope rhymes and handclap songs. The future created during jump rope is not one in which a girl is predestined to fill a traditional female role, but it is a world in which she has been exposed to traditional ideas about gender over a formative period of time. **Children also create mock societies during play**. In this society, children create rules and test them. As they make and break rules in tag and hide-and-seek, for example, they learn to use their own judgment and they experiment with the consequences of questionable behavior. It is up to the child decide which actions are acceptable and which are not as he or she move forward into adulthood. Finally, **play allows children to glimpse into the future by experimenting with fear and danger**. Playing imaginative, psychological games such as Bloody Mary provides children with a means of experimenting with power over the unknown. **The children enter the world with some experience and preparation, which has been achieved entirely through the paradoxical, real-but-not-real realm of play**. While many adults dismiss play as unimportant or frivolous, the truth is that **play is essential to human development**.

6 演　習

(1) あなたの知っている遊びについて，子供たちがする独自の工夫にはどんなものがあるでしょうか．具体的に説明し，なぜそうした工夫を子供が必要と思ったか，その工夫によって遊びにどんな意味のある変化が加わったかなどを，話し合ってください．
(2) 本書に引用した歌や他の遊び歌の音源を聞いて，あなたの気づいたことや分析できることを，英語の本文に習って文章に書いてみましょう．

ACTIVE LEARNING
What kinds of children's games do you know? What ideas or attitudes might

children be experimenting with in these games? Please be specific in your discussion.

第Ⅳ部
祝祭と地域
——地域共同体の営み

Part IV
Festivals and Celebrations

10章
ハロウィン——地域で異なる文化

Chapter 10
Halloween in New York City and California:
Regional Variations of a Single Celebration

1　10月31日，死者の祭り

　ハロウィンはアメリカ人の大好きな祭りです．近年では日本でもハロウィンを楽しむ人が増えたので，みなさんもご存知でしょう．もとは，救われなかった死者の幽霊や悪の魔術師たちの仮装をして行う夜の祭りでしたが，今ではさまざまな服装で日常からの逸脱を楽しむ機会になっています．「ジャコランタン」または「ジャック・オ・ランタン」と呼ばれる，カボチャをくり抜いて作るローソク立てはご存知ですか．顔に似せて目や鼻や口を切り抜きますが，幽霊やデーモンなどのあの世の者の顔を作ります．怖い顔も楽しい顔もありますね．こうした飾り物はハロウィンが秋の収穫に関連し，季節が（春・夏・秋）から死（冬）へと移る時期を示す祭りであることに由来します．

INTRODUCTION

Halloween is a popular celebration in the United States. **It is associated with the dead, with spookiness or evil, and it is celebrated on October 31**. The main way that people celebrate Halloween is by dressing up in costumes at night. A traditional Halloween costume is something a little bit scary, like a ghost, or a witch. A ghost is the spirit of a dead person that is not in the proper resting place (see Chapter 8). A witch is someone who has evil magic powers. However, people dress up in all kinds of costumes, from superheroes to animals to famous people to household objects. People can be anything they want on Halloween.

　Symbols connecting life and death are common in Halloween (Santino "Halloween"). **Halloween is associated with the harvest**. The fall harvest represents the fullness of life. The harvest also means it is time to prepare for winter, and winter symbolizes death. To represent life and death, people decorate their homes with vegetables that represent harvest, such as pumpkins, corn, hay, and dried corn. They also decorate with skeletons and ghosts, which represent death. A Jack-o'-lantern is a decoration that combines these elements. A Jack-o'-lantern is a pumpkin and pumpkins are associated with the harvest. To make a Jack-o'-lantern, people hollow out the pumpkin and carve it to look like a face. The face sometimes is associated with a spirit, demon, or ghost. A lighted candle is placed inside. The pumpkin represents the harvest, or life, while the face represents spirits, or death.

2　子供たちのハロウィン

　ハロウィンは，19世紀にアイルランド移民がアメリカへ伝えたものです．クリスマスとは異なり合衆国の祝日になっていないせいもあり，祝い方も地方や住民の文化的背景に応じてさまざまで，一般的には小さな子供の祭りとして知られています．「トリック　オア　トリート！」（美味しいものをくれなきゃ，いたずらするよ！）．ハロウィン用の衣装を着た子供たちが，大人にそう言ってはお菓子をもらい歩きます．近所の家の呼び鈴を鳴らすのが普通ですが，地域の特性に応じて方法はいろいろです．ショッピングセンターの店々を回るところや，大人が駐車場の車に待機してそこで集めさせたり，家が密集していない集落ではお菓子をもらって回る習慣がなかったり．でも，ともかく，ハロウィンは子供が普段の約束を破って自由になれる日です．遊びのある特別な衣装，夜になってから子供だけで出歩くこと，たくさんのお菓子を手に入れること，どれも夢のよう．かつては，10代の若者が悪さ（トリック）をしてもよい晩でもあったのですが，治安のために規制がかかり，いまでは「トリック　オア　トリート！」の本来の意味をわかっている人もあまりいなくなりました．一方で，ハロウィンがお菓子集めの祭りになったのは，戦後，砂糖の供給が豊富になったためなのです．

CHILDREN AND HALLOWEEN

Irish immigrants brought Halloween to the US during the nineteenth century. For most of the twentieth century, Halloween was a minor, unofficial holiday geared toward children. Even today, the US government does not officially recognize it. People do not get the day off from work for Halloween, like they do for other holidays, such as Christmas. Despite unofficial recognition, Hal-

Child trick-or-treating

loween is important and **represents different ideas to different groups of people**.

For children, Halloween traditionally represents a little extra freedom and excess because they go out at night in costume and eat a lot of candy. They are **symbolically free from the control of parents, who represent social norms**. Children usually celebrate Halloween by going trick-or-treating. Trick-or-treating means going to different houses in a neighborhood to collect candy, pencils, or other small treats. A child or a group of children dresses up in costume. They walk around the neighborhood in the evening. If a house has a light on, the children know it is OK to trick-or-treat at the house. They walk up the steps and ring the doorbell. When the person answers the door, the children say "trick-or-treat!" The person then gives a candy, pencil, or other treat to each child. The children then go to the next house. They collect the treats in a bag. At the end of the night, they have many different sweets and other treats.

The term "trick-or-treat" is interesting to think about. A "trick" is a prank or a joke. When the children say "trick-or-treat," they are telling the homeowner (in a playful way) to give them a treat or they will perform a trick on them. In the past, **Halloween was a night for mischief by children or teenagers**. This is another reason why Halloween is associated with freedom from social norms. Playing tricks and pranking was common. Teenagers might throw eggs at a building, put soap on a car, or string toilet paper around the trees on someone's property. In the 1930s and 1940s, local governments began to encourage children to trick-or-treat rather than play tricks. After World War II, trick-or-treating became a more common activity for children on Halloween because sugar was more easily available. The association of sugar and small treats with Halloween is partly why Halloween is considered a children's holiday. Sometimes children still play tricks on Halloween, but today, most children don't know the meaning of the phrase "trick-or-treat."

3 ハロウィンの歴史

　ハロウィンの起源はわかっていませんが，キリスト教が始まる以前のケルト文化の祝祭，サムハイン祭にちなむといわれています．ケルトの暦で一年の始まりがこの日にあたり，収穫を祝い冬の訪れを記したとも考えられています．サムハイン祭の期間には死者の霊がこの世に戻るとされている一方で（日本のお盆のようですね），キリスト教では現世に戻る死者の霊は天国へ行けなかった邪悪な悪霊だけと考えられているので，キリスト教文化がケルト文化を圧倒した後には，ハロウィンは魔女や幽霊と結びつけられるようになりました．この祭りを19世紀にアメリカへ伝えたのは，ケルト文化の伝統をもつアイルランドからの移民たちでした．アイルランドでは，ジャック・オ・ランタンをジャガイモやカブで作り悪霊を追い払っていたわけですが，アメリカではそれをカボチャで作ったのですね．

....

HISTORY OF HALLOWEEN

No one knows exactly how Halloween began. It is an ancient, pre-Christian holiday from the Celtic region of Europe. The term "Celtic" loosely refers to the region in Europe of Ireland, Wales, Scotland, Brittany, Cornwall, and the Isle of Man. These regions have related languages and cultures. Many people today admire the ancient traditions of music and poetry from this area, as well as the independent and fierce spirit of the peoples.

　The Celtic celebration of Halloween (or Samhain, pronounced "sow-when" in modern Irish), was associated with harvest and marked the beginning of winter. It may also have been the first day of the New Year in the Celtic calendar. It was a time when people needed to gather and store food and fuel for the winter and cattle were brought down from summer pastures (Santino, "Halloween"). Samhain also was associated with **the dead, who were thought to travel during this time**. Samhain was considered a magic, somewhat dangerous time of transition. Celtic peoples set out food and drink for the dead. It was also customary to light bonfires. As Christianity spread throughout Europe, **Samhain became associated with evil spirits. The traveling dead were considered wicked**, rather than just simply the spirits of the dead. In Ireland during the nineteenth century, people made Jack-o'-lanterns by hollowing out turnips, or sometimes potatoes or beets.

They carved faces into them, and put a lit candle inside. The purpose was supposedly to frighten away the spirits. When the Irish emigrated to the US during the nineteenth century, they found that pumpkins were better suited for making Jack-o'-lanterns. As a celebration of spirits, **Halloween evolved from Samhain traditions**.

4 地域で異なるハロウィン

ニューヨークのハロウィンパレード

　アメリカ随一のコスモポリタン都市，ニューヨーク．800もの異なる言語が話されているとさえいわれ，かつてはヨーロッパからの移民の玄関口でした．ここでは盛大に大人のハロウィンが祝われます．ニューヨーク市の中心，マンハッタン島の南部にあるグリニッジ・ヴィレッジは，「ザ・ヴィレッジ」とも呼ばれていて，かつては芸術家や演劇関係者，音楽家など，自由な生き方をする人々の居住地区でした．同性愛者の平等な権利を主張する運動もこの場所に拠点をおくなど，アメリカ社会の多様性を具現するような地域です．1974年に始まったヴィレッジのハロウィンパレードは，いまでは5，6万人が奇抜な仮装で練り歩く大人の祭りとなっています．それは，公共空間を劇場化した美術と音楽と社会批判のパレードで，なかには過激で性的な仮装もあります．エネルギッシュに多様性を主張する大人のハロウィンがニューヨークでますます異彩を放つのは，この懐の深い大都市が，自由を歓迎し逸脱を容認しつつ発展してきたという，歴史的事実に裏付けられているのでしょう．

HALLOWEEN IN NEW YORK CITY: AN ALTERNATIVE FESTIVAL

Halloween is still considered a children's holiday, but adults celebrate it more now than in the past. **The biggest adult celebration of Halloween is in New York City**. New York City is the largest, most diverse, and most cosmopolitan city in the United States. In 2016, the population was approximately 8.5 million people within the city itself, and about 20.6 million within the metro urban area (NYC Planning). New York also historically has been the most important entrance point into the US for immigrants. Some experts believe that over 800 different languages are spoken in New York City (Roberts 2010), making it one of the most linguistically diverse cities in the world.

Most Irish immigrants that came to the US landed in New York. Today New York still retains a large population with Irish roots. Given the prevalence of Irish immigrants in New York, it is not surprising that Halloween is important there.

New York City is made up of many different neighborhoods. **The biggest Halloween celebration in New York is located in a famous neighborhood called the "Village."** "The Village" is the casual nickname for the formal neighborhood name, which is "Greenwich Village." The Village is located on the west side of lower Manhattan (downtown New York City). Today it is a relatively wealthy, well-educated area, with a population of 72,000 people according to the 2010 census. The Village is a famous artists' colony. **It historically has been a haven for artists, writers, theater people, bohemians, drag queens, and other people interested in living a non-conformist lifestyle**. The Village has long been associated with the avant-garde. It also has been an important place for the gay rights movement. As noted above, New York City is very diverse. The Village represents one kind of diversity, which is diversity and freedom in thought and lifestyle. In short, the Village is a place where people are free to express themselves in any way they want.

The traditional idea of Halloween as a time of excess and freedom from social norms is magnified in the Village Halloween celebration. The Village Halloween celebration began in 1974 as a street pageant. Today, approximately 50,000-60,000 people dress up in costume and participate in a large parade. **The parade is a blend of theater, performance, music, and public art**. It includes giant, mechanical puppets, dancers, and many different kinds of musicians. The costumes can be quite clever, outrageous, or even offensive. For example, participants might join together in a group to create a moving costume. A group of people might dress as letters and then spell out various words as they march. Or they might dress as a deck of cards and shuffle themselves. Sometimes the costumes are sexual. People dress as up as sexual organs, or they may wear very little clothing at all. Everyone is a participant in the Village Halloween parade. It is a giant party in the streets. The parade lasts about three hours. Afterwards, people

Greenwich Village Halloween parade

go to bars and clubs to continue to celebrate.

　The parade is open to everyone, but since the costumes often have adult themes, **the atmosphere is not oriented towards children**. The Village is not a place where people with children traditionally live, and the Village Halloween celebration reflects this fact. Rather, the Village Halloween celebration is considered an alternative festival, as it does not conform to accepted social standards. The celebration **overturns social norms** through outrageous costumes, dance, performance, and theater. This reflects the orientation of the Village as a non-conformist, free-thinking, and bohemian neighborhood. Over the years, the Village Halloween parade has become somewhat similar to some Mardi Gras celebrations (see Chapter 11) and some people even call it "New York's Carnival." **Halloween as an alternative celebration thrives in New York City because New York is such a large and diverse place**. New York City accommodates a wide variety of lifestyles.

カリフォルニアのネオ・ペイガニズム

　ハロウィンを宗教的な行事として祝う人々もいます．カリフォルニアで、ネオ・ペイガニズムと呼ばれる宗教の信者たちです．カリフォルニアは3万9,000人を擁する大きな州で，アフリカ系，ヒスパニック系，先住民系のアメリカ人が多いことでも知られます．自由で開放的な文化風土のもと，1960年代には対抗文化（カウンター・カルチャー）の発信地となりました．既成の枠にとらわれない生き方をめざし，権威や抑圧に対抗する気風の中からネオ・ペイガニズムを始め新しい宗教がいくつも生まれました．ネオ・ペイガニズムとは，キリスト教以前のヨーロッパの古い宗教に回帰しながら信仰される新しい宗教だと考えられています．信者たちは，ケルトの祭りであったハロウィンを尊重し，ケルト時代と同じように「サムハイン」と呼んで彼らの祝日としています．自然や魔法を尊び季節の移り目を記す祭りであるとともに，死者と交信し生命を祝う行事でもあるのです．「リクレイミング」というフェミニストのネオ・ペイガニズム宗派では，サムハインの祭りに特別な衣装を着た1,000人ほどの人々が手をつなぎ，渦巻き状に丸くなって「スパイラル・ダンス」を踊ります．

....

HALLOWEEN IN CALIFORNIA: NEW RELIGIOUS MOVEMENTS
For some people, Halloween symbolizes religious ideas. Some communities, such as those belonging to new religious movements, celebrate Hallow-

een as a religious holiday. This is another way that adults have changed the meaning of Halloween.

New religious movements are modern religions that have been invented recently. Many new religious movements developed in California, a state along the coast of the western US. At 423,970 km², California is the third largest state in territory. It also has the most people, with a population of approximately 39 million people in 2016. **Like New York, California is very ethically and racially diverse**, with large African American, Latino, and Native American populations. The largest and most important cities are Los Angeles in the south and San Francisco in the north-central part of the state.

Importantly, **California is considered to be a more free and open culture than other parts of the US**. California was an important place during the 1960s counterculture movement. The counterculture movement was a period in history when young people rejected traditional values such as work and marriage and sought out alternative or experimental lifestyles, like living in communes. Many new religious movements also are associated with alternative lifestyles. Neopaganism, for example, is a new religious movement. The word "neopagan" is made up of the word "neo" and "pagan." "Pagan" refers to ancient European religious beliefs that existed before Christianity, while the term "neo" means "new." **Neopaganism refers to new religious groups that embrace presumably ancient, pre-Christian beliefs**. Neopagan groups reject Christianity, practice some form of magic, and embrace ancient European nature beliefs. Neopaganism became popular in California during the 1960s and today, many large Neopagan groups can be found there.

Neopagans have changed the meaning of Halloween from a spooky holiday associated with children to **a positive religious holiday that celebrates nature, magic, and the transition between seasons**. Neopagans are attracted to Halloween because of its roots in ancient Celtic traditions. They use the Irish term "Samhain" instead of Halloween. They have brought back many of the older meanings of Samhain, while also creating new ones. For many Neopagan groups, **Samhain is a time to pay respect to the ancestors, communicate with the dead, and to celebrate life**. People may build altars, say prayers and sing songs, conduct private and public rituals, and join others outside in the woods to celebrate nature.

One of the largest Neopagan celebrations in northern California is the

Reclaiming Spiral Dance. "Reclaiming" is the name of a feminist Neopagan group. The Reclaiming Spiral Dance began in 1979. Over 1000 people come to join this ritual and pageant during Samhain. The purpose of the Spiral Dance is to remember and honor the ancestors, mourn the recently deceased, celebrate new life, and reconnect to the Earth. Sometimes people dress in costume, but others may wear ritual clothing or specially made attire. **People join hands to dance the Spiral Dance and provide hope for the future.**

5 考察

アメリカにおけるハロウィン祭は実に多様であり，いくつかの方向から特徴をつかみ分析したり考察したりできます．まずそれは子供の祭りで，普段とは違う服装ができたくさんお菓子を食べられる，自由が楽しめる行事です．大人にとっては，ニューヨークやカリフォルニアといった多様性を許容する開放的な風土の地域で，既成概念にとらわれない創造性や精神の解放を表現する祭りになっています．ハロウィンには，古代の伝統と現代的な意味の両方が含まれているのです．

DISCUSSION

Halloween is a useful holiday that symbolizes important ideas for both adults and children. **For many American children, Halloween is traditionally a time to dress up in costume and eat a lot of candy.** It is also a time of a little bit more freedom and excess. In New York, a place where many different people and cultures mix, adults have taken the ideas of costuming, freedom, and excess further, creating a parade that celebrates the non-conformist, free, artistic, and bohemian personality of an important neighborhood called the Village. In California, which is associated with a more free and open society, new religious movements such as Neopaganism emphasize the traditional elements of life and death in Halloween. They celebrate interconnections between the living and the dead, and use Halloween as a holiday that supports religious beliefs. **Adults have extended and transformed the traditional elements of Halloween to create new meanings, accommodate adult needs, and fit the modern world.**

6 演 習

(1) 下の問いについて,英文を読み直して回答してください.
(2) 下の問いについて,各自で資料を集め,分析して答えを考え,その結果を持ち寄って討議してください.

ACTIVE LEARNING
How have holidays and festivals changed over time?
What meanings have stayed the same and what meanings have changed?
How do adults treat children's holidays and are they important to adults or not?

11章
マルディ・グラ——文化の重層性を理解する

Chapter 11
Mardi Gras: Cultural Diversity

1 華やかなマルディ・グラとその歴史

　アメリカ合衆国の祝祭のうちで，ニューオーリンズのマルディ・グラはひときわ華やかで有名です．仮装した人々と豪華な山車のパレードを見物するために，世界各地から観光客が訪れます．ニューオーリンズの周辺地域を最初に植民地としたのはフランス人でしたから，ここの文化は，初めから住んでいたアメリカ先住民の文化に加えフランスやスペインの文化と，奴隷として連れてこられたアフリカ人の文化が互いに影響しあって形成されました．マルディ・グラの色あざやかなコスチュームや仮面，羽やスパンコールに輝く装飾をみなさんもご覧になったことがあるかもしれませんね．山車の行列を見物する人混みには食べ物とお酒の匂いが漂い,「お恵みを！」と叫ぶ人々にマルディ・グラの女王が綺麗な色のビーズのネックレスやニセのコインを山車の上からばらまきます．

Mardi Gras masks

INTRODUCTION
Mardi Gras in New Orleans is one of the most important and famous traditional celebrations in the United States. Thousands of people come to this historic city from all over the world to watch people dress up in extravagant costumes and see the gorgeous floats of the Mardi Gras parades. Mardi Gras celebrations are mostly found in the southeastern region of the United States, where New

Orleans is located. The southeastern portion of the US is a warm, subtropical climate. **Much of this area was originally occupied by the French, and French, Spanish, Native American and African cultures heavily influence the region**. It is an area rich in cultural and ethnic diversity.

Mardi Gras is an overwhelming feast for the senses. Imagine walking down the narrow, crowded streets of New Orleans during Mardi Gras. Every single person you pass is wearing a glittering, elaborately decorated costume. Both men and women may wear wings three meters wide made of brightly-colored peacock and ostrich feathers, beaded collars that stand above the neck, sequined headdresses that tower two meters above the head, even glitter and feathers and sequins on their eyelashes! The women look like birds, butterflies, or flowers. People wear theater masks with happy and sad faces symbolizing comedy and tragedy. Others wear white, emotionless masks and look like statues. People dress like animals, or skeletons, or images of death. There is a slightly Renaissance or European style to the affair, echoing similar celebrations taking place across Europe. Many costumes suggest European royalty: people wear wigs that tower above their heads, similar to those worn in France in the eighteenth century. Or they wear gold crowns, and use hoops under women's gowns to make them stand out. Jesters, a kind of European royal clown, also are common. The streets are so crowded you can't move. Music is playing, confetti drifts down from above, and people are eating and drinking: "Throw me something mister!" you scream to the floats that pass by. Someone dressed as a Queen throws beads, or pretend golden coin, called a doubloon. You are at Mardi Gras, where **anything can happen**.

カーニバルを起源として

　マルディ・グラは，ヨーロッパの冬の祭り「カーニバル」のアメリカ版です．カーニバルは，ヨーロッパの他に南北アメリカやカリブ海地域，アジアやアフリカの一部でも行われている祭りです．特にニューオーリンズでは，衣装に何十万円もかけたり，贅沢に食べ贅沢に飲み，路上で見知らぬ人と友達になったりして，特別に羽目を外せる6週間です．そしてこの祝祭の期間が終わる頃，人々はまたいつもの生活に戻っていくのです．

....

Mardi Gras is an American version of a European winter celebration called **"Carnival" that is found in many parts of the world, including Europe, North and South America, the Caribbean, and parts of Asia and Africa**. During Mardi Gras people dress up in elaborate costumes, wear masks, hold balls, and march in large, extravagant parades. It is a time to put everyday life on hold, do other things, and become someone else. Traditional costumes include bright colors of gold, purple, and green, along with beads, feathers, sequins, and masks. **Mardi Gras is so important that people may spend thousands of dollars on a single costume. Excessive eating, drinking, and socializing in the streets also is very common**. Strangers talk to each other and even become friends just because it is Mardi Gras. The entire celebration lasts about six weeks. By the time it is over, people are ready to settle down for the rest of the year.

　カーニバルは，起源がわからないほど古い祭りで，中世には年中行事として定着していました．カーニバルの期間には日常ではできないことが許容され，庶民は権力者や聖職者を笑いものにしたりして普段の憂さ晴らしをしたのです．それが社会の安全弁として働いていました．カーニバルはまた，クリスマスやイースターと関連する宗教的な祭りでもあります．カーニバルは，クリスマスの祝いの期間が終わる1月6日に始まり，2月か3月の火曜日にくるマルディ・グラ・デイで終わります．そしてマルディ・グラ・デイからイースター（3月か4月の日曜日）までの40日間，人々は食事を慎み，祈りの時を過ごします．羽目をはずしたカーニバルの6週間というのは，その後にイースターまでの断食期間が控えていたからこそ意味があったといえます．

....

HISTORY
Carnival is a very old celebration. No one knows exactly how it originated. Some scholars think it may have Roman origins because it has some similarities to ancient Roman celebrations, such as a party-like atmosphere, inversion, and role reversals (discussed below). Carnival solidified in Europe during the medieval period. **People were allowed to say or do things during Carnival in Europe that were forbidden at other times of the year**. For example, the poor publically mocked the elite. People made jokes, dressed in costumes, sang funny songs, and used masks to ridicule or imitate their superiors, such as royalty and clergy. Sometimes the poor were made

"kings for day," as a kind of joke. Poor people **expressed pent-up hostilities against the rich and powerful by making fun of them** for a limited period of time. These activities served as a **safety valve for society**, meaning that this made poor people supposedly feel better and more willing to accept their humble station in life.

Carnival is also a religious time. **It links Christmas and Easter**, the two most important Christian holidays and bridges the deepest part of winter with early spring. Carnival season begins on January 06, which is the end of Christmas. People mark the beginning of Carnival by eating a special cake. The Carnival season ends on Mardi Gras day, which is in February or March and always on a Tuesday. After Mardi Gras day, people spend about forty days in prayer and fasting until Easter, which is a Sunday in March or April. This period of prayer and fasting is called Lent. One reason for the extreme eating, drinking, and partying during Carnival/Mardi Gras is that it is the last time people can eat and drink excessively before the long fasting period before Easter.

2 ニューオーリンズのマルディ・グラ

　1718年に建設されたニューオーリンズは，アメリカ合衆国の都市の中で最も古いものの一つです．メキシコ湾に面したミシシッピ川の河口に位置し，最初はフランス植民地でそれからスペインによる統治を経て，1803年にアメリカ合衆国の一部となりました．また，ニューオーリンズにはかつて，アフリカやカリブ海地域から連れてこられた奴隷を売買する市場がありました．こうした事情で，この都市には重層的な文化が発展しました．ニューオーリンズがマルディ・グラで有名なのはすでに述べましたが，マルディ・グラで人々は人種や民族や性の区別を超えた仮装を楽しみます．それは，文化が常識の規制を超えて交流し合う性質をもっているのだということを，象徴的に見せているといえるでしょう．ニューオーリンズにとって，マルディ・グラはとても重要で，2005年8月のハリケーン・カトリーナで甚大な被害を受けた翌年の1月でも，あらゆる困難を克服して実行されています（3章を参照してください）．

WHAT IS MARDI GRAS IN NEW ORLEANS?

The city of New Orleans, described above, is famous for its Mardi Gras celebration, which is the largest and most elaborate in the United States. **New Orleans was founded in 1718 and is one of the oldest cities in the US**. It is located on the Mississippi River near the Gulf of Mexico. New Orleans was originally founded by the French, but was sold to the Spanish for a period of time. Therefore the city is heavily influenced by European customs and traditions, including the celebration of Carnival. **New Orleans also was a center of slave trade**. Slaves from Africa and the Caribbean were taken to New Orleans to be sold in slave markets, and so the city is significantly shaped by African and Caribbean cultures. This mix of different peoples over the centuries has made New Orleans a very diverse city, famous for its food, music, and art. Although the city's population was nearly half a million people, today, due to the devastation of Hurricane Katrina (see Chapter 3), the city now has fewer people, approximately 343,000.

The diversity of New Orleans is reflected in Mardi Gras celebrations. One way in which Mardi Gras promotes diversity is the custom of changing one's identity through costumes. Sometimes people dress up as their opposites. For example, men might dress as women and women might dress as men. White people may dress up as African Americans. African Americans may dress up as white people, or they may dress up as Africans. A rich person may dress up as a beggar, and a poor person may dress up as royalty. **Dressing up as someone else can "reverse" ordinary social roles**. It allows people to become someone else temporarily. **Reversing ordinary social roles creates diversity symbolically**.

風刺と真実のメタファー

　マルディ・グラの衣装は単なる仮装ではなく，常識をはずれた組み合わせで日常を別の角度から示したり，ものまねや誇張を使って政治家や性的なタブーなどを風刺したりします．常識のタブーを踏み越えようとするお祭り騒ぎの雰囲気は，「カーニバレスク」（カーニバルのような）と形容されます．マルディ・グラの期間には 1,000 台もの山車が出るともいわれ，1 台の山車を作るのに 1 年かけることもあるそうです．それぞれの山車の行列にはテーマがあり，ファンタジーから神話までさまざまな設定がなされます．大がかりな行列は，「クルーズ」と呼ばれる組織がスポンサーとなっていて，クルーズは自分たちの行列の王様役と女王様役を指名する権利を持ちます．王族や貴族のいないアメリカ合衆国で，出資者組織が祭りの王や女王を指名するという構造もまた，マルディ・グラが現実を風刺し社会に潜む真実を暴くメタファー（暗喩）であることを示しています．

Mardi Gras costumes also create diversity by mixing up categories. Mardi Gras costumes frequently combine elements that do not go together. One example might be a man who dresses up as a nun and carries a large weapon. A nun is a female religious figure who represents charity and peace. A man cannot be a nun because nuns are always women. Additionally, nuns never carry guns, engage in war, or resort to violence. A man dressed as a nun with a large weapon combines elements that don't belong together. **Such costumes create diversity by putting elements together that are normally kept separate in ordinary life**. It helps people to think about life differently.

People also create diversity in Mardi Gras by behaving in ways that are unacceptable during the rest of the year. **Parody and political satire are common**. Parody means to make fun of something by imitation. People commonly parody politicians, or issues having to do with US politics. People might make fun of the President of the United States by dressing up as the President or giving funny speeches that don't make sense. This type of behavior is expected during Mardi Gras but less common during other times of the year. People also get drunk in public, wear sexy costumes, and talk to strangers, creating **a "carnival-esque" atmosphere. The term "carnivalesque" means "carnival-like" and suggests that the social world is temporarily out of order**. Such behavior is another way that **Mardi Gras creates diversity**.

Mardi Gras parades are also very important. **They feature large, elaborate floats, costumed dancers, and marching bands**. One website estimated that there are at least 53 parades and over 1000 floats during Mardi Gras. Thousands of people gather especially along the streets of St. Charles and Canal in order to see these exquisite, dream-like creations and to catch a "throw." "Throws" are small trinkets thrown by people riding the floats; they include plastic beads, candy, and fake doubloons (pretend gold pieces).

The floats are magnificent works that may take a year to build. The float themes are drawn from fantasy and mythology. For example, floats may feature fire-breathing dragons, gods depicted as the wind or the sun, or fantastic creatures from the sea, such as mermaids. Marching bands and dancers, also in brightly colored costumes, dance or march alongside the floats and play music.

Parades are organized by groups called **"krewes" [/kruz], which are tightly knit organizations that sponsor the large, elaborate floats**. Krewes may appoint Mardi Gras kings and queens, and build special floats for them to ride on. Mardi Gras kings and queens are chosen from wealthy, well-established members of society. **Mardi Gras kings and queens are another way that Mardi Gras temporarily reverses society, since the United States is a democracy and does not have kings and queens**.

3 アフリカ系アメリカ人のマルディ・グラ

　1865年に南北戦争が終結して南部の奴隷は解放されましたが，多くの黒人が南部を離れずニューオーリンズにも多数が留まりました．その後の100年間は「ジム・クロウ法」と呼ばれる一連の人種差別法と偏見が黒人たちを苦しめます．マルディ・グラにおいても，白人だけで組織されるクルーズには黒人が加われませんでした．そこで彼らは独自の伝統を作り上げました．それが結果的に，ニューオーリンズのマルディ・グラの多様性を増すことになります．

AFRICAN AMERICAN MARDI GRAS TRADITIONS

African Americans play an important role in Mardi Gras. As mentioned above, **New Orleans was a center of slave trade**. After slavery was abolished by the 13th amendment to the US Constitution in 1865, many slaves and their descendants stayed in New Orleans to live even though new laws emerged to keep white and black people apart. These laws, called segregation laws or Jim Crow laws, remained in place until civil rights laws were passed in 1964 and 1965. Segregation laws meant that African American people were not allowed to join the existing white-only parade organizations (krewes) in order to march in the main Mardi Gras parades. Instead, **African Americans developed their own unique parade traditions, adding to the overall diversity of Mardi Gras celebrations**.

ズールーズのパレード

　アフリカ系アメリカ人のパレードに Zulu Social Aid and Pleasure Club（日本語の正式名称はないようです）という団体によるものがあります．一般に「ズールーズ」と呼ばれ，1909 年の発足以来，ニューオーリンズのマルディ・グラで黒人のパレードを主催してきました．アフリカ系アメリカ人にマルディ・グラへの参加の機会を作りその存在を社会にアピールした反面，顔を黒く塗りステレオタイプ的なアフリカの衣装で行列する伝統は，19 世紀のミンストレルショーに由来していて差別的だという批判も浴びてきました．ミンストレルショーとは，白人芸人が顔を黒く塗ってステレオタイプ的なアメリカ黒人を演じたバラエティショーで，非常に人気がありましたが黒人のマイナスイメージを流布して定着させてしまうという弊害も大きかったのです．初代のズールーキングは，缶詰の缶で作った王冠にバナナの大きな葉がついた柄を笏として持ちました．そうした悪ふざけはマルディ・グラ・キングをパロディ化するもので，黒人を排除しステレオタイプ化している社会を風刺し暴露しているといえます．ステレオタイプ化を助長する点が問題であるとはいえ，ズールーズの歴史的重要性は揺るぎありません．多くの有名人がズールーキングに選ばれ，1949 年には，"What a Wonderful World" という代表曲で日本でも知られる世界的なジャズミュージシャンのルイ・アームストロングが王様になっています．

....

THE ZULU SOCIAL AID AND PLEASURE CLUB

One important African American parade tradition revolves around a club called the *Zulu Social Aid and Pleasure Club* (a very long title!). Most people call them "the Zulus" for short. Drawing on nineteenth century minstrel traditions, where white people dressed as black people for entertainment, the Zulus dress up as Africans by painting their faces black and wearing grass skirts. Their parade throws are hand-painted coconuts, which are highly prized.

　The *Zulu Social Aid and Pleasure Club* is an important but somewhat controversial parade organization. It is an important organization because it is one of the oldest and most historic African American Mardi Gras associations. It is controversial because the group invokes stereotypes of Africans. Despite this controversy, **the *Zulu Social Aid and Pleasure Club* offered an early opportunity for African Americans to participate in Mardi Gras their own unique way**.

　The term "Zulu" refers an ethnic group of the Bantu people who live in southern Africa. In 1909, a group of African Americans decided to dress up and march as Zulus because of a play they had seen about Zulus. Members drew on stereotyped images of Africa in order to make fun of white society. The first Zulus paraded informally around local neighborhoods. They also elected a King. **The first Zulu King, named William Story, wore a crown made of an old can and carried a banana stalk scepter**. The Zulu King was elected specifically to make fun of the Mardi Gras king associated with white people. The symbols of the Zulu King, such as the can and the scepter, evoked ideas about Africa at the time and suggested that Mardi Gras kings were a joke. **The Zulu King is a good example of the parody discussed above** and that continues today in Mardi Gras.

Though the *Zulu Social Aid and Pleasure Club* is an African American organization, not all African Americans have been happy about what they do during Mardi Gras, illustrating that diversity exists within African American communities as well. Many people have criticized the costumes and behaviors of the *Zulu Social Aid and Pleasure Club*. The Zulus began marching along the main parade route in 1968, during the Civil Rights era. People protested the organization because their costumes and actions **invoke negative stereotypes** of Africans and **reinforce damaging stereotypes of black Americans**. The costumes and behaviors of the Zulus remain controversial. At the same time, however, **the historic importance of the organization cannot be overlooked and many people are proud to belong to the Zulus**. Many prominent African Americans have been elected as Zulu King, including jazz musician Louie Armstrong in 1949.

マルディグラ・インディアン

　マルディグラ・インディアンとは，アメリカ先住民（ネイティヴ・アメリカン／インディアン）の仮装をして自分たちの居住地域をパレードするアフリカ系アメリカ人（黒人）のことです．小さなグループに分かれそれを「部族」と呼び，各部族の「酋長」は驚くほど豪華で派手な衣装を身につけます．マルディグラ・インディアンのパレードに披露される衣装は1年かけて作成される芸術品ともいわれるもので，重さが68キロに及ぶものもあるそうです．行列はただ動くのではなく，地域を劇場化して部族同士の衝突を演じたりするのですが，戦いの武器として音楽や踊り，詩を使います（銃や剣を使いません）．マルディグラ・インディアンの中にはそれを芸能活動としてツアーする人々もいるくらいです．それにしても，なぜアフリカ系の人々が先住民のフリをするのでしょう．一説に，

先住民が黒人奴隷の逃亡を助けてくれ差別時代には援助してくれたからといわれています．事実，先住民とアフリカ系の人々の混血は多いのです．「キング　オブ　ポップ」と称されたマイケル・ジャクソンの母親もネイティヴ・アメリカン（先住民）でした．先住民の仮装をしているアフリカ系アメリカ人のマルディグラ・インディアンは，先住民とともに差別され抑圧された歴史を共有している民族の文化表象です．

....

MARDI GRAS INDIANS

The Mardi Gras Indians are another important African American Mardi Gras parade tradition. **Mardi Gras Indians are groups of African American people who dress up in costume as Native American Indians and parade through their own neighborhoods**. The costumes do not accurately represent the historical clothing of Native

Mardi Gras Indians

Americans but rather are a symbolic representation. They are yet another example of how people transform their identity and create diversity in Mardi Gras.

It is a unique experience to encounter Mardi Gras Indians on the street. Groups of Mardi Gras Indians parade through their neighborhoods dancing, singing, and showing off, followed by a crowd of onlookers. Each group (or "tribe") of Mardi Gras Indians has a chief, who is magnificently outfitted in an elaborate headdress, with beads, sequins, rhinestones and feathers. Mardi Gras Indian costumes are works of art that may take a year to make. They weigh up to 68 kilos. Each tribe has its own special songs, music, and dances. When two chiefs meet in the street, they fight a pretend battle. They use their music, dance and poetry as weapons to taunt and insult their opponents, although it is all in good fun. It is a theater performance in the street. Some Mardi Gras Indian tribes even have become famous for their songs. They have record contracts, tour as musicians, and are featured in music festivals.

Why do people dress up as Mardi Gras Indians? One answer is that **many African Americans living in New Orleans feel kinship with Native American peoples of the southeast**. Native American tribes such as the Choctaw, Seminoles, and Chickasaws helped slaves who had escaped their owners. They fed or sheltered them. Sometimes escaped slaves married Native Americans. Some people who belong to Mardi Gras Indian tribes say that they dress up as a Mardi Gras Indian to honor and thank the Native Americans who helped their ancestors. When African American men dress up as Native Americans, **they remind people of the shared history of oppression and mutual aid that existed between these two groups**. Through costume, music, and dance, they also continue to mix and blend these two cultures, creating a unique Mardi Gras identity that is only found at special times of the year.

4 考　察

　マルディ・グラには普段と違うルールが持ち込まれ，人々は異なる自分を演じます．いつもと違う服を着て，違う行動をし，羽目をはずします．権威や社会や政治を風刺し，揶揄します．こうした祝祭は社会の安全弁ともなり，笑いが人々の活力源ともなります．しかし祭りが終われば，普段の生活が戻ってくるのです．

DISCUSSION

During Mardi Gras people look and behave differently than they do at other times of the year. **Mardi Gras is a traditional celebration that frees people from their ordinary roles and identities, and it creates diversity by changing the rules of everyday life**. Through costumes, people transform themselves into someone or something else, allowing them to take on roles not ordinarily available to them. People also behave differently during Mardi Gras. Regular social norms are suspended, and people are free to socialize, and eat and drink excessively. **People are also freer to criticize, comment on, or make fun of how society works**. They critique political structures, for example, by parodying political figures. They also critique economic differences, mocking members of the elite classes by dressing up as them. Nothing and no one escapes the laughter of Mardi Gras. **The freedom Mardi Gras offers, however, is only temporary**. Once Mardi Gras ends, society returns to its normal state of affairs.

5 演 習

　マルディ・グラで庶民が貴族を演じ風刺もするように，人々が立場を逆転してそれを劇場化する場面を，あなたは他に知っていますか．祝祭，芸能，行事，集団行動などに注目すると良いでしょう．

　その行為には，なにか得ることがあるのでしょうか．利益があるとしたら，それはどういう利益で，なぜ生じるのか，利益がないとしたらなぜ生じないのか，利益がないのになぜそのようなことをするのか，それぞれ考えてください．

　あなたが見出したその場面は，一時的な現象ですか，それとも永続的な効果を持つものですか．なぜそのように判断できるのでしょうか．あなたの言葉で説明してください．

....

ACTIVE LEARNING

What other ways does society symbolically enact reversals?
Do you think this is beneficial? If so, why? If not, why not?
Does this have any permanent effects?

12章
カントリーフェアとロデオ——農村の価値観を知る

Chapter 12
County Fairs and Rodeos:
Agricultural Roots and Rural Communities

1 農村の祭りの伝統

　アメリカの農村で行われる祭りは，先祖代々が同じ土地で農業をいとなみ神事にちなむ祭りがある日本とはだいぶ違っています．代表格はカントリーフェアとロデオです．カントリーフェアは，アメリカの食料庫ともいえる中西部で盛んで，8月末から9月にかけて行われます．家畜，農作物，地域の名産などの品評会があります．ロデオは主に7月に開かれる西部の夏のイベントで，カウボーイが牛や馬を扱う技術を競うものです．荒馬乗りや裸馬騎乗などのライディング競技，走って逃げる牛を投げ縄で捕まえるローピング競技などがあります．

INTRODUCTION

Many festivals and holidays have agricultural roots. **In the United States, the most common agricultural festivals and holidays are county fairs and rodeos**. County fairs showcase local animals, crops, and regional foods. They occur at the end of August or the beginning of September, when the crops are being harvested. They are very popular in the Midwest, where most of the food in the United States is grown.

　Rodeos are a type of spectator entertainment where cowboys show off their skills with ranch animals, such as cows, bulls, or horses. Rodeos occur anytime during the summer, but they are especially popular in July, which is the most patriotic month of the year. Rodeos are common in the western United States, which has strong ranching traditions.

2　中西部のカントリーフェア

　中西部は合衆国のほぼ中央に当たる地域で，肥沃な土地なので農業が盛んです．アメリカの農業人口は全体のわずか2%にすぎませんが，国土の41%が農作地で，そのほとんどが中西部に集中しています．アメリカの「パン籠(かご)」と呼ばれるゆえんです．この土地を肥沃にしたミシシッピ川は3,701キロで蛇行する大河で，マーク・トウェイン作『ハックルベリー・フィンの冒険』の舞台ですね．中西部の大都市といえばシカゴ．黒人系音楽を中心にしたアメリカ音楽の発信地です．

....

COUNTRY FAIRS IN THE MIDWEST
The Midwest is a region located in the middle of the country. It is best known for farming because it is especially fertile. Only about 2% of the population of the United States farms, but nearly 41% of the total landmass in the United States is considered to be farmland. Much of this land is located in the Midwest. It is sometimes called the "breadbasket" of America (a term similar to a nation's "rice bowl" in parts of Asia). Heavy manufacturing was also common in the Midwest for most of the twentieth century.

　The Midwest is home to the Mississippi River, which, at 3,701 km long, is one of the longest rivers in North America. **The Mississippi River is a historically important means of commerce and transportation** and is featured in a classic American novel, *The Adventures of Huckleberry Finn* (1884) by Mark Twain. The largest city in the Midwest is Chicago, which is located in northern Illinois and was a center for meat processing. **The Midwest is also known for its strong music traditions**, including blues, Motown, funk, and various rock and hip hop/rap styles.

....

　ヨーロッパ系の人々が中西部に定住したのは19世紀です．彼らの子孫は，率直で人懐っこく，保守的で，連邦政府の統治より地方の自治を重んじることで知られます．高い気温と湿度に恵まれた土地で栽培される作物のうち，最も重要なのがトウモロコシです．トウモロコシはさまざまに加工されて利用される他に，家畜の飼料としても欠かせない穀物です．

....

The Midwest was settled in the early nineteenth century primarily by northern Europeans who came to the region to farm. A large number of people living in the Midwest are descendants of German, Swedish, Norwegian and Irish peoples. The people living in the Midwest (called "Midwesterners") are considered to be straightforward, friendly, and politically conservative, meaning that they tend to embrace traditional gender and family roles and prefer less regulation by the federal government in matters of commerce, social services, and the environment.

The Midwest is an excellent region for farming because the soil is very rich, the days are hot, and there is usually plenty of rain. The majority of crops are grains, such as corn, which is largest crop grown in the US, along with soybeans and wheat. **Corn is the most important crop. It is used for food, animal feed, and ingredients in processed food, such as corn syrup, which is a replacement for sugar**. The Midwest also produces a lot of vegetables, such as tomatoes and pumpkins.

カントリーフェアが表す中西部の価値観

　カントリーフェアは農村の生活や伝統を楽しむ祭りです．収穫期後の２日間から７日間にわたって開かれ，映画やテレビのない時代には，農夫やその家族はカントリーフェアを特に楽しみにしていました．遠方の人々はワゴンやキャンピングカーで集まり，泊りがけで参加しました．フェアの中心でもあった家畜の品評会については，『シャーロットの贈り物』という児童小説を読んでみてください．クモのシャーロットに助けられた豚のウィルバーが，カントリーフェアで特別賞を勝ち取るファンタジーです．

....

A county fair is an agricultural festival that celebrates farming life and farming traditions. County fairs last between two days and a week. **They feature farm animals, agricultural products, and homemade domestic items**. County fairs usually are held in the fall because they are associated with the harvest. In the past, when there was no Internet and few movie theaters, television, or other commercial amusements, fairs were an important source of entertainment for people living in rural areas. **Fairs provided farmers a much-needed break after the hard work of the harvest**. They also provided a space for fun, socializing, and commerce at a time when few other options were available.

County fairs typically hold livestock shows where animals such as cows, pigs, sheep, goats, chickens and rabbits are exhibited for people to look at. The animals are judged and given prizes. The well-known children's book *Charlotte's Web*, by E.B. White, was published in 1952. It features a pig named Wilbur who is entered into competition at the county fair. Wilbur becomes famous with the help of a spider named Charlotte. He wins a special prize, which saves him from being slaughtered.

家畜の品評会で優勝する牛は見事に左右の均整がとれていて，清潔です．優勝する牛の様子には，その土地の価値観が見てとれます．家庭で作られる手芸品や焼菓子，瓶詰の食品も品評され，受賞作はそれぞれ，形，味，色，均一性などについて地域の人々が何をよいと判断するかに合格していなければなりません．

County fairs represent rural, Midwestern values by exhibiting livestock and awarding prizes to them. The award-winning animals allow people to see particular local values. In everyday rural farm life, for example, a cow might be valued if it is symmetrical and well balanced. A prize-winning cow at the county fair epitomizes these values by being extraordinarily symmetrical and well balanced. The prize-winning cow also will exhibit other important community values, such as cleanliness. **Values of symmetry, balance, and cleanliness are exaggerated in the prize-winning cow, making it easy for people see community values in a concrete, observable way** (Prosterman 1995).

Sheep waiting to be judged at county fair

County fairs also exhibit handmade domestic items, such as sewn objects, homemade cakes, cookies, and home canned goods. Prizes are awarded to the most perfect entries. These domestic objects also represent local values. In cookie-baking competitions, for example, prizes are given to plates of cookies that all look the same. There should not be big cookies alongside small cookies, and the cookies should be evenly baked. Judges evaluate uniformity, consistency, and overall taste. Fair-goers look at the prize-winning cookies and see visible representations of the values of uniformity, consistency, and taste. Different items represent different values. Good color, for example, is important in competitions featuring home canned vegetables. In each case, **local values are exaggerated and made obvious in the exhibited objects**.

農村の娯楽

カントリーフェアは，農村に欠かせない娯楽の機会でもあります．18世紀や19世紀の中西部では，農民は町や村から遠く離れてほぼ自給自足の生活をしていたので，一年に一度の祭りで家族以外の大勢の人に会うのも楽しみでした．変わった食べ物を売ったり，わざと車をぶつけ合うゲームをしたり，パイの大食いを競ったり．音楽演奏のショーも大事な楽しみで，カントリー音楽やカントリーダンスはこうした機会にも発展していったのです．カントリーフェアは，中西部の人々が自給自足をして自立性を保っていた頃に大事であった価値観に光を当て，地方自治の伝統をつなぐお祭りです．

....

In addition to honoring values associated with work, **county fairs also provide a space for people to play**. American farmers traditionally live near their fields and far away from the centers of villages and towns. In the past when popular entertainments were few, county fairs were an opportunity for farming families to experience novelty and to be entertained. Today mass entertainment is much more common, but contemporary fair-goers still go on **mechanical rides, eat unusual foods** such as deep-fried candybars, or **listen to musical performances** as they did in the past. There also may be **eating competitions**, such as a pie eating contest to see who can eat the most pie. One popular event is **the demolition derby**. Demolition derbies are shows where people drive old cars and crash into each other on purpose. The person with the car that lasts the longest wins. These fair-going activities are considered old-fashioned and nostalgic, hearkening back to the days before mass entertainment was readily available and farmers were more isolated.

County fairs are important cultural events. **During the eighteenth, nineteenth, and much of the twentieth centuries people living in rural areas in the United States had to be self-sufficient by making most of what they used in everyday life**. They did this by farming, raising animals, and homemaking. **County fairs present these ordinary activities as special by awarding prizes, highlighting the self-sufficiency and independence needed to survive. County fairs therefore highlight American values associated with farming and agriculture and they remind people of the ongoing importance of the country's agricultural traditions.

3 ロデオのある西部

　アメリカ合衆国の「西部」は，地理的な西側ということ以上の意味を持っています．日本でも西部劇映画を「ウェスタン」と呼びますが，「西部」は「フロンティア」のロマンチックな概念やイメージと強く結びついています．「フロンティア」（辺境地）とはヨーロッパ系アメリカ人が東から西に向けて居住地を拡大していった時の，ヨーロッパ系アメリカ人の勢力範囲と西側の「荒野」との境界域をさします．実際は，ヨーロッパ系が入植するはるか昔からアメリカ大陸全土にはアメリカ先住民（ネイティヴ・アメリカン）が，彼ら自身の法や秩序をもって暮らしていたのですが，18, 19世紀のヨーロッパ系アメリカ人にはそれを認識することができず，先住民の生活圏は無法の「荒野」と判断されたのでした．「西部」という言葉にまつわるロマンチックな印象は，いわゆる「未踏の地」へ西欧文明をもたらすという開拓精神に根ざしたものです．ですからアメリカ精神の表象を西部のイメージに求めることは，アメリカ先住民との厳しい関係を考慮しなければできないのですが，一方で，「西部」がアメリカ合衆国の文化的アイデンティティにおいて重要であることには変わりありません．

....

RODEOS IN THE WEST

Rodeos are commen in the western portion of the U.S. "The West" presumably refers to the western region of the United States. However, "the West" more accurately is defined as **a concept, or set of ideas, rather than a specific geographical area**. Primarily, the West is associated with **the frontier**. During the eighteenth and nineteenth centuries, most of the land that eventually became the United States was inhabited mainly by Native Americans. It was not yet settled by Euro-Americans. Euro-Americans first settled in the eastern portion of the New World (what became North America) and eventually spread westward. **The frontier was the outer edge of Euro-American settlement**, and the lands west of the frontier were not well known to Euro-American settlers. The western lands beyond the frontier had no centralized form of government, laws, stores, and few **Euro-American settlements. Euro-Americans considered this region to be wilderness**. Of course **Native Americans living in the western lands beyond the frontier had their own laws, settlements, and forms of government, but most Euro-Americans were unfamiliar with them**.

ここでいうロマンチックな見方とは，事実を無視して感情や想像でなされる判断をさします．西部について一般的に信じられているロマンチックな言説の一つは，西部には人が住んでいなかったというものです．事実は異なり，アメリカ大陸には先住民が 12,000 年にわたって暮らしていたのですが，西部が「未踏の荒野」であったという見方は根強く残っています．また，西部は男性原理のロマンチックイメージと結びついており，個人主義，暴力，自由，危険，無法といった言葉で形容されつつ，現代でも映画やテレビドラマ，西部をテーマにした（ディズニーランドのような）テーマパークで，現実とはズレのある「西部」が再生産され続けています（5 章も参照してください）．地理上の西部地域はアメリカ合衆国の西側約 3 分の 1 をさします．合衆国政府の国有地の 96％が西部にあり，国有地での個人の土地開発は禁じられているため，西部を旅行すると実に広大な自然のままの土地を目にすることができます．

....

The frontier and "the West" came to be associated with a cluster of romantic ideas. **A romantic idea is an idea based on emotional and imagined realities, rather than facts**. For example, **one romantic idea about the West is that it was uninhabited** (see Chapter 5). This is not true, since Native Americans have lived in parts of North America for nearly 12,000 years. However, the notion that huge swaths of land west of the frontier were wild and empty has remained a powerful idea. **Other romantic ideas about the West include individualism, violence, freedom, danger, and lawlessness**. Such romantic ideas continue to be highlighted in movies and shows about the west (called "westerns"), such as in the popular television show "Deadwood," which is about a mining town located in the west with few laws, as well as the show "Westworld," which is science fiction story about a realistic Western-style theme park inhabited by robots.

Today, "the West" loosely refers to the western third of the United States. It contains diverse landscapes, including desert, high mountains, rain forest, and agricultural regions. Traditional western economies include timber, ranching, and mining, while newer economies include technology industries and tourism. Many portions of the western US are less developed than in the east because the federal government owns much of the land there. **The federal government owns approximately 640 million acres of land in the United States（approximately 259,000,000 hectares）and 96% of these lands are located in the West（including Alaska）**. Government lands are considered public lands. They are not open to private development. The public (government) lands of the West contain large swaths of wilderness, as well as open, expansive landscapes.

ロデオと広大なラーンチ（ranch）

　ロデオは，カウボーイが馬や牛の扱いを競い合うスポーツイベントです．ロデオを見るには入場料が必要で，優秀な競技者には賞金が支払われます．ワイオミング，サウスダコタ，テキサスなど西部・中西部の州で公式なスポーツと認められています．荒馬乗りはロデオのハイライトです．出場するカウボーイやカウガールは，彼らを振り落とそうとする荒馬を片手で操って乗りこなさなければなりません．もう一方の手で馬に触ってはいけないことになっています．こうした競技は，「ラーンチ」と呼ばれる広大な牧場での仕事の中で，カウボーイが牛飼いの技術を磨き楽しむものとして発生しました．テキサス州には，3,339 平方キロにも及ぶラーンチがあります．東京都の面積が 2,190 平方キロ，23 区は 626 平方キロですから，いかに広いかがわかるでしょう．

....

　A rodeo is a sporting event where people watch cowboys demonstrate their expertise with horses, bulls, and other animals for entertainment. Rodeos are commonly held outside in a fairground, which is a large outdoor arena with benches for audience members and fences to contain animals. Audience members buy tickets to watch and rodeo contestants compete for prize money. Rodeo is the official sport of a number of western states, including Wyoming, South Dakota, and Texas.

　The most exciting rodeo event is the bucking bronco contest. A bucking bronco is a horse that tries to throw the rider off its back by jumping and kicking. Rodeo contestants (cowboys or cowgirls) attempt to stay on the bucking horse for at least eight seconds. They are only allowed to use one hand to hold onto the horse and are not allowed to touch the horse or him/

herself with the free hand. Riders are judged on style and skill to earn points.

The bucking bronco event evolved from authentic ranching skills of the past where cowboys tamed wild horses by riding them until they wore out. **A ranch is a very large farm where people raise livestock, such as cows, sheep, and horses for meat or wool**. Ranches are common in the western US because ranches require large tracts of land to graze the animals. Some ranches are enormous; one of the largest ranches in Texas, for example, is over 3339 km^2. Ranching was a common way for people to make a living in the West and remains closely connected to rural life in the region.

カウボーイ

　ラーンチで放牧されている家畜の世話をする男女を，カウボーイやカウガールと呼びます．カウボーイの服装には特徴があり，カウボーイハットやブーツやバンダナはその例です．20世紀の，特に映画の中でカウボーイはアメリカ文化の大事なアイコンとなり，荒くれた男っぽさ，自由，個人主義などの西部のイメージを体現しました．ジョン・ウェインは代表的な西部劇映画俳優です．ロデオに出場するのは，かつてはラーンチで働く一般の人々でしたが，いまは主に「ロデオ・カウボーイ」と呼ばれるプロの競技者です．それでもロデオが，人の思いのままにならない自然を手なずける技術を披露するショーだということに変わりはありません．

....

Rodeo cowboy riding a bucking bull

The people who work on ranches are called cowboys (or cowgirls). Cowboys are herders: they help herd animals. Other names in English for "cowboy" include "cowpoke," and "cowhand." In the past, cowboys rode horses to herd cattle; today, they still ride horses or they also might drive trucks. Cowboys wear western-style clothing that makes them quite recognizable, including cowboy hats, cowboy boots, a bandana, jeans, and chaps, which are leather coverings that protect the legs. **During the twentieth century, the cowboy became an important icon of American culture, symbolizing ideas about the West, such as freedom, rugged masculinity, and individualism**. An actor named John

Wayne made cowboys famous in his movies. He starred in 83 westerns (films about the West) between the 1930s and the 1970s.

In the past, most rodeo contestants were working cowboys and cowgirls who had regular jobs on ranches. Today, most large rodeos are professionally organized and contestants are trained athletes who specialize in rodeo skills. Rodeo constants are still considered cowboys (or cowgirls) but are identified as "rodeo cowboys" rather than cowboys who work on ranches. As spectators watch the rodeo cowboy ride a bucking bronco and admire his skill, people recall the idea of the West as place where nature, as represented by the bucking bronco, is untamed. **The idea of untamed nature is an idea specifically associated with the West** (see Chapter 3).

ロデオが表す西部の価値観

　激しく逃げ回る子牛を投げ縄で捕まえる競技はもう一つのハイライト種目で，野生の自然を人間がコントロールするという西部の理想の価値観を体現しています．他にも，体重が900キロにもなる獰猛な雄牛を乗り回す競技，走る馬に騎乗したままで去勢牛の角を捕まえ素早く牛に乗り移って地面に押し伏せる競技，馬のレースなどがあります．どの競技も，人間が自然を支配するまでのスリルとドラマを見せています．初期の西部入植者が生き延びるために自然を支配する力が欲しかったのですね．ロデオが保守的で愛国的な価値観を表現している理由もそこにあります．アメリカの独立と領土の拡大は，ロマンチックな価値観に従えば，手つかずの自然の征服だとみなされるからです．ロデオは7月4日の独立記念日に催されることが多く，会場では国旗が掲揚され国歌が高らかに歌われます．

....

　　Another important rodeo event is calf roping. Calf roping also evolved from actual ranching skills. Cowboys in the past had to catch wild cattle with a rope from their horses. During this rodeo event, calves are given a running head start. Riding a horse, the cowboy makes a lasso (a circle) over his head with a rope and throws the rope around the neck of the calf in order to stop it. He then jumps off the horse and ties up three of the calf's legs. The person with the fastest time wins the event. Other rodeo events including barrel racing, in which contestants race horses around large barrels to see who is the fastest; bull riding, which entails riding a bull that can weigh up to 900 kilos; and steer wrestling, where the cowboy leans off of a running horse to catch a steer behind the horns and wrestle it to the ground.

Most rodeo events pit a cowboy (or cowgirl) against an animal. **A rodeo is like a small drama where people compete against nature**. The animals represent nature, and the cowboys and cowgirls try to tame or subdue them. Watching cowboys race, subdue, or wrestle ranching animals reminds people of American history and the frontier of the past century, when there were places that were still very wild that settlers thought needed to be subdued or tamed.

Western values of freedom, untamed nature, rugged masculinity, and individualism are considered to be American values as well. This is why **rodeos tend to be conservative and patriotic**. People sing the national anthem (see Chapter 6) and fly the American flag. Rodeos are commonly held during July. July 04 is national Independence Day, when the United States celebrates its independence from England and July is the most patriotic month of the year.

メキシコとスペインの影響

カウボーイや牛の放牧はアメリカ独自のものと思われがちですが，メキシコやスペインの影響を強く受けています．それというのも，アメリカの南西部から西部にかけた240万平方キロという広大な土地はかつてメキシコの領土で，19世紀の中葉には，先にメキシコからの独立を果たしたテキサス共和国が合衆国に併合され，次いで広大な土地がメキシコから割譲されたのでした．カウボーイの活躍した土地は，こうした歴史を背景にメキシコ文化との深いつながりを保っており，カウボーイはメキシコ風に「バケーロ」，ロデオも「チャレアダ」と呼ばれることがあります．ほかにもスペイン語由来の用語がたくさん使われています．

....

American cowboys and herding traditions are largely derived from Mexican and Spanish influences, since most of the western United States used to belong to Mexico. During the nineteenth century, the US acquired 2,400,000 km^2 in territory from Mexico. This land became much of the current western portion of the US. Mexican and Spanish influences are still found in this region. One alternative English word for "cowboy," for example, is "buckaroo." This word is likely derived from the Spanish word for cowboy, which is "*vaquero.*" Rodeos are likely derived from the Mexican version of rodeo, which is called a *charreada*.

4 考　察

　カントリーフェアとロデオは，アメリカ人の自然に対する接し方と価値観をそれぞれに表しています．カントリーフェアでは，農作業や日常生活で達成されることを競い合って，勤労をたたえるとともに，自然が人々の生活にもたらす豊かさと美を喜び，自給自足や独立心が賞賛されます．これに対してロデオでは，動物を手強い自然に見立てそれを手なずける技を競い合うことで，自然を征服する意志が象徴的に表現されています．そのようにどちらの祭りも，自然と人間の関係についてのアメリカ人の価値観を体現しているのです．

....

DISCUSSION

County fairs and rodeos represent different kinds of ideas and values that Americans have about their relationship with nature. **County fairs highlight agricultural activities related to farming and domestic life**, such as raising livestock, cooking, and sewing. These activities harness **the abundance of nature, transforming it into something both useful and beautiful for people**. The agricultural activities exhibited and given prizes in county fairs also exemplify **values of self-sufficiency and independence**.

　Rodeos also symbolically place Americans in a particular relationship to nature. **In rodeos, nature is presented as a wild and untamed entity, symbolized by animals** such as the bucking bronco, and recalling romantic notions about the frontier. Instead of working with nature to channel abundance, as in agricultural activities, here **the cowboy symbolically conquers nature by subduing or outlasting the animals**. In both events, regional values with respect to man and nature are made manifest.

5 演　習

　祭りや祝い事の多くは，人間と自然の関係を象徴的に見せています．あなたがよく知っている祭りを取り上げ，人間と自然の関係がどう表されているか，その象徴的表現を指摘して，説明してください．人間が自然をどう考え，自然に何を望み，自然とどういう関係を結びたいと思っているかは，祭りで行われる一連の儀式やしきたりや，人々の参加の仕方のどういう部分に表れているでしょうか．

以上のような点を，宗教的な祭りと，観光を盛んにするために行うような世俗的な祭りの両方で検討してください．

....

ACTIVE LEARNING

Many festivals and celebrations symbolically articulate the relationship of people to nature. Choose a festival that is familiar to you. How are human/nature relationships symbolized? What role do animals play? Try to examine these themes in both religious and non-religious or tourist festivals.

第V部
デジタル時代に生きる伝統文化と新世代文化
——未来への文化を透視する

Part V
Living Traditions in the Digital Age

13章
インターネット・ミーム——越境する文化を把握する

Chapter 13
Internet Memes: Investigating Borderless Culture/s

1 ミームとは？

　インターネットは現代に欠かせないメディア（意思伝達媒体）となりました．インターネット上に続々と登場する新たな文化を通して，人々の生活や価値観，考え方などを知ることができます．こうした文化の一つにあげられるのがミームです．ミームとは，ごく日常的な写真や言葉を組み合わせて，見た人を笑わせるように作られたデジタルコンテンツのことです．「ミーム」とは，もともとは，模倣されることで人間の脳から脳へと伝達され増殖していく仮想の遺伝子をさします．メッセージ性を加えた画像や映像がインターネット上にあげられ，それをもとに誰かが中味を少し変えたものを作り，また誰かが少し変えて……というように，まるで遺伝か感染のように，ある一連のコンテンツが広がっていく時，そのコンテンツをミームと呼ぶのです．そして，多くの場合，ミームは笑いを誘うジョーク（おふざけ）になっています．それをたくさん集めて分析すると，ネットでつながっている特定の人々に共通する関心事や考えがわかります．

INTRODUCTION

The Internet is a new medium for the creation and expression of culture. What traditions exist on the Internet and what might we learn about American values and ideas by examining them? **One of the most common forms of culture on the Internet is a "meme."** Internet memes are videos, pictures, animations, or other digital content that express an idea and circulate widely. The content often is drawn from ordinary activities and experiences. There are thousands of different memes, so it is difficult to make generalizations about them. The memes discussed in this chapter **combine words and pictures to make a joke or statement. They reflect a particular per-**

spective, and the purpose often is to make people laugh**.

The term "meme" is drawn from the study of genetics and refers to small, cultural ideas (or units) that replicate themselves by being passed from person to person (McNeill 2009). As Internet memes circulate (known as "going viral," that is, spreading like a virus), people change them in order to make a new, or slightly different version of the same meme. For example, people insert different pictures with the same set of words, or they use the same picture, but change the words. The newly-created meme refers to the original meme, and **by comparing multiple versions of a particular meme, scholars can identify what important themes or ideas are expressed** (see Chapter 1).

ミームはたいてい平凡なものに題材をとり，動物はその代表格です．動物を擬人化し，あたかも動物が言ったり思ったりしているかのようにして，人が実際には発言できないことを表現します．次にあげるのは，犬と猫のミームです．日本と同じくアメリカでも犬と猫は好まれるペットで，犬と猫のミームにはアメリカ人の生活や文化の特徴が読み取れます．他方，インターネットミームという文化を共有するのは，インターネット環境に親しんだ人々です．ですからミームは，これまでの文化のように，「アメリカ」「日本」などの地理的境界や「英語」「日本語」などの言語的境界でくくるのではなく，「インターネットユーザー」かどうかという境界線で文化の担い手や享受者が仕分けられる新しい文化なのです．そして，ミームは同じ文化的知識を共有する人々の間に広がっていきます．本章では，犬と猫について笑いを誘うミームを扱います．ユーモアの大事な部分が，アメリカ文化において共有されている動物と人間の関係性を土台としていることを見ていきましょう．その関係性とは，どういったものなのでしょうか．

....

Most memes are banal, having to do with ordinary activities and daily life. Animals are popular meme subjects. People like to take pictures of their pets (or other animals) in strange positions or doing funny things, and then add words to indicate what the animal is thinking. **Attributing human characteristics, actions, and thoughts to animals is called "anthropomorphism" and makes animals seem human. These "humanized" animals express feelings or thoughts in memes that people can't otherwise say**.

The examples below are humorous memes about dogs and cats, which are the most common animals Americans keep as pets. **Memes about dogs and cats reveal cultural attitudes about animals**. Dogs are considered to be highly social members of the family. They are teachable, eager to please, and get in trouble because they lose control of themselves. Cats also are members of the family, but are more independent. They do what they want and are unconcerned with pleasing people and getting along with others.

Internet memes are "borderless," meaning they are not bound by territory. Memes hypothetically can circulate globally. Yet memes are bounded in ways other than region. People who don't use the Internet, for example, will be unfamiliar with Internet memes: **memes are specific to people with Internet access**. Additionally, memes in English may not travel much beyond the English-speaking world of Internet users. Most importantly, **memes presume shared cultural knowledge. In the memes for this chapter, the "shared cultural knowledge" is shared ideas about the personalities of dogs and cats, as well as presumptions about appropriate social behavior**. Let's see how this works in a few examples.

2 社会規範を示す：ワンちゃんを辱めるミーム

「犬を辱めるミーム」は，アメリカで人気があります．犬の写真の横に「僕は／私は……をしました」と罪の告白をしたかのような但し書きが置いてある写真です．但し書きではその犬のダメなところや失敗が暴露され，犬は深く自らの行いを恥じ入っているように見えます．その自虐的な演出がユーモラスです．多くは，猫に負けた犬を表しています．猫が怖いとか，猫に餌を取られるとかいうシチュエーションが笑いを誘う背景に，犬が猫より弱いのは不名誉であるという共通認識を読み取ることができます．

....

REINFORCING SOCIAL NORMS: DOG-SHAMING MEMES
One popular cycle of memes is "dog-shaming memes." People create these memes by taking pictures of dogs that have misbehaved, or that have bad habits, and posting them to the Internet. The photograph includes a handwritten note clarifying the situation as if it was written by the dog. The pattern for these notes is "I did ..." or "I am ....", along with an explanation of the

13章　インターネット・ミーム――越境する文化を把握する　　167

bad behavior. The idea is that **the dog has admitted to its bad behavior and is punished by being publically shamed. These memes are funny because the dog is put in the role of a guilty person**.

　The first meme is very straightforward. It shows the dog, who looks ashamed or guilty, accompanied by a note explaining that it is afraid of the cat. **Many dog-shaming memes place dogs in inferior positions to cats**. Americans typically think that dogs should dominate cats because many dogs are bigger and stronger than cats. Although many dogs are wary of cats, **one cultural idea is that being dominated by a cat is dishonorable for a dog**. The second meme is funny because dogs love food. The note explains that the dog is upset because the cat is eating its food, but the dog is too scared to chase the cat away. The dog looks sad or unhappy as the cat eats its food.

　もう一つの犬のミームによくあるのは，不適切なものを食べてしまう犬の写真です。口紅やお札を食べてしまう犬，ゴミをあさって台所を散らかす犬，何度叱られても熱帯魚の餌を食べてしまう犬など．こうしたミームが楽しまれる背景には，犬は食いしん坊で何でも食べてしまう動物だという共通の理解があります．

··

　Many dog-shaming memes are about inappropriate, disgusting, or off-limit items that the dog has eaten. **Another cultural idea about dogs is that dogs are greedy or gluttonous** and will eat nearly anything. These

memes suggest that, **as gluttons, dogs can't control themselves even though they know better**. This is another example of anthropomorphism, the attribution of human characteristics to animals.

In the first example on this page, the dog has eaten lipstick and money from a woman's purse. These memes partly are funny because of the mess the dog makes. The dog has been caught and photographed "red-handed," a phrase meaning that the dog has been caught with obvious evidence of guilt. The evidence in this example is the coloring on the dog's mouth and feet, and the mess on the couch. Along with the letter of explanation, this dog-shaming meme suggests a convict picture, a police photograph in which a guilty person is photographed with an identifying number to inform the public of his or her guilt. In the next example, the dog has eaten the garbage. The note indicates this is a common behavior for this dog and also suggests a convict picture.

Other examples depict dogs eating vomit, feces, clothing, and food belonging to other species. In the next meme, the note says that the dog lasted only three days before it once again ate the fish food. A variation of this same meme says it has been zero days since this dog has eaten the kitty litter.

では，こうした犬のミームに人気がある理由を考えてみましょう．そこには，

犬と人間の間のどんな関係性が読み取れるのでしょうか．アメリカでは犬は人間と同じ家に住み，一緒のベッドで寝たりもします．ですから，家族の一員として人間のルールに基づいた行動が求められるのです．「私は……をしました」という告発のサインをつけられて公共の場にさらされる「辱めの罰」を受ける理由も，犬は教えれば人間の生活ルールを学べると考えられているためです．そして，これらのミームを見た人たちは，犬のいたずらを笑うと同時にいたずらな犬をしつけなければならない犬の主人たちに同情を寄せ，共感を育んでいるのです．

....

Why do people make dog-shaming memes and why are they popular? What can they tell us about attitudes towards animals? Dogs are considered to have very sociable, people-like qualities. Americans often think of dogs as members of the family. Dogs often live indoors with the family and even sleep in the same bed. **As members of the family, dogs are expected to behave according to the rules a person would follow**.

The dogs in these examples have broken expected rules of behavior. Because the dog is expected to behave as a person, the dog is "punished" by being placed in the role of a convict. Unlike cats, **dogs are seen as teachable and eager to please and so discipline is considered appropriate**. In contrast, people discipline cats less often, because cats are seen as less teachable. Of course, dog-shaming memes don't really punish the dog but rather mimic punishment. Instead, **these memes allow the viewer to laugh at the bad behavior, feel sorry for the dog, and sympathize with the dog owner**, who must deal with the mess and teach the dog to behave appropriately.

3　社会規範をくつがえす：超不機嫌猫，グランピー・キャット

「グランピー・キャット」と呼ばれている不機嫌な顔の猫のミームも人気があります．但し書きは，猫の内心のつぶやきです．人間の行動に従う能力のある犬のミームが公共への罪の告白だったのに対し，自分中心に行動する猫のミームは，社会規範が気に入らない思春期の子供たちの不満を代弁する独白口調です．これが見る人の笑いを誘う背景には，優れた人間は前向きで積極的かつ満足して生きている，そうでなければならないという前提が，アメリカで強力に受けいれられていることがあります．

SUBVERTING SOCIAL NORMS: GRUMPY CAT

Cats also are popular subjects. One widespread cat meme is called "Grumpy Cat." Grumpy Cat memes feature a picture of an irritable-looking cat alongside words or phrases that represent Grumpy Cat's "interior monologue," what Grumpy Cat is supposedly thinking. Grumpy Cat always sounds like a cranky person or a rebellious teenager with a bad attitude towards life. **Grumpy Cat's negative outlook directly contradicts the prevalent American idea that people should be positive, optimistic, and happy. Grumpy Cat is funny because she subverts social norms by being socially inappropriate and rude**.

　グランピー・キャットは実在の飼い猫で，本名（？）をターダー・ソースといいます．生まれつき身体に障害があり，口の形から不機嫌に見えてしまうのですが実際は人懐っこい猫なのだそうです．でもターダー・ソースの写真を使ったミームは，そのイラついて見える表情を利用して，とても人気があります．最初の例は，"Row, row, row your boat"（ボートを漕ごう）で始まる子供の歌の歌詞が上に，"No"という拒否の一言が下にありますね．グランピー・キャットが「イヤだね」と言っているのは，一緒に仲良く歌うことなのかボートを漕ぐことなのか，わからないけれど，この歌が持つ予定調和的な気分を共有したくないと断固拒否しています．次の例は，"A little bird told me it was your birthday"（小鳥があなたの誕生日だって教えてくれたよ）という文章が上にあります．"A little bird told me"というフレーズは，「ある人が教えてくれたんだが」という決まり文句なので，正しくは「あなたの誕生日なんだってね」という意味で，当然その後には「ハッピー・バースディ」とお祝いの言葉が続くはずなのに，"I ate him [the bird]"（で，その小鳥は食べちゃった）と言っている，というか，グランピー・キャットが心の中で思っていることになっている．誕生日を教えてくる奴なんか食べちゃった，というひねくれた反抗心と，小鳥を食べるいかにも猫らしい無遠慮な行動のマッチングが笑いを誘います．さて，最後のミームの説明は，みなさんが英語の説明を読んでからにしましょうね．

　Grumpy Cat is an actual cat named Tardar Sauce. Tardar Sauce has a real deformity from a condition called "dwarfism" that makes her mouth look

like a human frown. Tardar Sauce is quite affectionate, but to viewers, Grumpy Cat's mouth makes it look like she is very bad-tempered. Because of her unusual looks, many memes have emerged that feature Grumpy Cat being annoyed.

The first cat meme refers to a well-known, happy children's song called "Row, Row Row Your Boat" (see Chapter 6). It **presumes shared cultural knowledge** of this song. The first line of the meme begins the first line of the song. Grumpy Cat, who is sitting in a boat, interrupts the happy song by saying "no." It is unclear whether Grumpy Cat doesn't want to sing the song, doesn't want to row the boat, or both. This meme is funny to viewers, however, because children's songs sometimes are annoying to adults, who may find them overly sentimental or cloying. **Grumpy Cat says what people might think but don't usually say**.

The second meme begins with the phrase "a little bird told me it was your birthday." **"A little bird" is another example of the shared cultural knowledge** necessary for understanding memes. It is way of saying that the person speaking has important information but won't reveal the source. The little bird isn't real, it just means "someone told me." In this meme, Grumpy Cat is saying she knows it's the viewer's birthday. Usually, when a person knows it is someone's birthday, she or he will wish the person "happy birthday." It is considered polite. The first line therefore sets up the expectation that Grumpy Cat will wish the viewer a customary "happy birthday" (see Chapter 6). In this case, however, Grumpy Cat says, "I ate him." This meme is funny because Grumpy Cat does what a cat would do, which is eat the bird (even though the bird isn't real), rather than what a human would do (wish the person "happy birthday.") The meme also is funny because it suggests that Grumpy Cat hates birthdays. Again, **Grumpy Cat breaks social con-**

ventions by saying and doing what a polite person would not.

The next meme follows the same pattern as the ones above. The first line sets up a happy or pleasant expectation, while the second line reveals Grumpy Cat's bad attitude and lack of respect. In this case, the first line suggests that Grumpy Cat likes long walks. The second line, however, reveals that Grumpy Cat likes people (rather than herself) to take long walks. When people take walks, Grumpy Cat does not have to be around them.

最後の例も、2番目の例と同じく、写真の上にある文章には社会規範内で期待される良い反応、「長い散歩が好きです」とあります。ところが、下のところで「人間が（長い散歩を）している時がいちばんよい」と付け加えられている。ここで意味が転覆します。「実は散歩が好きというわけじゃない」という、社会的な期待に反した猫の本心と、「人間がそばにいないほうが快適だ」というもう一つの猫の本心が巧みに表されておかしいのです。猫は犬よりも冷淡で自律していると一般的には受け止められていて、人間の思うようには行動しないから犬のようにしつけるのは無理だとされます。この共通理解を背景に、グランピー・キャットは期待される人間社会の規範に「イヤだね」と言って笑いを誘うのです。機嫌よくポジティブでいつも礼儀正しくしているのなんてイヤだと、実は人々が内心思っていることを、しかめ面でむっつりと表現するから人気なのですね。

....

Is it possible to learn about American culture from something as ordinary, silly, and presumably unimportant as Grumpy Cat memes? **Grumpy Cat memes—and cat memes generally—are common and widespread. We must presume, therefore, that they are important in some way.**

Grumpy Cat memes primarily reveal attitudes about cats. Americans view cats and dogs as having different personalities. Dogs are perceived as friendly, exuberant, and eager to please people, while **cats are perceived as aloof and independent** (even though this is not necessarily true). Cats also are thought to be less teachable than dogs; they do what they want and people have little influence on them. Americans even divide themselves into "dog people" and "cat people," people who prefer and relate to one animal over the other. The behavior and attitude of cats also is thought to be more mysterious, unpredictable, and unfathomable than dogs. These are some of the reasons why people like them.

Grumpy Cat memes embody these cultural ideas about cats. Grumpy Cat is independent, aloof, and irritable. As a cat, she is unpredictable, independent, and says and does exactly what she wants. Unlike a dog, she does not care about pleasing people and no one attempts to teach her to behave. **Grumpy Cat's bad attitude directly contradicts American cultural norms that dictate people should be happy and optimistic. She breaks common rules of politeness, articulating what people may feel or think but usually don't say**. People laugh at and admire Grumpy Cat for her bad attitude because she is honest and just being herself (a cat).

4 考　察

　インターネット上で大流行しているミームは，集めて分析すると，ある特定のミームを楽しむ人々に共通の価値観や知識，共有されている認識や社会規範，また隠された問題などを観察することができます．動物が擬人化されたミームを解釈するには，その文化に共有された動物と人間との関係性を知っておく必要があります．この章で取り上げた犬のミームでは，犬が人間と家族のように暮らすことから，社会規範の学習を犬に期待することが前提になっています．しつけに逆らった犬は，大人の言うことをきかなかった子供の立場に置き換えて見ることができます．一方，猫のミームでは，自分の思うように生きたい人々の気持ちの代弁者としてグランピー・キャットがいます．背景には，常に肯定的であることを求めるアメリカ社会の無言の圧力があるのです．

DISCUSSION

Memes are a new form of culture that circulates primarily on the Internet. Many people think memes are trivial, but like other forms of culture, memes **presume shared cultural knowledge** and reveal important concepts. In these examples, viewers must know the qualities attributed to dogs and cats and how people view themselves in relation to dogs and cats in order to understand these memes.

The dog and cat memes examined here place animals in the role of people, though in different ways and with different characteristics. Dog-shaming memes are about reinforcing social behavior and rules of appropriateness. **They frame dogs as beings who are happy and eager to please, but who also are easily overcome by their urges and must be controlled. These memes place the dog in the role of a person who must be taught to behave and the dog owner in the role of a parent.**

In contrast, Grumpy Cat memes subvert normal social rules of behavior. Grumpy Cat is rude or negative, but no one attempts to teach Grump Cat anything or change her ways because cats are considered independent, aloof, and less concerned with what people think. **Grumpy Cat memes represent the viewpoint of people who appreciate the independent qualities attributed to cats, and who may chafe against American standards of decorum that dictate a positive outlook on life.**

5 演　習

インターネット上には，きわめて多数のミームサイクル（連続して変化していく一連のミーム群）があります．一つのミームサイクルを選び出し，以下の問いを参考に分析してください．その結果を発表し，クラスで話し合ってください．ミームを見ることのできるリンクを，本書の専用サイト（p.viii）に掲載してあります．

ACTIVE LEARNING

There are hundreds of different meme cycles. Choose a cycle of memes and examine the different variations, and share your ideas with the class.
What do you learn?
What kind of knowledge is presumed in order to understand the meme?
What pattern or structure does the meme follow?
What cultural ideas, attitudes or values does this meme cycle evoke?

14章

デジタル時代のヴァナキュラー・カルチャー
——これから文化を学ぶ人のために

Chapter 14
Vernacular Culture in the Digital Age:
For Those Who Study Culture, a Conclusion

1 新たな挑戦

　デジタル環境の発達により，日常的な文化（ヴァナキュラー・カルチャー／フォークロア）は大きく変化しました．そして文化の研究者は，新たな挑戦を迫られています．これまでは，人と人とが出会う環境で文化が生成されたり拡散したりしてきたので，個人は，人種やジェンダー，社会階層，居住地域など顔の見えるレベルで特定できるアイデンティティ（ここに自分は属しているという認識，自分はどういう立場の個人かという認識）を共有できる人々と連帯して文化を育んできました．本書のI部からIV部で扱った物語や歌や祝祭の習慣などは，どれもそうした文化です．ところが，前章で扱ったミームのようなインターネット上の文化においては,対面で確認できるアイデンティティは曖昧になります.ネット上でのみつながる個人のアイデンティティは，誇張も縮小も自由自在で，架空の個人になりすますことさえできてしまいます．また，インターネット上の共同体に加わるかどうかも，それぞれの判断に任されています．こうした環境で従来の文化は変質を迫られ，新たな文化が活発に発信されてきています．私たちは，その研究に挑む必要があるのです．

INTRODUCTION
Digital environments pose interesting challenges to people interested in studying culture. In face-to-face environments, culture is tied to specific groups or communities that interact with each other on a regular, face-to-face basis, share specific identity features such as race, gender, and class, or that are bound together by region, territory, or geography.　Many of the cultural forms discussed in this book, for example, are tied to specific groups, such as the celebration of Halloween among Neopagans; specific re-

gions, such as rodeos in the West; or even a broad, national culture, such as songs and disaster stories. But such associations are more elusive online. As discussed in the last chapter on memes, **digital environments connect people who would never meet across great geographical distances. They also allow people to minimize, enhance, or entirely transform their personal identity**. Finally, **people actively choose whether or not to join digital communities**. They may participate as much or as little as they like, and they can leave at any time. As the Internet grows and changes, new forms of culture emerge that challenge, change, or extend the conventional characteristics associated with culture and cultural groups.

2　オンライン・コミュニティ

　「ファンダム」とも呼ばれる，物語ファンのオンライン上の共同体（コミュニティ）があります．これは，ある作家や作品のファンが，お気に入りの作品の設定や登場人物を使いながら自分で作った話を互いに見せ合い意見を交換するつながりで，たとえば『ハリー・ポッター』シリーズのファンダムは最大級です．1960年代70年代に日本で盛んだった同人誌も，同じ文学傾向の仲間が集い作品を世に出す，という点では似たところはあるかもしれません．従来型の文学ファンの同人誌とファンダムでの発表が最も異なっている点は，アマチュア作者が自分の作品を（印刷を待たずに）瞬時に公開できるスピードや手軽さと，ファンダムのコミュニティが寄せるコメントやフィードバックで作品の評価が決まることです．同時に，ファンダムは職業作家への登竜門にはなりにくくファンのコミュニティという性格が強いので，印刷によるアマチュア出版とは作品公開の目的やメディアとしての用途を異にしているともいえます．

ONLINE COMMUNITIES
One kind of popular online community is fanfiction communities, which are sometimes called "fandoms." These online groups consist of amateur writers who are fans of a work by a published professional author. Fans write their own stories about the author's characters, or they use the original work's settings as a backdrop for their own writing. Fans come together online to share their own work, talk about their favorite authors, read the work of others, and share ideas and criticism. Fandoms also provide sup-

port and allow people to interact socially with others who share similar interests. There are hundreds of fanfiction communities. One of the largest fandoms is Harry Potter fanfiction, based on the popular Harry Potter series by J.K. Rowling.

The idea of writing fanfiction is not new. In Japan, for example, dōjinshi, which is similar to fanfiction, existed in the 1960s and 1970s. The scope of interaction, and means for circulating fanfiction, however, was limited in the past. Fanfiction writers shared their writing in print, through published magazines. The process of publishing such magazines was slow, writers often did not receive feedback on their work, and readership was small.

In contrast, **digital environments expand networks of interactions among participants and speed up processes of publishing**. Harry Potter fans, for example, are not limited by geography—they connect to other Harry Potter fans across the world. Time-consuming activities such as production layout, typesetting, and printing, which print publication requires, are no longer necessary: publishing one's work entails simply uploading it to a website. Digital environments also offer fanfiction writers an instantaneous, interactive forum for receiving feedback and criticism about their work.

Online fanfiction communities have democratized the writing and publishing process. In the past, only the best or most well-known writers were published, making it difficult for new or unknown authors to circulate their work. In digital environments, anyone can publish. The online community collectively decides what is acceptable and what is not through comments and feedback. The power to decide what is good and what is not lies in the hands of the fanfiction community, rather than a few well-positioned individuals with access to formal publication methods. The writing and publishing process is open and accessible to all.

　オンライン・コミュニティには負の側面もあります．ある考えを共有する人々がインターネット上でつながることにより，社会全体から自分たちを切り離しがちで，客観性を失い，自分たちだけの考えに固まる傾向があるということです．一つの例が，アメリカのワクチン反対者のグループです．急進的なメンバーの主張は，ワクチン接種は危険であるのに，政府や医療関係企業が結託して利潤追求のためにワクチン接種を推進しているというものです．医学的に証明されているワクチン接種の効果や副作用例の数の少なさといった客観的情報は，彼らの不安

を払拭する役に立ちません．オンライン・コミュニティに公開される個人的な被害体験談や反ワクチンの考え方は，あっという間に共感者を集め，科学的証拠を視野に入れないまま人々の偏見を固めてしまいます．このプロセスを「確証バイアス」と呼びます．自分の考えを補強する情報だけを信用し，自分の考えに沿わない情報は軽視したり否定したりする，偏見（バイアス）強化の行動です．

....

Online communities may have negative effects as well (Howard 2013). When large numbers of people voluntarily join together online to share ideas, they may isolate themselves from the larger world and reinforce pre-existing beliefs. Anti-vaccine groups, for example, are groups of people who believe that medical vaccines potentially are harmful. Radical members of these groups believe that vaccines are a conspiracy between the medical establishment and the government to gain control of the population, or that they exist merely as a way for pharmaceutical companies to make money. These fears persist, despite the fact that extensive medical research on different kinds of vaccines concludes that adverse effects by vaccines are extraordinarily rare (Maglione et al. 2014).

In offline environments, groups of people who hold beliefs that contradict traditional sources of authority such as science, the government, or mainstream news sources likely are to be small. **Online communities, however, allow such individuals to connect with hundreds, or even thousands, of other people who share similar ideas**. Like fanfiction communities, anti-vaccine communities share ideas, beliefs, and conversations online. They share stories about people who allegedly have been harmed by vaccines and circulate articles that argue vaccines are harmful (Kitta 2011). Information is not taken from conventional scientific evidence, but rather personal experience, rumor, or alternative news sources. These online interactions reinforce people's belief that vaccines are harmful. Scientists call this process "**confirmation bias**," **which means the tendency to select information that confirms pre-existing beliefs and to reject evidence that does not support it.**

　ロブ・ハワードは，オンライン・コミュニティが「ヴァナキュラーな権威者」を形成するとしました．日常的なレベルで何かに関わる普通の人々が，良し悪しにかかわらず，かつては職業的な専門家が担っていた権威を持つようになったと

いうことです．アナログの時代には，人気作家と認められるためには権威ある有名作家や出版社に認められる必要がありましたが，いまではファンダムが人気や評価を左右します．加えてアメリカでは，麻疹や百日咳といった子供の深刻な感染症はほぼ根絶していたにもかかわらず，近年ふたたび流行している背景に，反ワクチンコミュニティの拡大があるとも指摘されています．活発なインターネット・コミュニティやネット上での人々の行動には，このように功罪入り混じった文化的側面があり，私たちはその内容を見極めていかねばなりません．

・・・

Rob Howard (2013) postulates that online communities constitute a form of **"vernacular authority,"** meaning that in certain situations people may place themselves in the position of expert. Fandoms place themselves in the position of author and publisher, while anti-vaccine groups place themselves in the position of researcher or expert authority. In the case of fandoms, the emergence of vernacular authority has had positive effects by expanding publishing options for amateur writers. In the anti-vaccine community, the results have been less positive. In the US, serious childhood diseases such as measles and pertussis (whooping cough) nearly had been eradicated. Recent resurgences of both these diseases have been associated with refusal to vaccinate (Phadke, et al. 2016), posing increased risks to children. **The dynamics of Internet communities and online interaction have both positive and negative consequences**.

3 流言パニック

インターネット上で容易に起こるもう一つの現象例に，流言パニックがあります．何かの脅迫的な刺激（流言・うわさ）によって，恐怖やヒステリックな反応が広範囲に及ぶことを流言パニックといいます．2章で述べた同時代伝説に似ていますが，物語やよく構成されたナラティヴはありません．何らかの出来事が発端となって社会に潜む緊張や不安が呼び起こされ，恐怖を招き，集団的な行動につながるのが特徴です．

・・・

RUMOR-PANICS

Rumor-panics are another form of culture that spread easily over the Internet. **A rumor-panic is widespread fear and hysteria based on a perceived threat**. Rumor-panics are similar to contemporary legends (see Chapter 2), but there is less of a story or well-defined "narrative." Rather, **pre-existing social tensions are triggered by an event, which leads to widespread fear and collective action** (Ellis 2002).

　2016年に,「不気味なピエロ<ruby>クリーピー・クラウン</ruby>」のパニックが起こりました．夏の初め，ゾッとする姿のピエロが各地で目撃されたという不確実情報がネット上に流れます．ピエロがなにか悪いことをしたという書き込みはなかったのに，子供の誘拐，傷害や殺人などがあったという噂が流れました．ウェブサイトやソーシャルメディアには不気味なピエロを「見た」というニュースが溢れ，人々は恐怖におののきました．学校が休校になり警察は警戒を呼びかけ，職業としてピエロを演じている人たちは命の危険さえ感じるほどでした．その後の詳しいことは英文を読んでいただきたいのですが，ホワイト・ハウスまでも巻き込んだこのピエロ・パニックは，アメリカ合衆国以外の18を超える国々に波及し，ドイツでも政府の対応が求められる事態となりました．

....

A promotional photo of Gags, a character in a horror movie made in Green Bay, Wisconsin. People presumed that these promotional photos, which circulated on social media, were real, spawning the international creepy clown rumor-panic of 2016.

One recent example of a rumor-panic is **the "creepy clown" phenomenon of 2016**. Beginning in the summer of that year, unsubstantiated reports of frightening clowns appeared online. People across the country supposedly began sighting fierce, maniacal-looking clowns in their hometowns, in malls, in the woods, or other places. Nobody reported the clowns as having done anything bad, but rumors circulated that the clowns were abducting children, or wanting to hurt or kill people. People posted pictures of scary clowns on websites and social media, and both real and fake news outlets reported the "sightings" as real. People became so frightened that schools were closed down, police issued warnings, and real, professional clowns were afraid for their lives. By October of 2016, fear of clowns was so widespread in the United States that people were banned from dressing like clowns for Halloween (see Chapter 10) and stores that sold Halloween items removed clown costumes from the shelves. White House Press secretary Josh Earnest even answered a question about clown sightings during a press conference in October (Morris 2016). The creepy clown phenomenon eventually spread to more than eighteen countries, including the United Kingdom, Australia, Canada, Singapore, Chile and Sweden. In São Paulo, Brazil, professional clowns marched to demonstrate their innocence and protest against evil clowns (Nauman 2016), while the German Interior Ministry apparently issued a "zero-tolerance policy" against anyone dressing up as a creepy clown (Noack 2016).

　発端はこうです．2016年8月2日，ウィスコンシン州のグリーンベイで製作されたホラー映画のオンライン宣伝戦略として，「ギャグズ」と名付けられた邪悪な雰囲気のピエロの写真がフェイスブックに掲載されました．ギャグズは黒い風船を手に持って，グリーンベイのダウンタウンを徘徊しています．地方の映画制作会社のこの宣伝写真が，映画広告の目的とは関係なく，一週間でオンライン上に拡散したのです．ブラジル，アイルランド，ドイツといったふうに国境も難なく超えて「目撃報告」が相次ぎました．自ら不気味なピエロの姿をする人が現れたり，500人超の大学生が「ピエロ狩り」に出るなど様相は混乱を極めますが，だれも本物に出会うことはありませんでした．そして，11月初旬にはパニックは収束し，年末には人々の関心はすっかり別のことに移っていました．

....

　As with nearly all rumor-panics, there was no basis for the widespread fear. The origin of the creepy clown phenomenon was an online marketing ploy designed by promoters of a locally produced horror film in Green Bay, Wisconsin. Promoters created a Facebook page on Aug. 02, 2016. They posted photographs of a sinister-looking clown dubbed "Gags" (an actor dressed as a clown) clutching a bunch of black balloons and wandering through the streets of downtown Green Bay. Film promoters hoped their photographs would attract the attention of people in order to promote their film. Within a week, however, photos of Gags had been shared online tens of thousands of times. News reports of scary clown sightings appeared in countries as far away as Brazil, Ireland, and Germany. A few "copycats" even dressed up as frightening clowns as a joke, spreading the rumor-panic even further. In some instances, people took action by guarding themselves against clowns. As an example, more than five hundred students at Penn State University went "clown hunting," scouring the university campus for creepy clowns. While they obviously found none, such group behavior can easily become quite dangerous.

The creepy clown phenomenon died down as quickly as it had emerged. By early November of 2016, few creepy clown sightings were reported. By the end of the year, it was hardly mentioned and the world had moved on other things.

　すでに述べたように，流言パニックは社会に潜在する緊張や不安を呼び覚まします．恐怖に駆られた人々は集団的なヒステリー状態となり，警察が出動したり自警団ができたり，逆に「不気味なピエロ」のふりをする人が出たりという現象があらわれます．このように，流布した「ナラティヴ」(噂話／物語) に対して人々が実際に行動して参与すること（行動によってナラティヴを支持しさらに内容を付け加えること）を，「オステンション」と呼びます．この場合のナラティヴは，「不気味なピエロ」に関する一連の情報とその関連事件です．アメリカでピエロのパニックが起こった理由としては，「邪悪な雰囲気がある」ということと「ピエロ」の幸せで楽天的なイメージの矛盾が，人々に潜在する不安を刺激したといえるでしょう．邪悪なピエロとは，無垢な子供の要素を社会が失ったことの表れと感じられ，子供の誘拐が噂され，恐怖を招きました．あるいは，2016年にアメリカ合衆国を二分した大統領選挙の不安な行方が，混沌とした社会に対する国民の恐怖を覚醒し，邪悪なピエロがその象徴であったという研究者たちもいます．インターネットが普及する前にも流言パニックはありましたが，「不気味なピエロ」のように，多数の国々であっという間に広がるものはありませんでした．デジタル環境下では，不確かなものを多数含むありとあらゆる種類の考えや情報が，膨大な数の人々にごく短時間で広まるのです．

As mentioned above, rumor-panics exacerbate pre-existing social tensions. These pre-existing social tensions erupt when a triggering event occurs, and motivate people to collective action. In this case, the triggering event was the posting of frightening clown pictures online. The collective action was widespread fear and panic, leading to police action, vigilante groups, and copycat behavior. **Scholars call the acting out of such ideas "ostension," meaning that people may participate in widespread narratives by acting them out in the real world**. But why clowns and what were the pre-existing tensions that the original Facebook post made manifest?

Most people in the US have ambivalent feelings towards clowns. On the one hand, clowns are considered to be cheerful, happy figures, and clowns usually are associated with children. On the other hand, many people don't like clowns or feel nervous around them. **Terrifying or homicidal clowns exploit this ambivalence**. They invert the presumption that clowns are happy and positive. Scary clowns suggest a loss of childhood innocence or that something is terribly wrong with the world. Because many people reported creepy clowns chasing children, the creepy clown phenomenon might reflect pre-existing tensions about the presumed safety of children (see Chapter 2). Other scholars have hypothesized that the creepy clown phenomenon reflected the state of national politics at the time, since it occurred during a contentious presidential election. In other words, the frightening clown, symbolizing fear and chaos, was a real-life representation of the chaos and fear happening in national politics.

While rumor-panics existed before the Internet, they have become much more common and widespread. Before the Internet, rumor-panics did not spread as quickly and they were limited to a local or national level. **The creepy clown rumor-panic emerged quite suddenly, spread very swiftly, and reached international proportions**. It may be one of the first international rumor-panics spread by the Internet. **Digital environments spread all kinds of ideas very quickly and to enormous numbers of people.**

4 考　察

インターネットは急速に変化していますから，デジタル環境下の文化研究は新しく刺激的な分野といえます．そこで以下にいくつか，研究を始める時のポイントを書きます．

(1)　ウェブサイトの管理者をよく確認すること．大学や政府系の機関など既存の権威・信用がある団体や組織によるものか，ウィキペディアのように多数の人が比較的自由に書き込めて掲載内容に関われるものかどうか．参加型のサイト

には，ヴァナキュラーな（日常的な）人々の視点や考えが反映されています．
⑵　オンライン・コミュニティを研究する場合は，そのコミュニティがオフラインでも活動しているかどうかを確かめる．デジタル環境のみでつながっているコミュニティもあれば，主にオフラインで活動し，連絡を取ったり活動報告をする目的だけでインターネットを利用している団体もあります．
⑶　サイトの中身を調べるときに，コメント欄も読むこと．そのコミュニティに属する人たちのものの見方や考え方が読み取れます．

　ヴァナキュラー・カルチャーの研究は，興味深く，楽しく，多くを学べる学問分野です．文化のどの側面でも詳しく観察すれば，社会や人間について洞察することができます．繰り返される日々の営みと人々のすることを軽んじないで，有名な文学や美術や音楽を研究するように詳しく観察すれば，私たちは自分についても他人についても，自分が属すると思う文化についてもそうでないと思う文化についても，深く理解することができるようになるのです．

....

DISCUSSION

Because the Internet changes so rapidly, it can be an exciting arena for the study of new and emerging forms of culture. Ways to study Internet culture are still developing. Below are a few suggestions.

　First, **choose your sites with care**. Are the sites maintained only by large organizations, or are they active, participatory sites where many people contribute? Websites and media maintained by large organizations that do not allow active contributions will reflect the perspective of that particular organization. A corporate or government website, for example, will be tightly controlled and reflect the perspective of those in power. In contrast, participatory sites (such as Wikipedia) allow the general public or members of that group to actively contribute and share content. Participatory sites provide a broader, more vernacular (or "everyday") perspective about what a group of people thinks.

　Additionally, **when choosing an online community to study, consider whether or not that community or group interacts offline**. Some online communities exist solely in the digital realm. Others may exist primarily offline and simply use digital environments for facilitating communication and coordinating offline activities. An example of such a group might be a bicycling club that gathers together for bicycle rides, but coordinates efforts online among its members.

Finally, in addition to examining the content of a site, be sure to examine the comments section. **People share their responses to the content itself, or a particular issue, and debate ideas in the comments section, providing an audience perspective**. For example, while a set of YouTube videos about a game might be good to analyze, the comments section provides insights into an audience response. The comments section cannot take the place of oral interviews, but it provides a researcher an excellent overview of general trends or ideas.

The study of vernacular culture is exciting, entertaining, and informative. Any aspect of culture can provide insights into society, provided we look closely enough. People often dismiss the everyday, traditional forms of culture such as the food we eat, the clothes we wear, and the conversations we have with friends and family as too ordinary and mundane to be important. We presume that because they are ordinary, repetitive, and unexciting, they are not worthy of attention or scholarly examination. While it is important to study the best cultural productions a society has to offer, such as great works of literature, important art, and music, **let us not forget that insights emerge from more ordinary things as well. Upon close inspection, the small activities that make up our everyday lives can reveal important discoveries about ourselves and others**.

5 演 習

(1) オンラインゲームとコスプレのコミュニティは，現代のコミュニティとしては代表的なものでしょう．それぞれの活動を調べ，コミュニティの特徴を，オンラインとオフラインの両方から説明してください．この二つを大きなコミュニティにしたと思われる特徴を，それぞれについてあげて，説明してください．

(2) 偽（フェイク）ニュースサイトが，インターネット上で盛んになっています．既存のニュースメディアそっくりに作られていて，実は嘘の情報やプロパガンダを掲載しています．こうした現象を，本文で述べた「ヴァナキュラー権威」(多数の普通の人々の参加が評価や真偽の印象を決めていくこと，決める権威を持つこと）と関連させて考察，分析・説明，議論してください．

ACTIVE LEARNING

Online gaming and Cosplay communities are two well-developed and active communities to study. Check on the Internet to find out what they do. Describe briefly what each community does online and offline. Which elements do you think have made each of these communities so large?

Fake news sites have recently become much more common on the Internet. These sites imitate traditional news media, because they look and sound like real news. The stories they post, however, are either entirely false, propaganda, or only partly true. Can you draw connections between this phenomenon and the concept of vernacular authority?

参考文献　References

1章

Afanas'ev, Aleksandr.［1855-1863］1945. *Russian Fairy Tales*. Translated by Norbert Huterman. New York: Pantheon Books.

Ashliman, D.L. 1998-2015. Cinderella. Accessed January 20, 2017. http://www.pitt.edu/~dash/type0510a.html.

Basile, Giambattista.［1634, 1636］1999. Cinderella Cat. Translated by Nancy L. Canepa. *Marvels & Tales: Journal of Fairy-Tale Studies* 13/2: 201-10.

The Cinderella Bibliography. 2017. Robbins Library Digital Project, University of Rochester. Accessed January 21, 2017. http://d.lib.rochester.edu/cinderella.

Dundes, Alan, ed. 1982. *Cinderella: A Casebook*. Madison: University of Wisconsin Press.

Lüthi, Max. 1982. *The European Folktale: Form and Nature*. Translated by John D. Niles. Bloomington: Indiana University Press.

Perrault, Charles.［1697］2009. *The Complete Fairy Tales*. Translated by Christopher Betts. Oxford: Oxford University Press.

Rooth, Anna Birgitta. 1951. *The Cinderella Cycle*. Lund.

Stone, Kay. 1975. Things Walt Disney Never Told Us. *Journal of American Folklore* 88:42-50.

Toelken, Barre. 1996. *The Dynamics of Folklore*. Logan: Utah State University Press.

Grimm, Jacob, and Willhelm.［1857］1987. *The Complete Fairy Tales of the Brothers Grimm*. Translated by Jack Zipes. Vol. 1. New York: Bantam Books.

2章

Bennett, Gillian, and Paul Smith. 1996. *Contemporary Legend: A Reader*. New York: Garland.

Brunvand, Jan. 1981. *The Vanishing Hitchhiker: American Urban Legends and their Meaning*. New York: Norton.

——. 1984. *The Choking Doberman and Other "New" Urban Legends*. New York: Norton.

——. 2001. *Encyclopedia of Urban Legends*. ABC-CLIO.

Fine, Gary Allen. 1992. *Manufacturing Tales: Sex and Money in Contemporary Legends*. Knoxville: University of Tennessee Press.

Fine, Gary Allen, Véronique Campion-Vincent, and Chip Heath, eds. 2005. *Rumor Mills: The Social Impact of Rumor and Legend*. New Brunswick, NJ: Aldine Transaction.

Mikkelson, David. 2008a. The Microwaved Pet. Snopes.com, August 08. Accessed January 01, 2017. http://www.snopes.com/horrors/techno/microwavedpet.asp.

——.2008b. Tressed to Kill. Snopes.com, August 08. Accessed January 15, 2017. http://www.snopes.com/horrors/vanities/hairdo.asp.

Snopes.com http://www.snopes.com.

US Department of Labor. 100 Years of U.S. Consumer Spending for 1950. Available online as .pdf. U.S. Bureau of Labor Statistics. https://www.bls.gov/home.htm.

de Vos, Gail. 2012. *What Happens Next? Contemporary Urban Legends and Popular*

Culture. Santa Barbara, CA: Libraries Unlimited.

3章

9-11 Memorial and Museum. 2017. Accessed January 22. https://www.911memorial.org/oral-histories-0.

Ancelet, Barry Jean, Marcia Gaudet, and Carl Lindahl, eds. 2013. *Second Line Rescue: Improvised Responses to Katrina and Rita*. Jackson: University Press of Mississippi.

Anonymous. "Gutted." Hurricane Digital Memory Bank. Hurricanearchive.org. Accessed March 11, 2016. http://hurricanearchive.org/items/show/45985.

Anonymous. "Our Lives Changed Right Before Our Eyes." Hurricane Digital Memory Bank. Hurricanearchive.org. Accessed March 8, 2016. http://hurricanearchive.org/items/show/45998.

Antoine, Rebeca, ed. 2008. *Voices Rising: Stories from the Katrina Narrative Project*. New Orleans: University of New Orleans Publishing.

Bauman, Richard. 1986. *Story, Performance, and Event: Contextual Stories of Oral Narrative*. Cambridge: Cambridge University Press.

Cody, Cornelia. 2005. Only in New York: The New York City Personal Experience Narrative. *Journal of Folklore Research* 42/2: 217–44.

Di Marco, Damon. 2007. *Tower Stories: An Oral History of 9–11*. 2d ed. Santa Monica, CA: Santa Monica Press, LLC.

Fink, Mitchell and Lois Mathias. 2002. *Never Forget: An Oral History of September 11, 2001*. New York: Harper Collins.

Folklife in Louisiana. 2016. Louisiana Folklife Program. Accessed July 06. http://www.louisianafolklife.org/katrina.html.

Hurricane Digital Memory Bank. 2016. Accessed November 03. http://hurricanearchive.org.

Jasper, Pat, and Carl Lindahl. 2006. *The Houston Survivor Project*. A special issue of *Callalo* 29/4.

Lindahl, Carl. 2012. Legends of Hurricane Katrina: The Right to Be Wrong, Survivor-to-Survivor Storytelling, and Healing. *Journal of American Folklore* 125/496: 139–76.

Marotte, Mary Ruth, and Glenn Jellenik, eds. 2015. *Ten Years after Katrina: Critical Perspectives of the Storm's Effect on American Culture and Identity*. Lanham, MD: Lexington Books.

New Orleans Disaster and Oral History Memory Project. 2016. Aliveintruth.com. Accessed June 15. http://www.aliveintruth.com.

Penner, D'Ann R., and Keith C. Ferdinand. 2009. *Overcoming Katrina: African American Voices from the Crescent City and Beyond*. New York: Palgrave.

September 11, 2001 Documentary Project. 2016. Library of Congress. Accessed Aug. 09. https://www.loc.gov/collections/september-11th-2001-documentary-project/about-this-collection.

Stahl, Sandra Dolby. 1989. *Literary Folkloristics and the Personal Narrative*. Bloomington: Indiana University Press.

Storr, Nona Martin, Emily Chamlee-Wright, and Virgil Henry Storr. 2015. *How We Came*

Back: *Voices from Post-Katrina New Orleans*. Arlington: George Mason University.

4章

Afro-American Work Songs in a Texas Prison. 1966. Folklore Research Films. Produced by Pete and Toshi Seeger with Bruce Jackson. http://www.folkstreams.net/film, 122.

Burns, Richard Allen. 2012. Where Is Jody Now? Reconsidering Military Marching Chants. In *Warrior Ways: Explorations in Modern Military Folklore*, ed. Eric A. Eliason and Tad Tuleja, 79-98. Logan: Utah State University Press.

Hawes, Bess Lomax. 1974. Folksongs and Function: Some Thoughts on the American Lullaby. *Journal of American Folklore* 87/344: 140-148.

Lomax, Alan. 1997. *Prison Songs, Vol. 1: Murderous Home*. Recorded 1947-1948. Rounder, compact disc.

Trnka, Susanna. 1995. Living a Life of Sex and Danger: Women, Warfare, and Sex in Military Folk Rhymes. *Western Folklore* 54/3: 232-41.

Warner, Maria. 1998. 'Hush-a-Bye-Baby': Death and Violence in the Lullaby. *Raritan: A Quarterly Review* 18/1: 93-114.

ウェルズ恵子『魂をゆさぶる歌に出会う：アメリカ黒人文化のルーツへ』岩波ジュニア新書，2014

5章

Burnett, John. 2009. Narcocorridos: Ballads of the Mexican Cartels. NPR.org, October 10. Accessed January 23, 2017. http://www.npr.org/2009/10/10/113664067/narcocorridos-ballads-of-the-mexican-cartels.

Cohen, Michael C., ed. 2016. *The Ballad: A Special Issue on Historical Poetics and Genre*, a special issue of *Nineteenth Century Literature* 71/2.

Edwards, Carol D., ed. 1986. *The Ballad in Context: Paradigms of Meaning*, a special issue of *Western Folklore* 45/2.

Fields, Polly Stevens. 1988. "And He Laid Poor Jesse in His Grave": A Study of Selected Ballads about Jesse James. *Mississippi Folklore Register* 22/1-2: 33-46.

McNeill, William K. 1980. Ballads about Jesse James: Some Comments. *Mid-America Folklore* 8/1-2: 44-52.

Nelson, Scott Reynolds. 2008. *Steel-Driving Man: The Untold Story of an American Legend*. London: Oxford University Press.

Polenberg, Richard. 2015. *Hear My Sad Story: The True Tales that Inspired "Stagolee," "John Henry," and Other Traditional American Folk Songs*. Ithaca: Cornell University Press.

Toelken, Barre. 1986. Ballads and Folksongs. In *Folk Groups and Folklore Genres: An Introduction*, ed. Elliott Oring, 147-74. Logan: Utah State University Press.

Waltz, Robert B., ed. 2016. The Traditional Ballad Index: An Annotated Bibliography of the Folk Songs of the English Speaking World. Accessed January 23, 2017. http://www.csufresno.edu/folklore/BalladIndexTOC.html.

※その他については，次の本の参考文献をみてください．
ウェルズ恵子『フォークソングのアメリカ：ゆで玉子を産むニワトリ』南雲堂，改装版 2007

6章

Barbash, Fred, and Travis M. Andrews. Aug. 30, 2016. A Brief History of 'The Star-Spangled Banner' Being Played at Games and Getting No Respect. *The Washington Post*. Accessed Nov. 14, 2016. https://www.washingtonpost.com/news/morning-mix/wp/2016/08/30/a-brief-history-of-the-star-spangled-banner-being-played-at-games-and-getting-no-respect/?utm_term=.feb24af7b920.

Cyphers, Luke, and Ethan Trex. Sept. 19, 2011. The Song Remains the Same. *ESPN: The Magazine*. Accessed Nov. 08, 2016. http://www.espn.com/espn/story/_/id/6957582/the-history-national-anthem-sports-espn-magazine.

History.com. History of the Christmas Carol. Accessed January 24, 2017. http://www.history.com/topics/christmas/history-of-christmas/videos/history-of-the-christmas-carol.

Pew Research Center. Religious Landscape Study. Accessed December 12, 2016. http://www.pewforum.org/religious-landscape-study.

Spitzer, Nick. February 15, 2012. The Story of Woody Guthrie's "This Land Is Your Land." Accessed December 15, 2016. http://www.npr.org/2000/07/03/1076186/this-land-is-your-land.

7章

Buhs, Joshua Blu. 2009. *Bigfoot: The Life and Times of a Legend*. Chicago: University of Chicago Press.

Dorson, Richard. 1982. *Man and Beast in American Comic Legend*. Bloomington: Indiana University Press.

Meurger, Michel. 1989. *Lake Monster Traditions: A Cross-Cultural Analysis*. London: Fortean Tomes.

Napier, John. 1973. *Bigfoot: The Yeti and Sasquatch in Myth and Reality*. New York: Dutton.

8章

Bennett, Gillian. 1999. *Alas, Poor Ghost! Traditions of Belief in Story and Discourse*. Logan: Utah State University Press.

de Caro, Frank. 2015. The Lalaurie Haunted House, Ghosts, and Slavery: New Orleans, Louisiana. In *Putting the Supernatural in Its Place: Folklore, the Hypermodern, and the Ethereal*, ed. Jeannie Banks Thomas, 24–48. Salt Lake City: University of Utah Press.

Goldstein, Diane, Sylvia Ann Grider, and Jeannie Banks Thomas. 2007. *Haunting Experiences: Ghosts in Contemporary Folklore*. Logan: Utah State University Press.

Irving, Washington. The Legend of Sleepy Hollow. Accessed January 04, 2017. http://www.eastoftheweb.com/short-stories/UBooks/LegSle.shtml.

Morrison, Toni. 1997. *Beloved*. New York: Alfred A. Knopf.

Tucker, Elizabeth. 2007. *Haunted Halls: Ghostlore of American College Campuses*. Jackson: University Press of Mississippi.

9章

Bateson, Gregory. 1972. "A Theory of Play and Fantasy." In *Steps to an Ecology of Mind*,

177-193. Chicago: University of Chicago Press.
Bradbury, Ray. [1946] 2009. *Dandelion Wine: A Novel*. Reprint. New York: William Morrow.
Bronner, Simon J. 1988. *American Children's Folklore*. Little Rock, Ark.: August House, Inc.
Chagall, Irene. 2014. "Let's Get the Rhythm: The Life and Times of Miss Mary Mack." Produced by Irene Chagall, Steve Zeitlin, and City Lore. 54 min. New York, DVD.
Glass, Ira. 1998. 109: Notes on Camp. *This American Life*, August 28. Accessed December 20, 2016. https://www.thisamericanlife.org/radio-archives/episode/109/notes-on-camp.
Knapp, Mary, and Herbert. 1978. *One Potato, Two Potato: The Folklore of American Children*. W.W. Norton and Company.
Sutton-Smith, Brian, et al., eds. 1999. *Children's Folklore: A Sourcebook*. Logan: Utah State University Press.
Tucker, Elizabeth. 2005. Ghosts in Mirrors: Reflections of the Self. *Journal of American Folklore* 118/468: 186-203.
Tucker, Elizabeth. 2008. *Children's Folklore: A Handbook*. Westport, CT: Greenwood Press.

10章

Bannatyne, Leslie Pratt. 1998. *Halloween: An American Holiday, An American History*. Pelican Press.
Kugelmass, Jack. 1994. *Masked Culture: The Greenwich Village Halloween Parade*. New York: Columbia University Press.
NYC Planning. Department of City Planning, Current Population Estimates. Accessed 05 January, 2017. https://www1.nyc.gov/site/planning/data-maps/nyc-population/current-future-populations.page.
Roberts, Sam. 20 April, 2010. Listening to (and Saving) the World's Languages. *New York Times*, Section: NY/Region. Accessed March 16, 2017. http://www.nytimes.com/2010/04/29/nyregion/29lost.html.
Santino, Jack. 1994. *Halloween and Other Festivals of Death and Life*. Knoxville: University of Tennessee Press.
——. Halloween: The Fantasy and Folklore of All Hallows. Library of Congress. Accessed January 22, 2016. http://www.loc.gov/folklife/halloween.html.

11章

Abrahams, Roger D. 2006. *Blues for New Orleans: Mardi Gras and America's Creole Soul*. Philadelphia: University of Pennsylvania Press.
The History and Traditions of Mardi Gras Promo. 2017. Accessed January 25. https://www.youtube.com/watch?v=mo5ClQDKnqk.
Kinser, Samuel. 1990. *Carnival, American Style: Mardi Gras at New Orleans and Mobile*. Chicago: University of Chicago Press.
Mauldin, Barbara, ed. 2004. *Carnival!* Seattle: University of Washington Press.
Mardi Gras New Orleans. 2016. Accessed October 25. http://www.mardigrasneworleans.com.
Santino, Jack. 1995. *All Around the Year: Holidays and Celebrations in American Life*.

University of Illinois Press.

12章

Applebome, Peter. June 18, 1989. Wrangling Over Where Rodeo Began. *New York Times*. Accessed March 16, 2017. http://www.nytimes.com/1989/06/18/travel/wrangling-over-where-rodeo-began.html?pagewanted=all.

Fredriksson, Kristine. 1993. *American Rodeo: From Buffalo Bill to Big Business*. College Station: Texas A&M University Press.

PRCA Prorodeo. 2017. Official Home Page of the Professional Rodeo Cowboys Association. Accessed January 22. http://www.prorodeo.com.

Prosterman, Leslie. 1995. *Ordinary Life, Festival Days: Aesthetics in the Midwestern County Fair*. Washington: Smithsonian Institution Press.

Stoeltje, Beverly. 1989. Rodeo: From Custom to Ritual. *Western Folklore* 48/3: 244–255.

13章

McNeill, Lynne. 2009. The End of the Internet: A Folk Response to the Provision of Infinite Choice. In *Folklore and the Internet: Vernacular Expression in a Digital World*, ed. Trevor J. Blank, 80–97. Logan: Utah State University Press.

Pimple, Kenneth. 1996. The Meme-ing of Folklore. *Journal of Folklore Research* 33/3:236–40.

Schrempp, Gregory. 2009. Taking the Dawkins Challenge, or the Dark-side of the Meme. *Journal of Folklore Research* 46/1: 91–100.

14章

Blank, Trevor J. 2014. *Toward a Conceptual Framework for the Study of Folklore and the Internet*. Logan: Utah State University Press.

Blank, Trevor, J., ed. 2012. *Folk Culture in the Digital Age: The Emergent Dynamics of Human Interaction*. Logan: Utah State University Press.

Ellis, Bill. 2002. Hitler's Birthday: Rumor-Panics in the Wake of the Columbine Shootings. *Children's Folklore Review* 24/1–2:

Howard, Robert Glenn. 2013. Vernacular Authority: Critically Engaging Tradition. In *Tradition in the Twenty-First Century: Locating the Role of the Past in the Present*, ed. Trevor J. Blank and Robert Glenn Howard, 72–99. Logan: Utah State University Press.

Kitta, Andrea. 2011. *Vaccinations and Public Concern in History: Legend, Rumor, and Risk Perception*. New York: Routledge Press.

Maglione, Margaret A., et al. 2014. Safety of Vaccines Used for Routine Immunization of US Children: A Systematic Review. *Pediatrics* 134/2: 325–337. Accessed February 05, 2017. http://pediatrics.aappublications.org/content/134/2/325.long.

Morris, J.D. 07 October, 2016. "Creepy clown" Threats Lead to Investigations in Sonoma County. *The Press Democrat*. Accessed 05 February, 2017. http://www.pressdemocrat.com/news/6171472-181/creepy-clown-threats-lead-to.

Nauman, Zoe. 26 October, 2016. Not Clowning around: Big Hearted Clowns Stage Peaceful Protest in Sao Paulo to Prove They Aren't All Evil and Scary. *The Sun*. Accessed 05 February, 2017. https://www.thesun.co.uk/news/2057082/big-hearted-clowns-stage-

peaceful-protest-in-sao-paulo-to-prove-they-arent-all-evil-and-scary/.
Noack, Rick. 29 October, 2016. Germany Announces "Zero Tolerance" against Creepy Clowns Ahead of Halloween. *The Washington Post*. Accessed 05 February, 2017. https://www.washingtonpost.com/news/worldviews/wp/2016/10/29/germany-announces-zero-tolerance-policy-against-creepy-clowns-ahead-of-halloween/?utm_term=.c472f6691fa0.
Phadke, Varun K., et al. 2016. Association between Vaccine Refusal and Vaccine-Preventable Diseases in the United States: A Review of Measles and Pertussis. *JAMA* 315/11: 1149-1158. Accessed 05 February, 2017. https://www.ncbi.nlm.nih.gov/pmc/articles/PMC5007135/.

図版出典一覧

Chapter 1 photos

Photo #1:
Caption: Cinderella tries on the slipper
Attribution: Illustration by Carl von Offterdinger is licensed under CC BY 2.0 via Wikimedia Commons

Photo #2
Caption: Cinderella asking tree for help
Attribution: Illustration by Elenore Abbott is licensed under CC BY 2.0 via Wikimedia Commons

Chapter 2 photos

Photo #1:
Caption: Many Americans eat fast food in thier cars
Attribution: Shutterstock stock photo

Photo #2:
Caption: The Talking Angela app has been the topic of contemporary legends
Attribution: By ونام بوراس (Own work) ［CC BY-SA 4.0 (http://creativecommons.org/licenses/by-sa/4.0)］, via Wikimedia Commons

Chapter 3 photos

Photo #1:
Caption: Flooding in New Orleans after Hurricane Katrina
Attribution: Photo by NOAA Images is licensed under CC BY 2.0

Photo #2
Caption: Terrorist attack on World Trade Center buildings in New York City
Attribution: Photo by 9-11 Photos is licensed under CC BY 2.0

Chapter 4 photos

Photo #1:
Caption: The American military uses chants and calls to help soldiers march in time together
Attribution: By U.S. Navy photo ［Public domain］, via Wikimedia Commons

Photo #2:
Caption: Mothers around the world sing lullabies to soothe children to sleep
Attribution: published in the U.S. before 1923 and public domain in the U.S.

Chapter 5 photos
    Photo #1:
    Caption: John Henry with hammer
    Attribution: US commemorative stamp

    Photo #2
    Caption: Portrait of Jesse James
    Attribution: CC BY 2.0 (http://creativecommons.org/licenses/by/2.0)], via Wikimedia Commons

Chapter 6 photos
    Photo #1:
    Caption: Singing "Happy Birthday to You"
    Attribution: Picture by Dark Dwarf is licensed under CC BY 2.0

    Photo #2
    Caption: Baseball player leading fans to sing "Take Me out to the Ballgame"
    Attribution: Picture by Eric Molina is licensed under CC BY 2.0

Chapter 7 photos
    Photo #1:
    Caption: Bigfoot beer, an example of Bigfoot marketing
    Attribution: Photo by Edwin is licensed under CC BY 2.0

    Photo #2
    Caption: Lake monster sculpture created in ice and snow
    Attribution: Photo by Lisa Gabbert

Chapter 8 photos
    Photo #1:
    Caption: A typical haunted house with ghosts
    Attribution: Picture by Liz West is licensed under CC BY 2.0

    Photo #2
    Caption: A typical American ghost
    Attribution: Picture is licensed under CC BY 2.0

Chapter 9 photos
    Photo #1:
    Caption: Children playing tag
    Attribution: By EJ Fox ("pseudoplacebo") from Circleville, United States (Playing snatch the fish) [CC BY-SA 2.0 (http://creativecommons.org/licenses/by-sa/2.0)], via Wikimedia Commons

Photo #2
Caption: Looking for Bloody Mary in a bathroom mirror is an old children's game. What will she do?
Attribution: Permission by Damla, creator. Deviantart.com.

Chapter 10 photos
  Photo #1:
  Caption: Child trick-or-treating
  Attribution: Photo by Colleen McMahon is licensed under CC BY 2.0

  Photo #2
  Caption: Greenwich Village Halloween parade
  Attribution: Photo by Joe Shlabotnik (Flickr: Bananas) [CC BY 2.0 (http://creativecommons.org/licenses/by/2.0)], via Wikimedia Commons

Chapter 11 photos
  Picture #1:
  Caption: Mardi Gras masks
  Attribution: Photo by Tyler is licensed under CC BY 2.0

  Picture #2:
  Caption: Mardi Gras Indians
  Attribution: Photo by Derek Bridges is licensed under CC BY 2.0

Chapter 12 photos
  Picture #1:
  Caption: Sheep waiting to be judged at county fair
  Attribution: Photo by Randy Robertson is licensed under CC BY 2.0

  Picture #2:
  Caption: Rodeo cowboy riding a bucking bull
  Attribution: Photo by Kate Ure is licensed under CC BY 2.0

Chapter 13 photos
  Picture #1:
  http://www.collegehumor.com/post/6856437/dog-shaming-meme
  Picture #2:
  http://thumbpress.com/dogs-with-notes-the-best-of-dog-shaming-50-funny-pictures/
  Picture #3:
  http://www.just4petcare.com/dog-shaming-funny-pics-meme/
  Picture #4:
  http://runt-of-the-web.com/dog-shaming
  Picture #5:

https://www.pinterest.com/pin/184084703492026693/
Picture #6:
http://thumbpress.com/dogs-with-notes-the-best-of-dog-shaming-50-funny-pictures/
Picture #7:
http://www.memecommunity.com/row-row-row-your-boat/
Picture #8:
https://memegenerator.net/instance/66914439/grumpy-cat-a-little-bird-told-me-it-was-your-birthday-i-ate-him
Picture #9:
http://www.complex.com/style/2013/03/the-50-funniest-grumpy-cat-memes/long-walks

Chapter 14 photo
Picture #1:
Caption: A promotional photo of Gags, a character in a horror movie made in Green Bay, Wisconsin. People presumed that these promotional photos, which circulated on social media, were real, spawning the international creepy clown rumor-panic of 2016.
Attribution: Photo by Adam Krause. Printed with permission.

索　引

数字
9-11　　　　　　　　　　　　　　　35

あ行
愛国的な歌　　　　　　　　　　　75
アイデンティティ　　　iv, 34, 71, 155, 175
アウトロー　　　　　　　　　　　64
アメリカ先住民　　　　　　　　109
アンダードッグ　　　　　　　　　63
一人称の語り　　　　　　　　　　31
鬼ごっこ　　　　　　　　　　　118
オンライン・コミュニティ　　　176

か行
カーニバル　　　　　　　　　　139
カウボーイ／カウガール　　　　158
確証バイアス　　　　　　　　　178
カリフォルニア　　　　　　　　134
境界（線）　　　　　　　27, 100, 165
グランピー・キャット　　　　　169
クリスマス　　　　　　　　　　　73
クリスマス・キャロル　　　　　　73
グリム童話　　　　　　　　　　　8
コール・アンド・レスポンス　　　46
黒人霊歌　　　　　　　　　　　　79
個人的経験　　　　　　　　　　　29
子供の歌　　　　　　　　　　　　80
コミュニケーション　　　　　　113
子守唄　　　　　　　　　　　　　52

さ行
ジェシー・ジェイムズ　　　　　　64
ジェンダー　　　　　　　　22, 103
宗教歌　　　　　　　　　　　　　79
ジョン・ヘンリー　　　　　　　　59
シンデレラ　　　　　　　　　　　3
ズールーズ　　　　　　　　　　145
スリーピー・ホロウ　　　　　　101
西部　　　　　　　　　　　64, 155

た行
男女の役割分担　　　　　　　　　22
中西部　　　　　　　　　　　　150
デジタルコンテンツ　　　　　　164
伝承遊び歌　　　　　　　　　　117

電子レンジ　　　　　　　　　　　24
伝説　　　　　　　　　　　　　　16
伝統　　　　　　　　　　　　iv, 3
同時代伝説の要素　　　　　　　　24
同時多発テロ　　　　　　　　　　35
トーキング・アンジェラ　　　　　25
奴隷制（奴隷制度）　　　65, 79, 106

な行
南部　　　　　　　　　45, 57, 106, 144
ニューオーリンズ　　　　　30, 138
ネオ・ペイガニズム　　　　　　134

は行
バジーレ　　　　　　　　　　　　10
「ハッピー・バースディ」の歌　　　72
ハヌカ　　　　　　　　　　　　　74
バラッド　　　　　　　　　　　　58
ハリケーン・カトリーナ　　　　　30
ハロウィンパレード　　　　　　132
ビッグフット　　　　　　　　　　87
『ビラヴド』　　　　　　　　　　107
ファストフード　　　　　　　　　20
ファンダム　　　　　　　　　　176
フェアリーテイル　　　　　　　　2
フォークロア　　　　　　　iii, 175
フォーミュラ　　　　　　　　　　4
「フック」　　　　　　　　　　　　17
ブラディ・メアリ　　　　　　　121
判官びいき　　　　　　　　　　　63

ま行
ミリタリー・カデンス　　　　　　49
メディア　　　　　　　　　　　　33
モチーフ　　　　　　　　　　　　5

ら行
ルール　　　　　　　　　　　　118
レジェンド　　　　　　　　　　　16

わ行
ワークソング　　　　　　　　　　44

ウェルズ恵子（Keiko Wells）
　立命館大学文学部教授

リサ・ギャバート（Lisa Gabbert）
　ユタ州立大学英文科（フォークロア）准教授

多文化理解のための
アメリカ文化入門――社会・地域・伝承

平成29年4月30日　発　　　行
令和2年4月10日　第3刷発行

著作者　ウェルズ恵子
　　　　リサ・ギャバート

発行者　池田和博

発行所　丸善出版株式会社
　〒101-0051　東京都千代田区神田神保町二丁目17番
　編集：電話(03)3512-3264／FAX(03)3512-3272
　営業：電話(03)3512-3256／FAX(03)3512-3270
　https://www.maruzen-publishing.co.jp

© Keiko Wells, Lisa Gabbert, 2017

組版印刷・株式会社 日本制作センター／製本・株式会社 松岳社
ISBN 978-4-621-30152-4 C1082　　　Printed in Japan

JCOPY 〈(一社)出版者著作権管理機構 委託出版物〉
本書の無断複写は著作権法上での例外を除き禁じられています。複写される場合は、そのつど事前に、(一社)出版者著作権管理機構(電話03-5244-5088, FAX03-5244-5089, e-mail：info@jcopy.or.jp)の許諾を得てください。